Y: THE LAST MAN — KIMONO DRAGONS

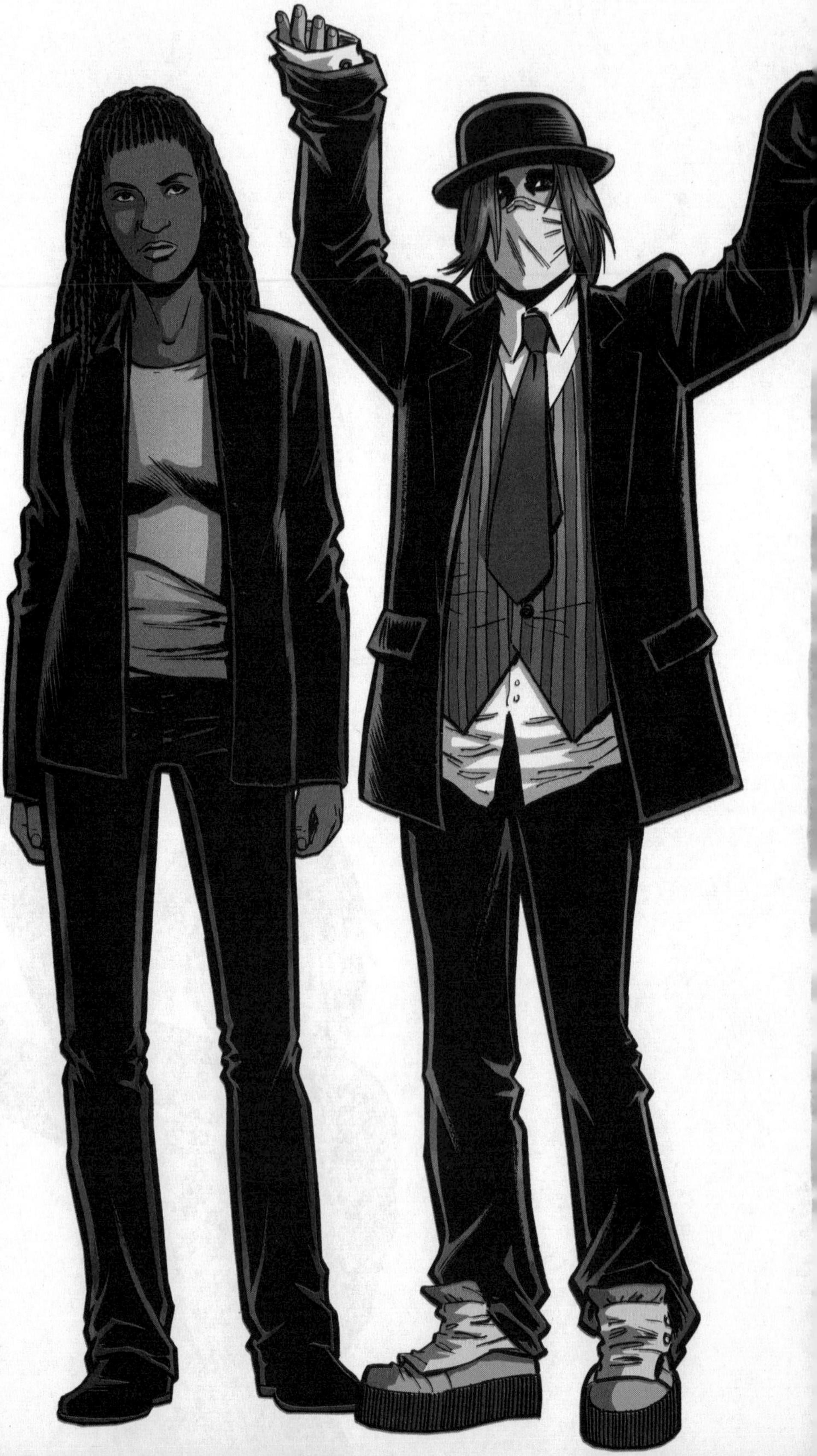

THE LAST MAN — KIMONO DRAGONS

Brian K. Vaughan
Writer

Pia Guerra
Goran Sudžuka
Pencillers

José Marzán, Jr.
Inker

Zylonol
Colorist

Clem Robins
Letterer

Massimo Carnevale
Original series covers

Y: THE LAST MAN created by Brian K. Vaughan and Pia Guerra

Y: THE LAST MAN — KIMONO DRAGONS

Published by DC Comics. Cover and compilation copyright © 2006 DC Comics.
All Rights Reserved.

Originally published in single magazine form as Y: THE LAST MAN 43-48.
Copyright © 2006 Brian K. Vaughan and Pia Guerra. All Rights Reserved.
All characters, their distinctive likenesses and related elements featured in
this publication are trademarks of Brian K. Vaughan and Pia Guerra.
VERTIGO is a trademark of DC Comics. The stories, characters and incidents
featured in this publication are entirely fictional. DC Comics does not read
or accept unsolicited submissions of ideas, stories or artwork.

DC Comics, 1700 Broadway, New York, NY 10019
A Warner Bros. Entertainment Company.
Printed in Canada. First Printing.
ISBN: 1-4012-1010-4
ISBN 13: 978-1-4012-1010-6
Cover illustrations by Massimo Carnevale.
Logo designs by Terry Marks.

Y THE LAST MAN — Contents

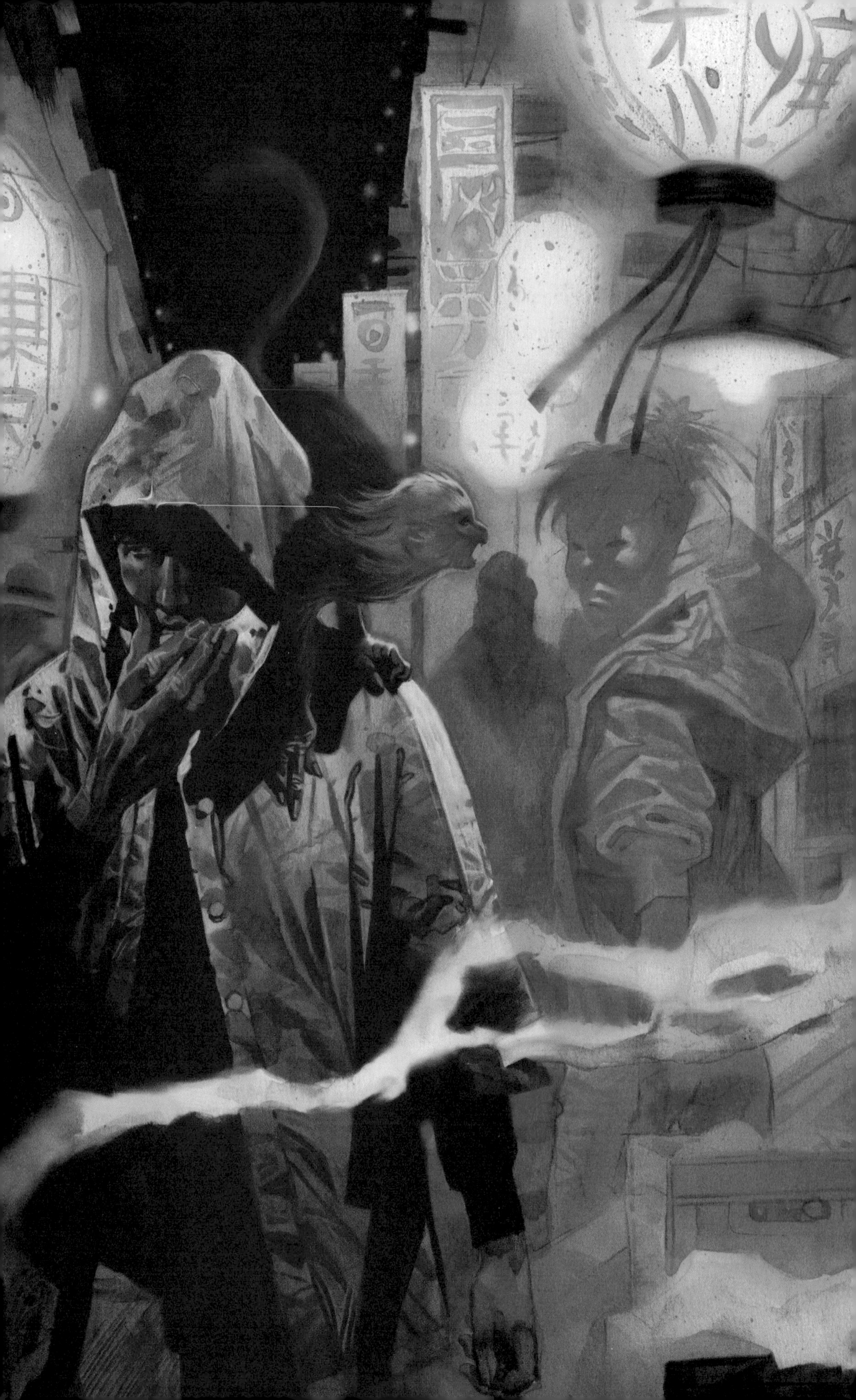

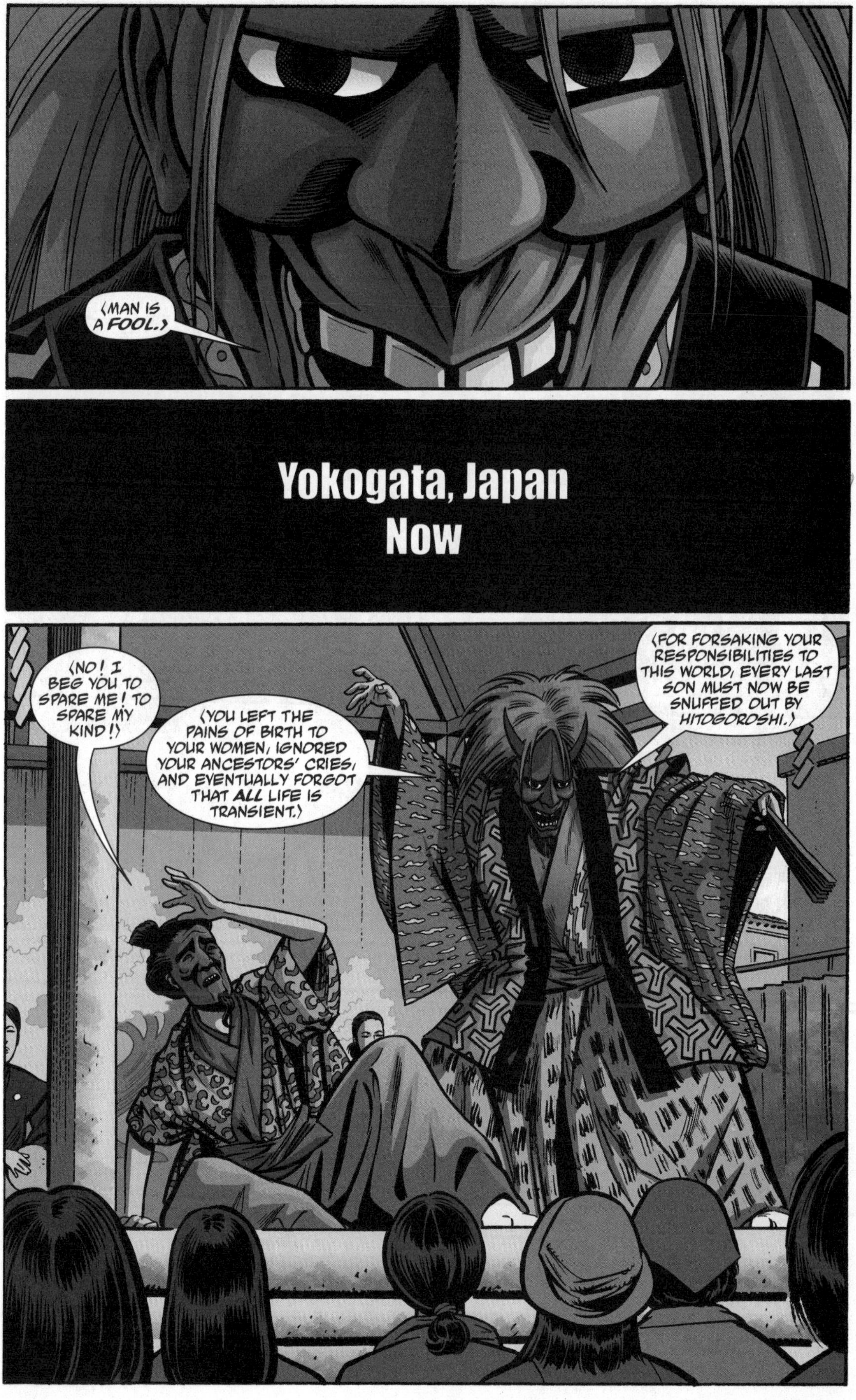
⟨MAN IS A FOOL.⟩
Yokogata, Japan
Now
⟨NO! I BEG YOU TO SPARE ME! TO SPARE MY KIND!⟩
⟨YOU LEFT THE PAINS OF BIRTH TO YOUR WOMEN, IGNORED YOUR ANCESTORS' CRIES, AND EVENTUALLY FORGOT THAT ALL LIFE IS TRANSIENT.⟩
⟨FOR FORSAKING YOUR RESPONSIBILITIES TO THIS WORLD, EVERY LAST SON MUST NOW BE SNUFFED OUT BY HITOGOROSHI.⟩

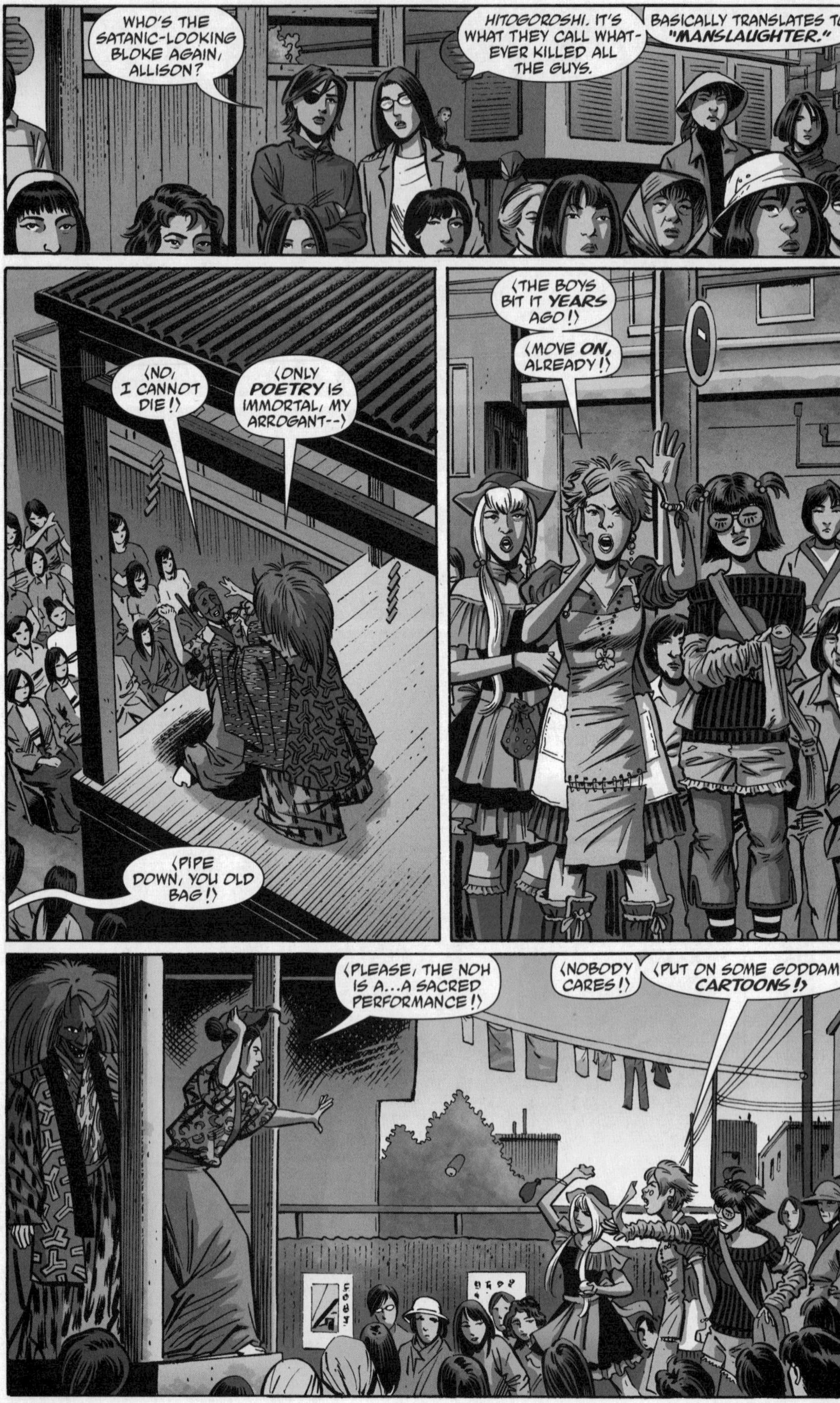
WHO'S THE SATANIC-LOOKING BLOKE AGAIN, ALLISON?
HITOGOROSHI. IT'S WHAT THEY CALL WHATEVER KILLED ALL THE GUYS.
BASICALLY TRANSLATES TO "MANSLAUGHTER."
⟨NO, I CANNOT DIE!⟩
⟨ONLY POETRY IS IMMORTAL, MY ARROGANT--⟩
⟨PIPE DOWN, YOU OLD BAG!⟩
⟨THE BOYS BIT IT YEARS AGO!⟩
⟨MOVE ON, ALREADY!⟩
⟨PLEASE, THE NOH IS A...A SACRED PERFORMANCE!⟩
⟨NOBODY CARES!⟩
⟨PUT ON SOME GODDAMN CARTOONS!⟩

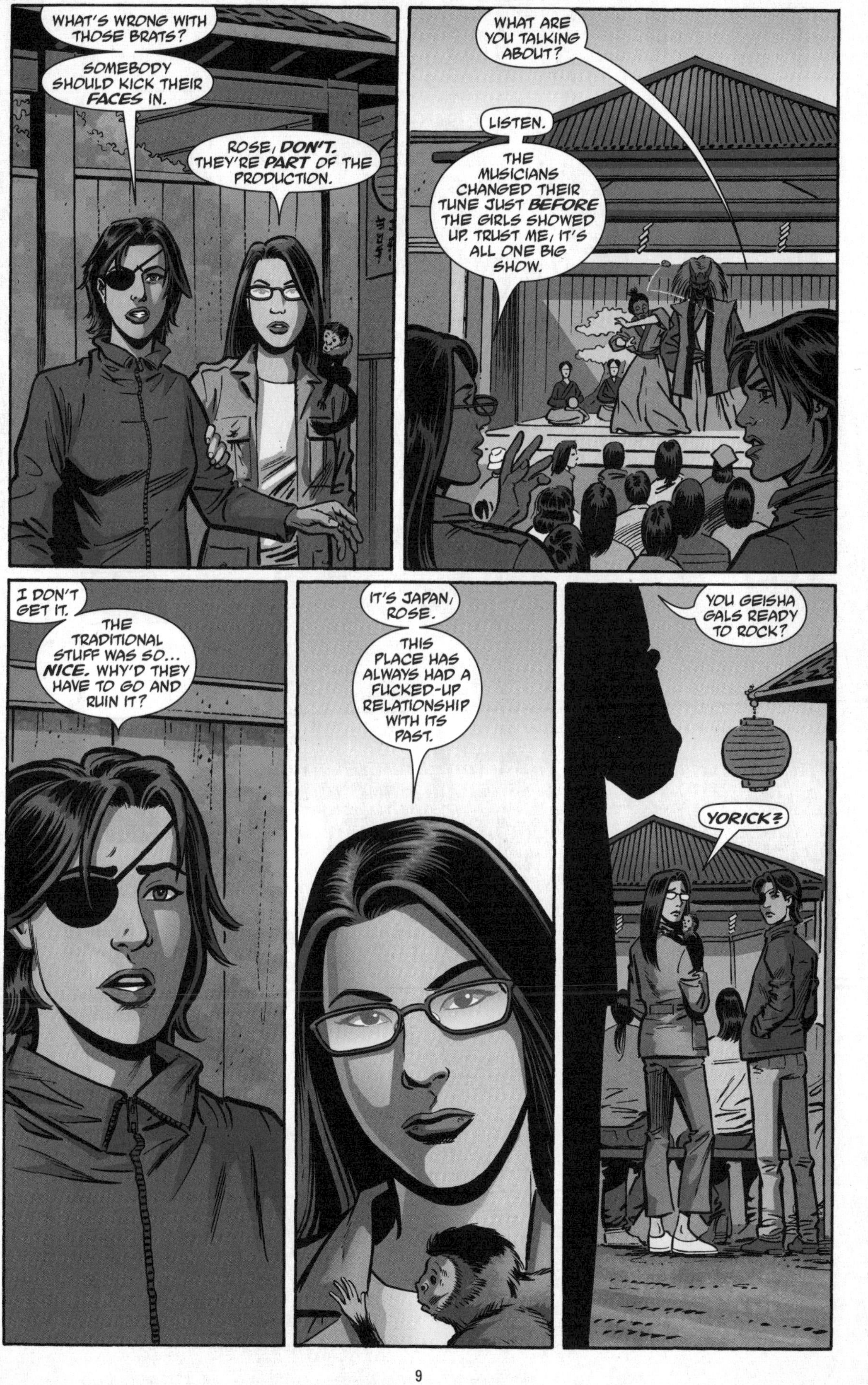
WHAT'S WRONG WITH THOSE BRATS?
SOMEBODY SHOULD KICK THEIR FACES IN.
ROSE, DON'T. THEY'RE PART OF THE PRODUCTION.
WHAT ARE YOU TALKING ABOUT?
LISTEN.
THE MUSICIANS CHANGED THEIR TUNE JUST BEFORE THE GIRLS SHOWED UP. TRUST ME, IT'S ALL ONE BIG SHOW.
I DON'T GET IT.
THE TRADITIONAL STUFF WAS SO... NICE. WHY'D THEY HAVE TO GO AND RUIN IT?
IT'S JAPAN, ROSE.
THIS PLACE HAS ALWAYS HAD A FUCKED-UP RELATIONSHIP WITH ITS PAST.
YOU GEISHA GALS READY TO ROCK?
YORICK?

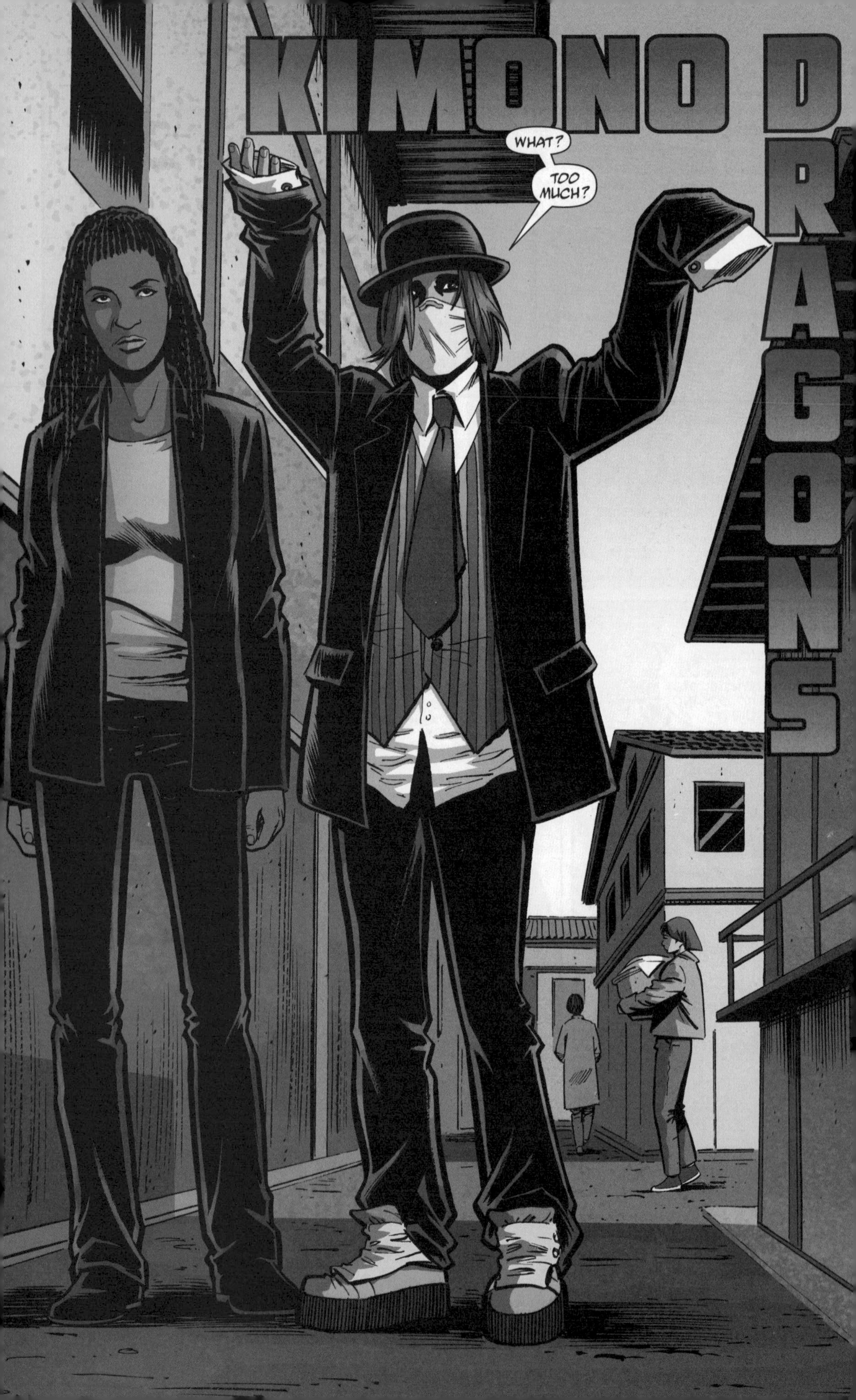
KIMONO DRAGONS
WHAT?
TOO MUCH?

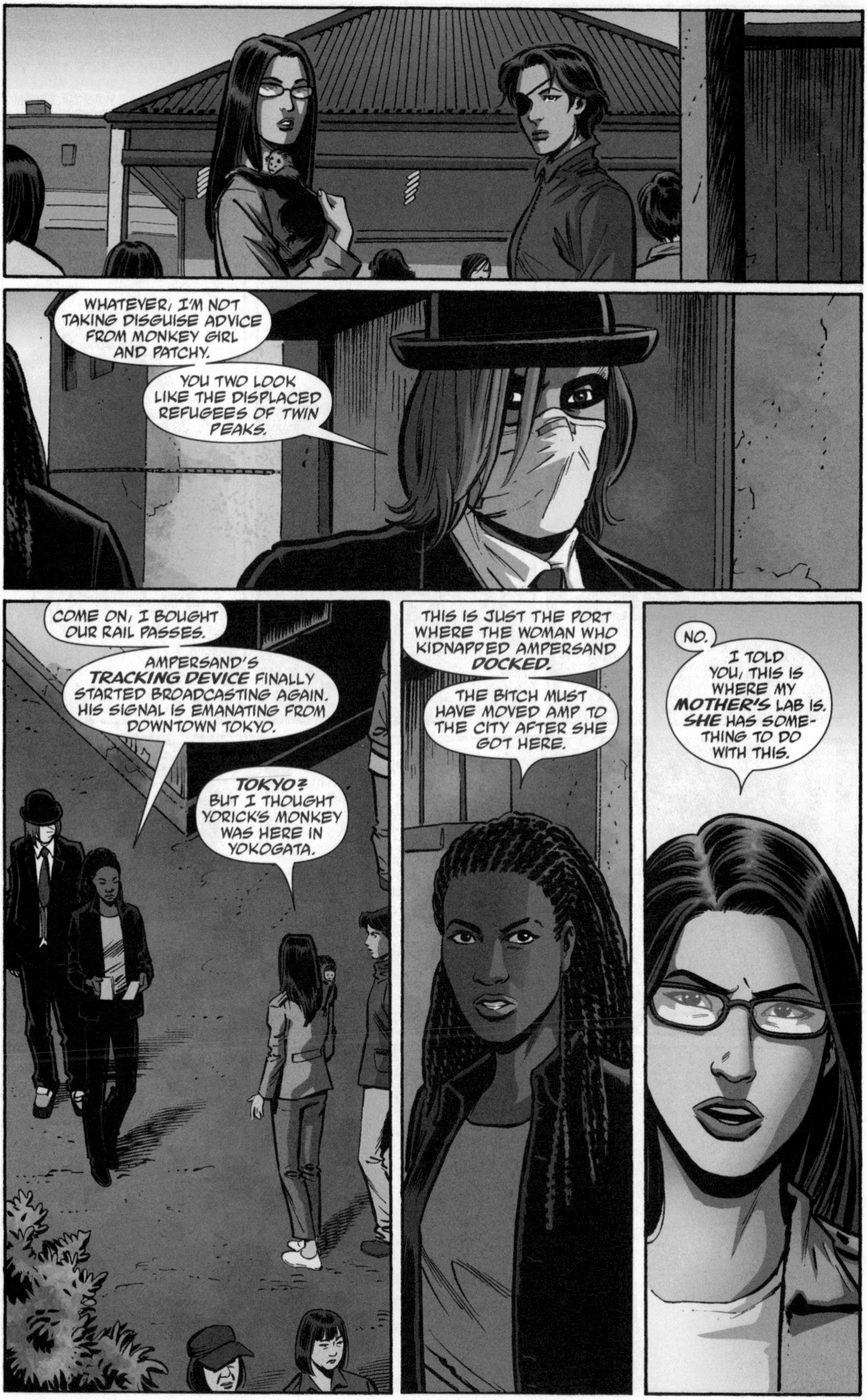
WHATEVER, I'M NOT TAKING DISGUISE ADVICE FROM MONKEY GIRL AND PATCHY.
YOU TWO LOOK LIKE THE DISPLACED REFUGEES OF TWIN PEAKS.
COME ON, I BOUGHT OUR RAIL PASSES.
AMPERSAND'S TRACKING DEVICE FINALLY STARTED BROADCASTING AGAIN. HIS SIGNAL IS EMANATING FROM DOWNTOWN TOKYO.
TOKYO? BUT I THOUGHT YORICK'S MONKEY WAS HERE IN YOKOGATA.
THIS IS JUST THE PORT WHERE THE WOMAN WHO KIDNAPPED AMPERSAND DOCKED.
THE BITCH MUST HAVE MOVED AMP TO THE CITY AFTER SHE GOT HERE.
NO.
I TOLD YOU, THIS IS WHERE MY MOTHER'S LAB IS. SHE HAS SOMETHING TO DO WITH THIS.

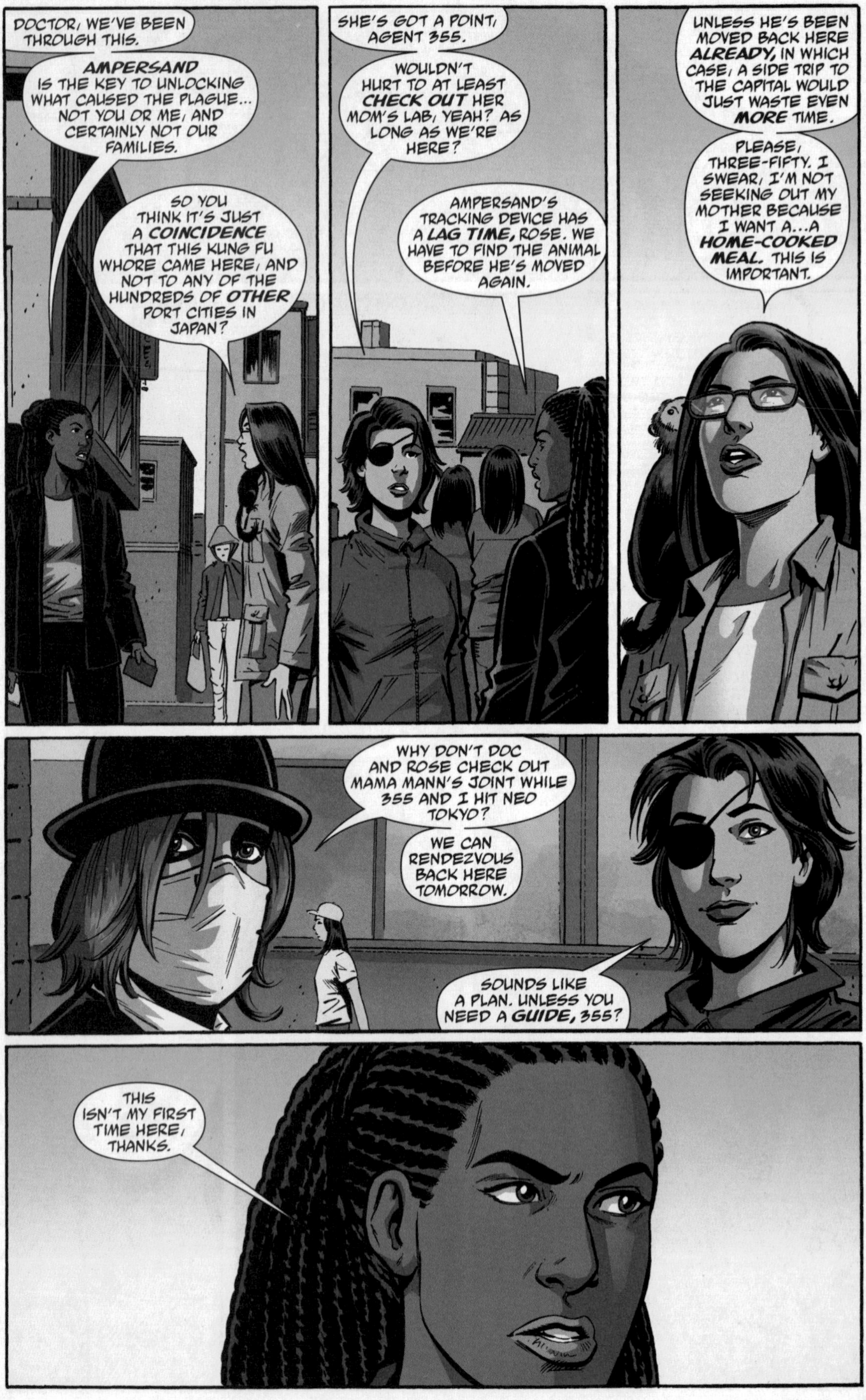
DOCTOR, WE'VE BEEN THROUGH THIS.
AMPERSAND IS THE KEY TO UNLOCKING WHAT CAUSED THE PLAGUE... NOT YOU OR ME, AND CERTAINLY NOT OUR FAMILIES.
SO YOU THINK IT'S JUST A COINCIDENCE THAT THIS KUNG FU WHORE CAME HERE, AND NOT TO ANY OF THE HUNDREDS OF OTHER PORT CITIES IN JAPAN?
SHE'S GOT A POINT, AGENT 355.
WOULDN'T HURT TO AT LEAST CHECK OUT HER MOM'S LAB, YEAH? AS LONG AS WE'RE HERE?
AMPERSAND'S TRACKING DEVICE HAS A LAG TIME, ROSE. WE HAVE TO FIND THE ANIMAL BEFORE HE'S MOVED AGAIN.
UNLESS HE'S BEEN MOVED BACK HERE ALREADY, IN WHICH CASE, A SIDE TRIP TO THE CAPITAL WOULD JUST WASTE EVEN MORE TIME.
PLEASE, THREE-FIFTY. I SWEAR, I'M NOT SEEKING OUT MY MOTHER BECAUSE I WANT A...A HOME-COOKED MEAL. THIS IS IMPORTANT.
WHY DON'T DOC AND ROSE CHECK OUT MAMA MANN'S JOINT WHILE 355 AND I HIT NEO TOKYO?
WE CAN RENDEZVOUS BACK HERE TOMORROW.
SOUNDS LIKE A PLAN. UNLESS YOU NEED A GUIDE, 355?
THIS ISN'T MY FIRST TIME HERE, THANKS.

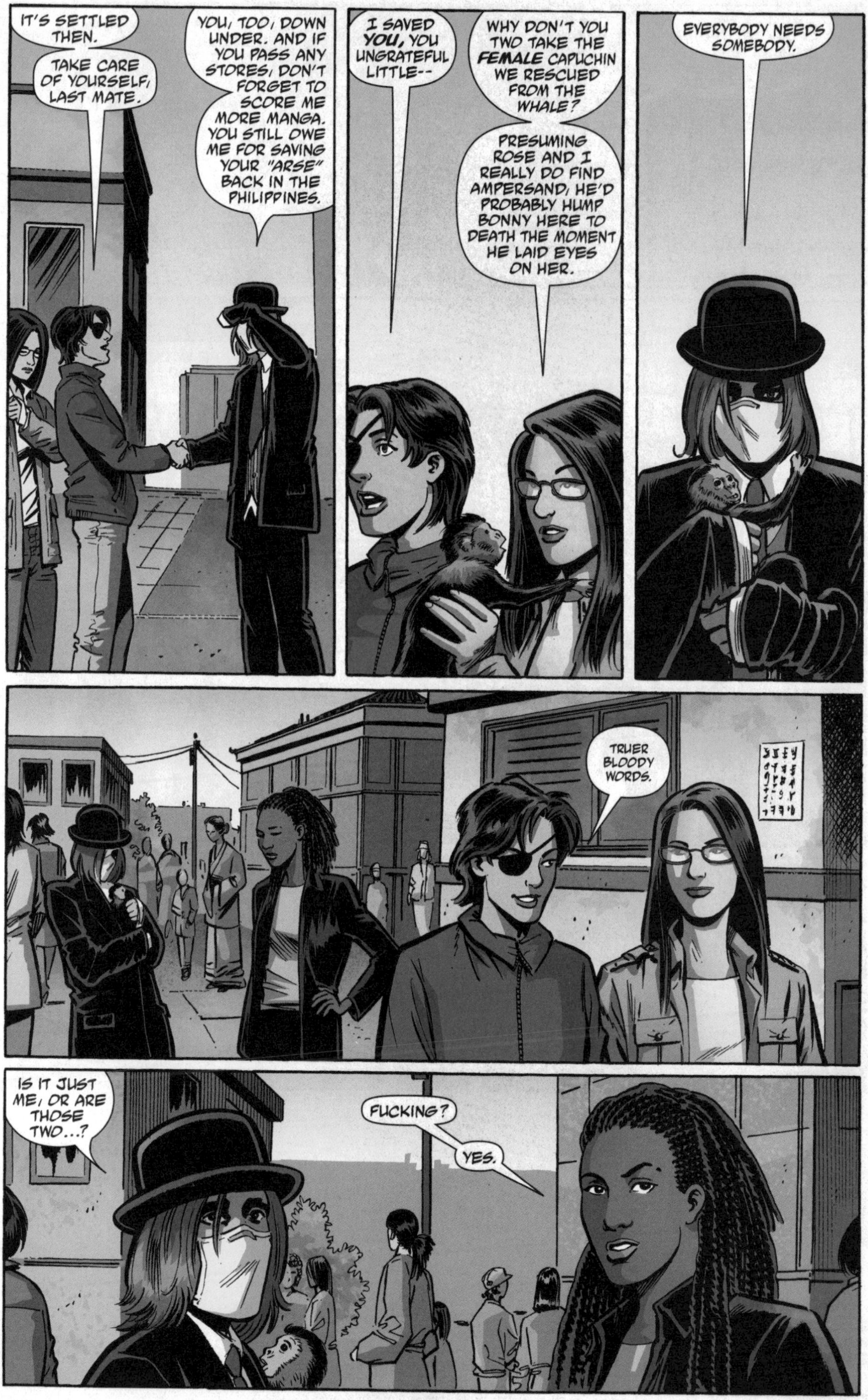
IT'S SETTLED THEN.
TAKE CARE OF YOURSELF, LAST MATE.
YOU, TOO, DOWN UNDER. AND IF YOU PASS ANY STORES, DON'T FORGET TO SCORE ME MORE MANGA. YOU STILL OWE ME FOR SAVING YOUR "ARSE" BACK IN THE PHILIPPINES.
I SAVED **YOU,** YOU UNGRATEFUL LITTLE--
WHY DON'T YOU TWO TAKE THE **FEMALE** CAPUCHIN WE RESCUED FROM THE WHALE?
PRESUMING ROSE AND I REALLY DO FIND AMPERSAND, HE'D PROBABLY HUMP BONNY HERE TO DEATH THE MOMENT HE LAID EYES ON HER.
EVERYBODY NEEDS SOMEBODY.
TRUER BLOODY WORDS.
IS IT JUST ME, OR ARE THOSE TWO...?
FUCKING?
YES.

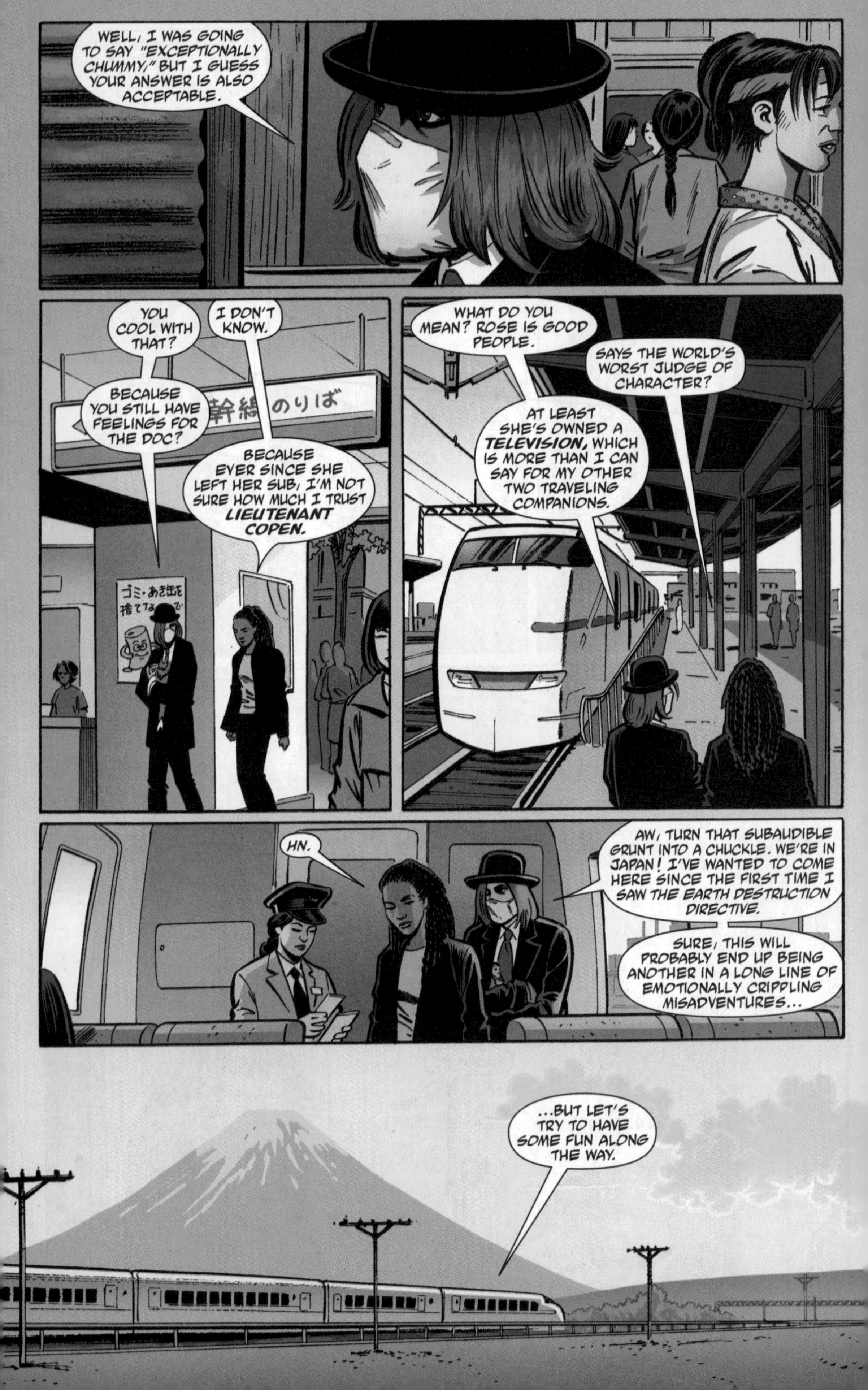

WELL, I WAS GOING TO SAY "EXCEPTIONALLY CHUMMY," BUT I GUESS YOUR ANSWER IS ALSO ACCEPTABLE.
YOU COOL WITH THAT?
BECAUSE YOU STILL HAVE FEELINGS FOR THE DOC?
I DON'T KNOW.
BECAUSE EVER SINCE SHE LEFT HER SUB, I'M NOT SURE HOW MUCH I TRUST **LIEUTENANT COPEN.**
幹線のりば
ゴミ・あき缶を
WHAT DO YOU MEAN? ROSE IS GOOD PEOPLE.
SAYS THE WORLD'S WORST JUDGE OF CHARACTER?
AT LEAST SHE'S OWNED A **TELEVISION,** WHICH IS MORE THAN I CAN SAY FOR MY OTHER TWO TRAVELING COMPANIONS.
HN.
AW, TURN THAT SUBAUDIBLE GRUNT INTO A CHUCKLE. WE'RE IN JAPAN! I'VE WANTED TO COME HERE SINCE THE FIRST TIME I SAW THE EARTH DESTRUCTION DIRECTIVE.
SURE, THIS WILL PROBABLY END UP BEING ANOTHER IN A LONG LINE OF EMOTIONALLY CRIPPLING MISADVENTURES...
...BUT LET'S TRY TO HAVE SOME FUN ALONG THE WAY.

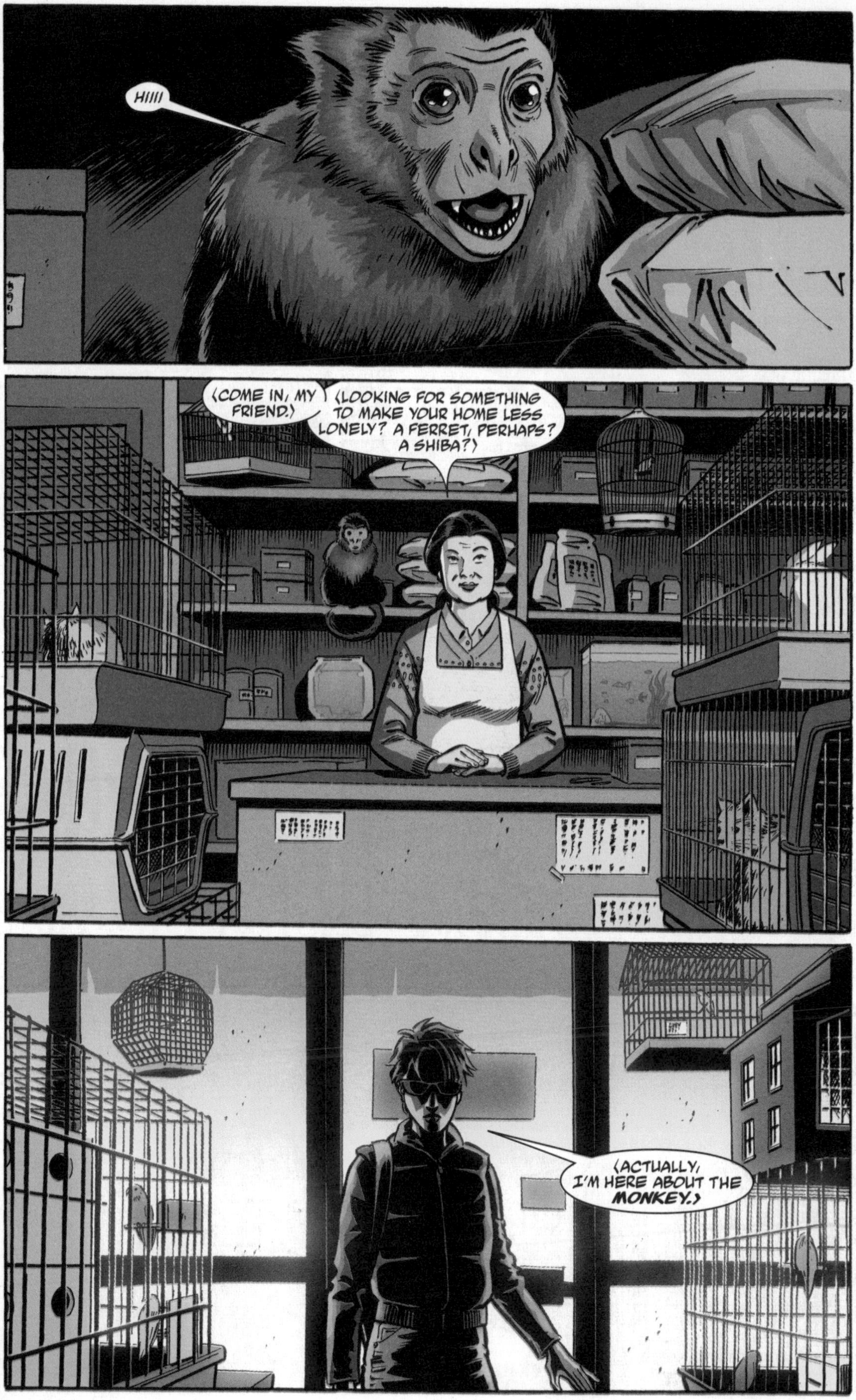
HI!!!
‹COME IN, MY FRIEND.›
‹LOOKING FOR SOMETHING TO MAKE YOUR HOME LESS LONELY? A FERRET, PERHAPS? A SHIBA?›
‹ACTUALLY, I'M HERE ABOUT THE MONKEY.›

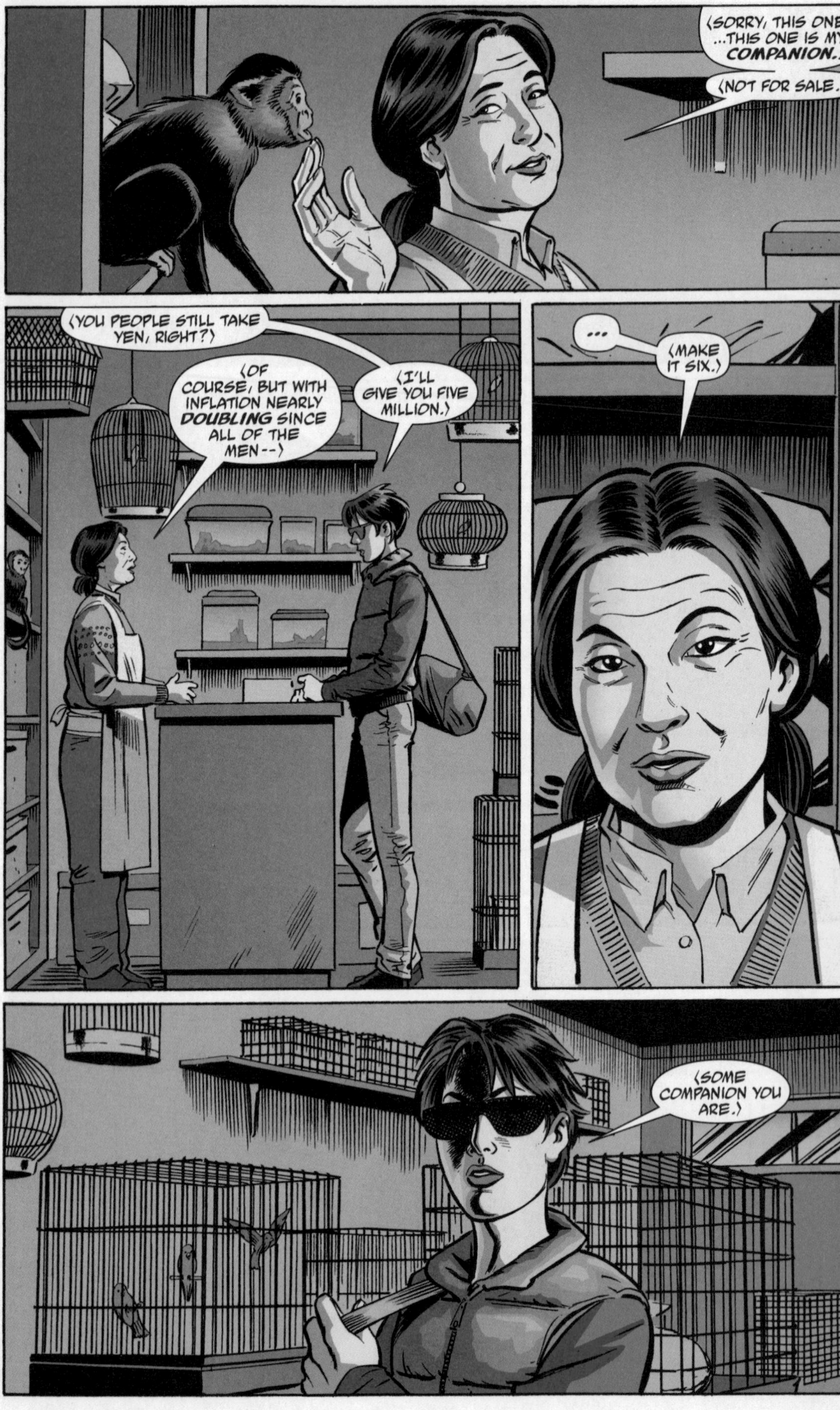
⟨SORRY, THIS ONE ...THIS ONE IS MY COMPANION.⟩
⟨NOT FOR SALE.⟩
⟨YOU PEOPLE STILL TAKE YEN, RIGHT?⟩
⟨OF COURSE, BUT WITH INFLATION NEARLY DOUBLING SINCE ALL OF THE MEN--⟩
⟨I'LL GIVE YOU FIVE MILLION.⟩
...
⟨MAKE IT SIX.⟩
⟨SOME COMPANION YOU ARE.⟩

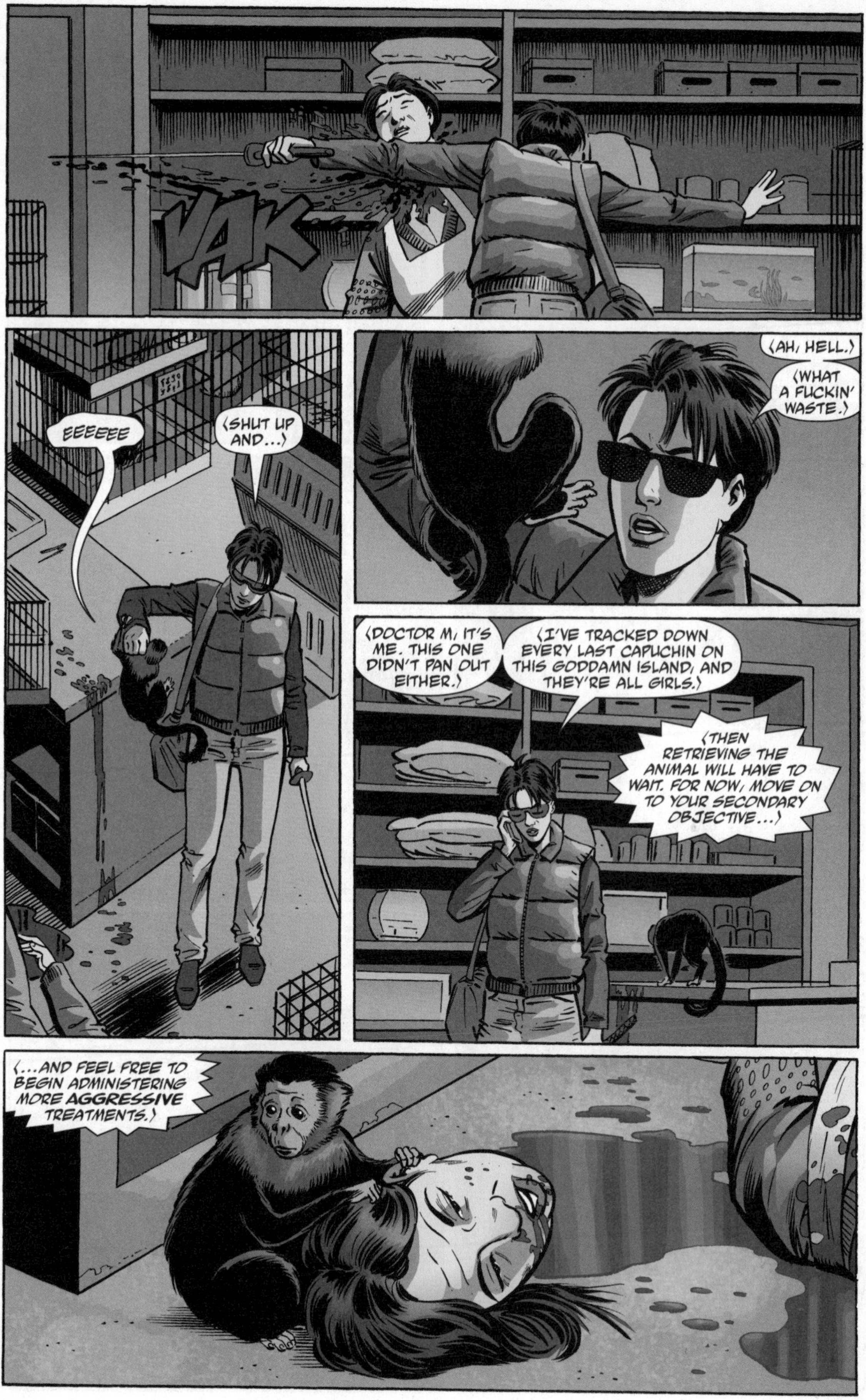
VAK
EEEEEE
⟨SHUT UP AND...⟩
⟨AH, HELL.⟩
⟨WHAT A FUCKIN' WASTE.⟩
⟨DOCTOR M, IT'S ME. THIS ONE DIDN'T PAN OUT EITHER.⟩
⟨I'VE TRACKED DOWN EVERY LAST CAPUCHIN ON THIS GODDAMN ISLAND, AND THEY'RE ALL GIRLS.⟩
⟨THEN RETRIEVING THE ANIMAL WILL HAVE TO WAIT. FOR NOW, MOVE ON TO YOUR SECONDARY OBJECTIVE...⟩
⟨...AND FEEL FREE TO BEGIN ADMINISTERING MORE **AGGRESSIVE** TREATMENTS.⟩

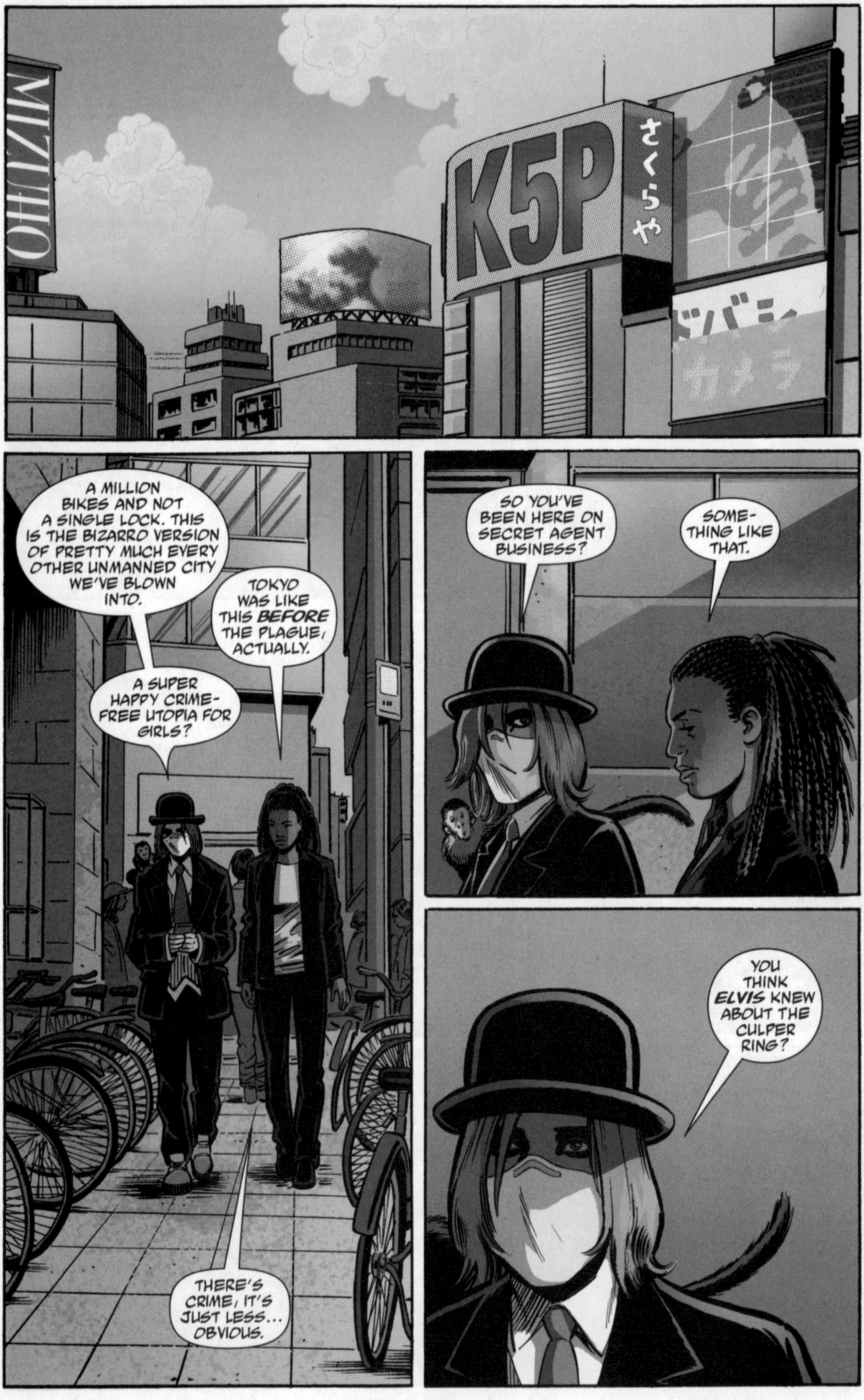
MIZUHO
K5P
さくらや
カメラ
A MILLION BIKES AND NOT A SINGLE LOCK. THIS IS THE BIZARRO VERSION OF PRETTY MUCH EVERY OTHER UNMANNED CITY WE'VE BLOWN INTO.
TOKYO WAS LIKE THIS ***BEFORE*** THE PLAGUE, ACTUALLY.
A SUPER HAPPY CRIME-FREE UTOPIA FOR GIRLS?
THERE'S CRIME; IT'S JUST LESS... OBVIOUS.
SO YOU'VE BEEN HERE ON SECRET AGENT BUSINESS?
SOME-THING LIKE THAT.
YOU THINK ***ELVIS*** KNEW ABOUT THE CULPER RING?

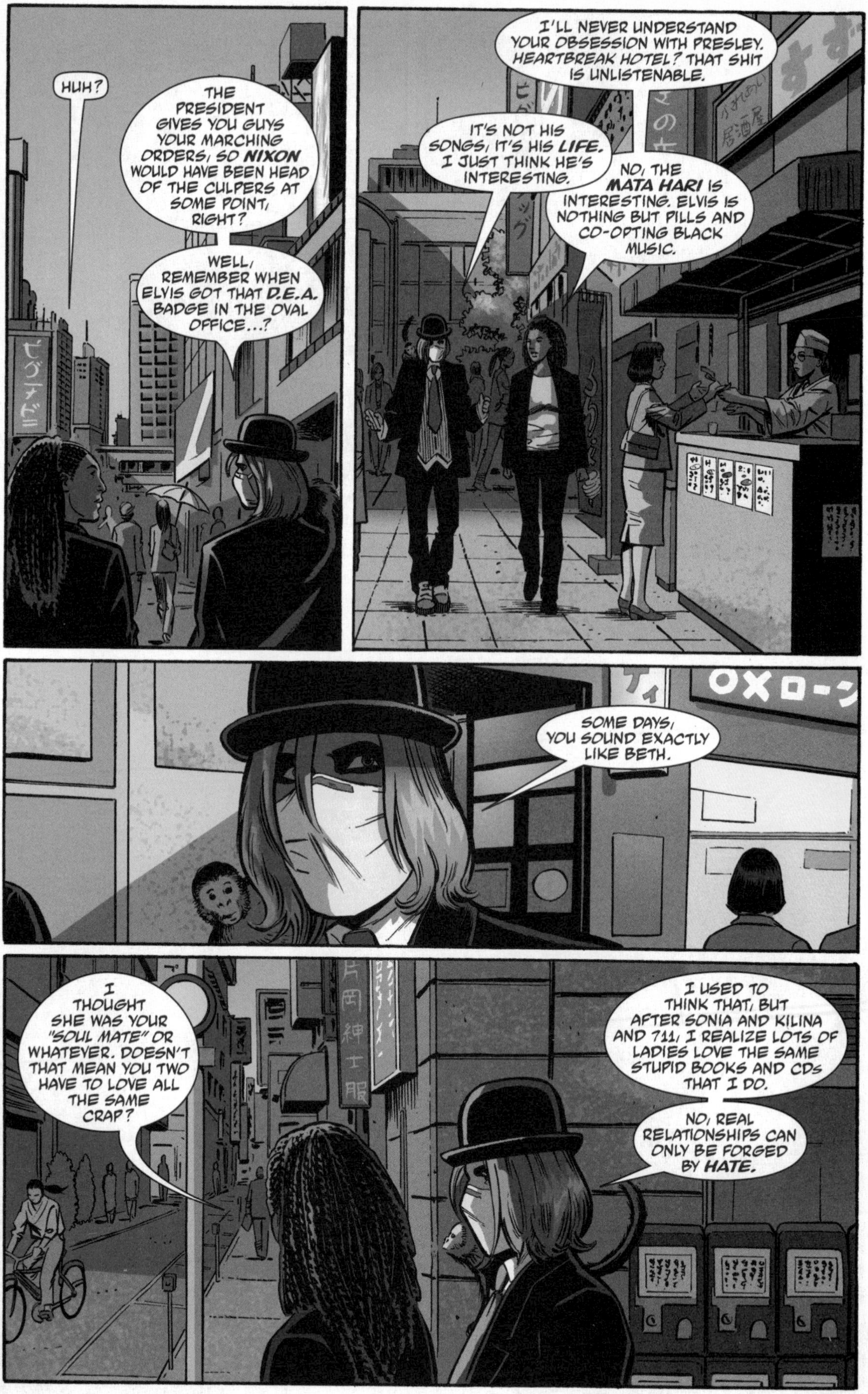
HUH?
THE PRESIDENT GIVES YOU GUYS YOUR MARCHING ORDERS, SO **NIXON** WOULD HAVE BEEN HEAD OF THE CULPERS AT SOME POINT, RIGHT?
WELL, REMEMBER WHEN ELVIS GOT THAT **D.E.A.** BADGE IN THE OVAL OFFICE...?
I'LL NEVER UNDERSTAND YOUR OBSESSION WITH PRESLEY. HEARTBREAK HOTEL? THAT SHIT IS UNLISTENABLE.
IT'S NOT HIS SONGS, IT'S HIS **LIFE.** I JUST THINK HE'S INTERESTING.
NO, THE **MATA HARI** IS INTERESTING. ELVIS IS NOTHING BUT PILLS AND CO-OPTING BLACK MUSIC.
SOME DAYS, YOU SOUND EXACTLY LIKE BETH.
I THOUGHT SHE WAS YOUR "SOUL MATE" OR WHATEVER. DOESN'T THAT MEAN YOU TWO HAVE TO LOVE ALL THE SAME CRAP?
I USED TO THINK THAT, BUT AFTER SONIA AND KILINA AND 711, I REALIZE LOTS OF LADIES LOVE THE SAME STUPID BOOKS AND CDs THAT I DO.
NO, REAL RELATIONSHIPS CAN ONLY BE FORGED BY **HATE.**

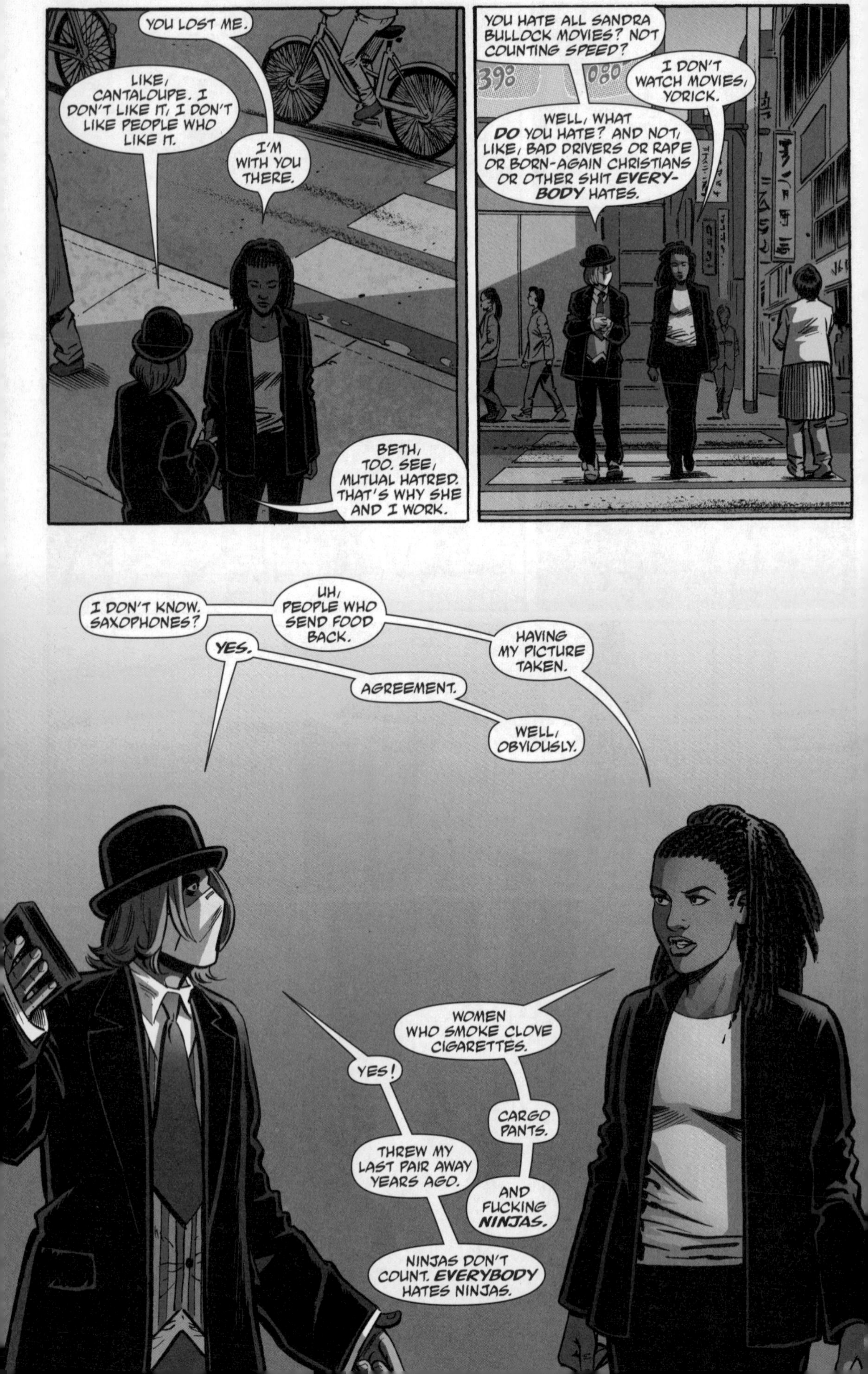
YOU LOST ME.
LIKE, CANTALOUPE. I DON'T LIKE IT, I DON'T LIKE PEOPLE WHO LIKE IT.
I'M WITH YOU THERE.
BETH, TOO. SEE, MUTUAL HATRED. THAT'S WHY SHE AND I WORK.
YOU HATE ALL SANDRA BULLOCK MOVIES? NOT COUNTING SPEED?
I DON'T WATCH MOVIES, YORICK.
WELL, WHAT DO YOU HATE? AND NOT, LIKE, BAD DRIVERS OR RAPE OR BORN-AGAIN CHRISTIANS OR OTHER SHIT EVERYBODY HATES.
I DON'T KNOW. SAXOPHONES?
UH, PEOPLE WHO SEND FOOD BACK.
HAVING MY PICTURE TAKEN.
YES.
AGREEMENT.
WELL, OBVIOUSLY.
WOMEN WHO SMOKE CLOVE CIGARETTES.
YES!
CARGO PANTS.
THREW MY LAST PAIR AWAY YEARS AGO.
AND FUCKING NINJAS.
NINJAS DON'T COUNT. EVERYBODY HATES NINJAS.

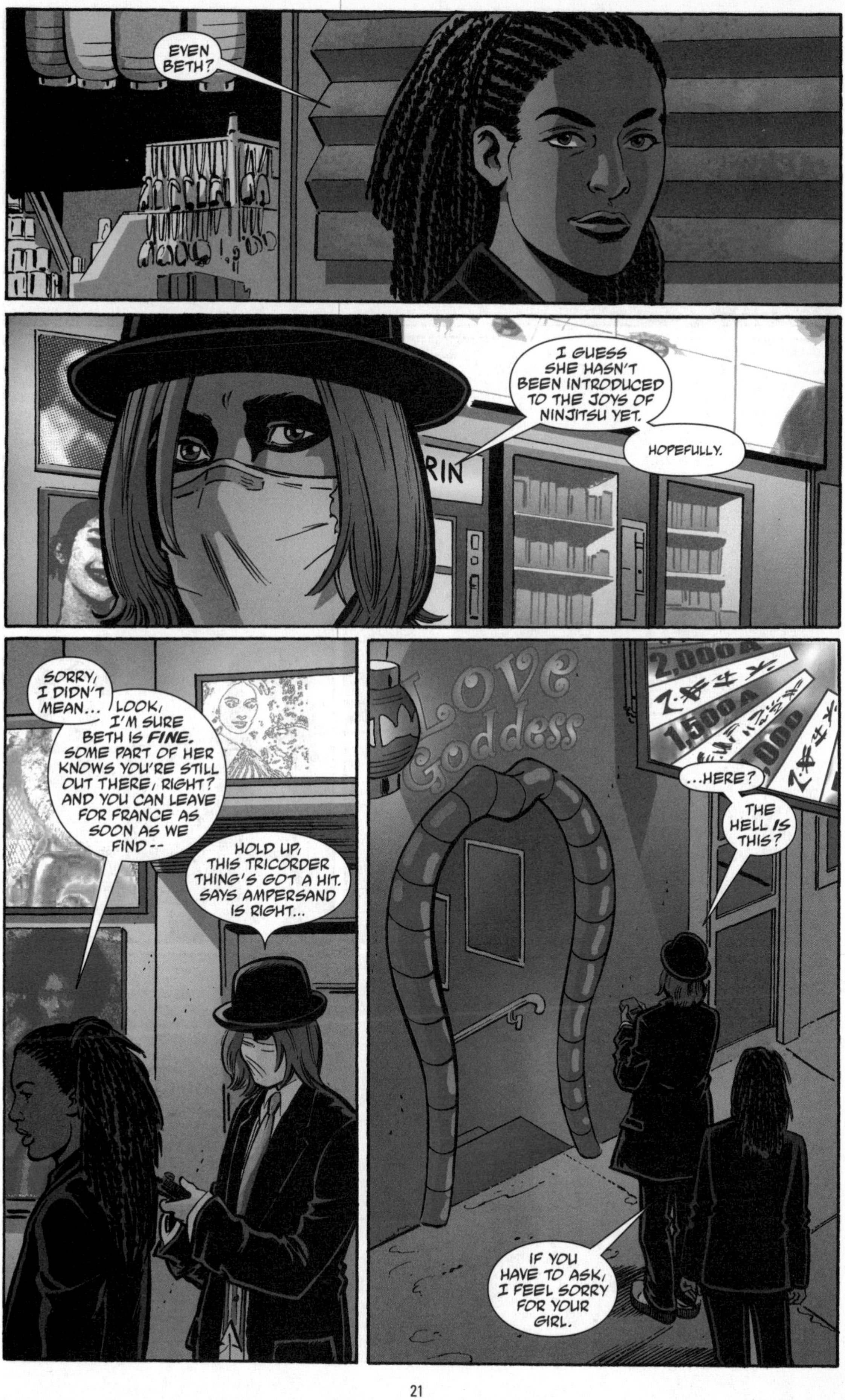
EVEN BETH?
I GUESS SHE HASN'T BEEN INTRODUCED TO THE JOYS OF NINJITSU YET.
HOPEFULLY.
RIN
SORRY, I DIDN'T MEAN...
LOOK, I'M SURE BETH IS **FINE.** SOME PART OF HER KNOWS YOU'RE STILL OUT THERE, RIGHT? AND YOU CAN LEAVE FOR FRANCE AS SOON AS WE FIND--
HOLD UP, THIS TRICORDER THING'S GOT A HIT. SAYS AMPERSAND IS RIGHT...
Love Goddess
2,000
1,500
...HERE?
THE HELL *IS* THIS?
IF YOU HAVE TO ASK, I FEEL SORRY FOR YOUR GIRL.

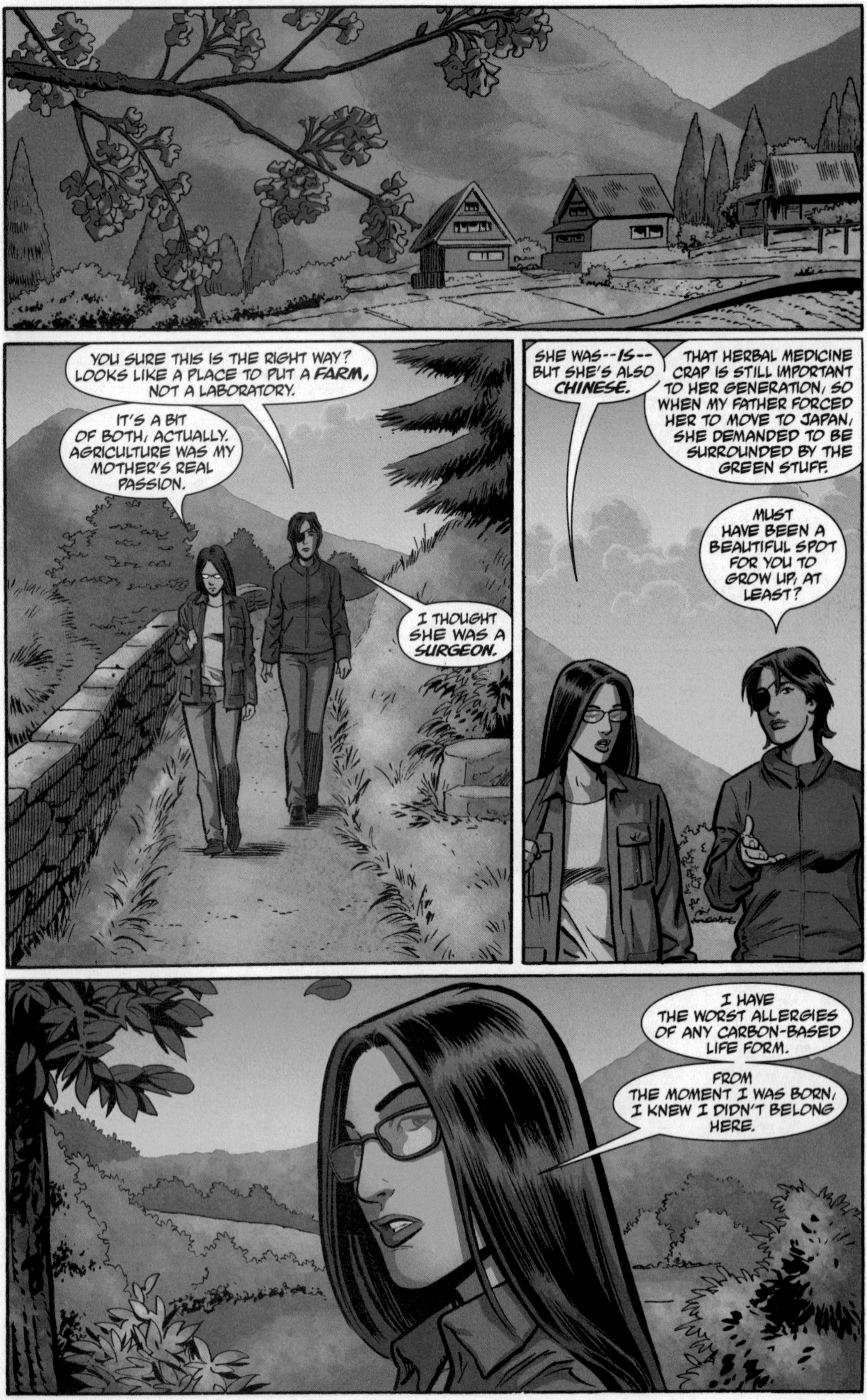
YOU SURE THIS IS THE RIGHT WAY? LOOKS LIKE A PLACE TO PUT A FARM, NOT A LABORATORY.
IT'S A BIT OF BOTH, ACTUALLY. AGRICULTURE WAS MY MOTHER'S REAL PASSION.
I THOUGHT SHE WAS A SURGEON.
SHE WAS--IS--BUT SHE'S ALSO CHINESE.
THAT HERBAL MEDICINE CRAP IS STILL IMPORTANT TO HER GENERATION, SO WHEN MY FATHER FORCED HER TO MOVE TO JAPAN, SHE DEMANDED TO BE SURROUNDED BY THE GREEN STUFF.
MUST HAVE BEEN A BEAUTIFUL SPOT FOR YOU TO GROW UP, AT LEAST?
I HAVE THE WORST ALLERGIES OF ANY CARBON-BASED LIFE FORM.
FROM THE MOMENT I WAS BORN, I KNEW I DIDN'T BELONG HERE.

WAIT, IF YOUR OLD MAN'S JAPANESE, HOW'D HE HOOK UP WITH YOUR MUM?

SOME CONFERENCE IN SHANGHAI. THOUGHT I ALREADY TOLD YOU THAT?

YEAH, BUT WHAT *KIND* OF CONFERENCE?

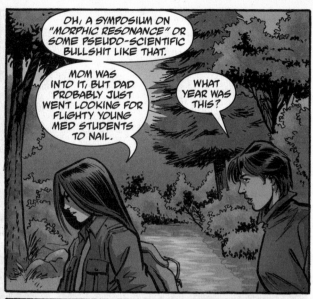

OH, A SYMPOSIUM ON "MORPHIC RESONANCE" OR SOME PSEUDO-SCIENTIFIC BULLSHIT LIKE THAT.

MOM WAS INTO IT, BUT DAD PROBABLY JUST WENT LOOKING FOR FLIGHTY YOUNG MED STUDENTS TO NAIL.

WHAT YEAR WAS THIS?

WHAT'S WITH THE INTERROGATION ALL OF A SUDDEN?

WHAT? NO, I...I JUST WANT TO KNOW EVERYTHING ABOUT YOU, ALLISON.

I *LIKE* YOU.

I THINK I'M STARTING TO...TO...

23

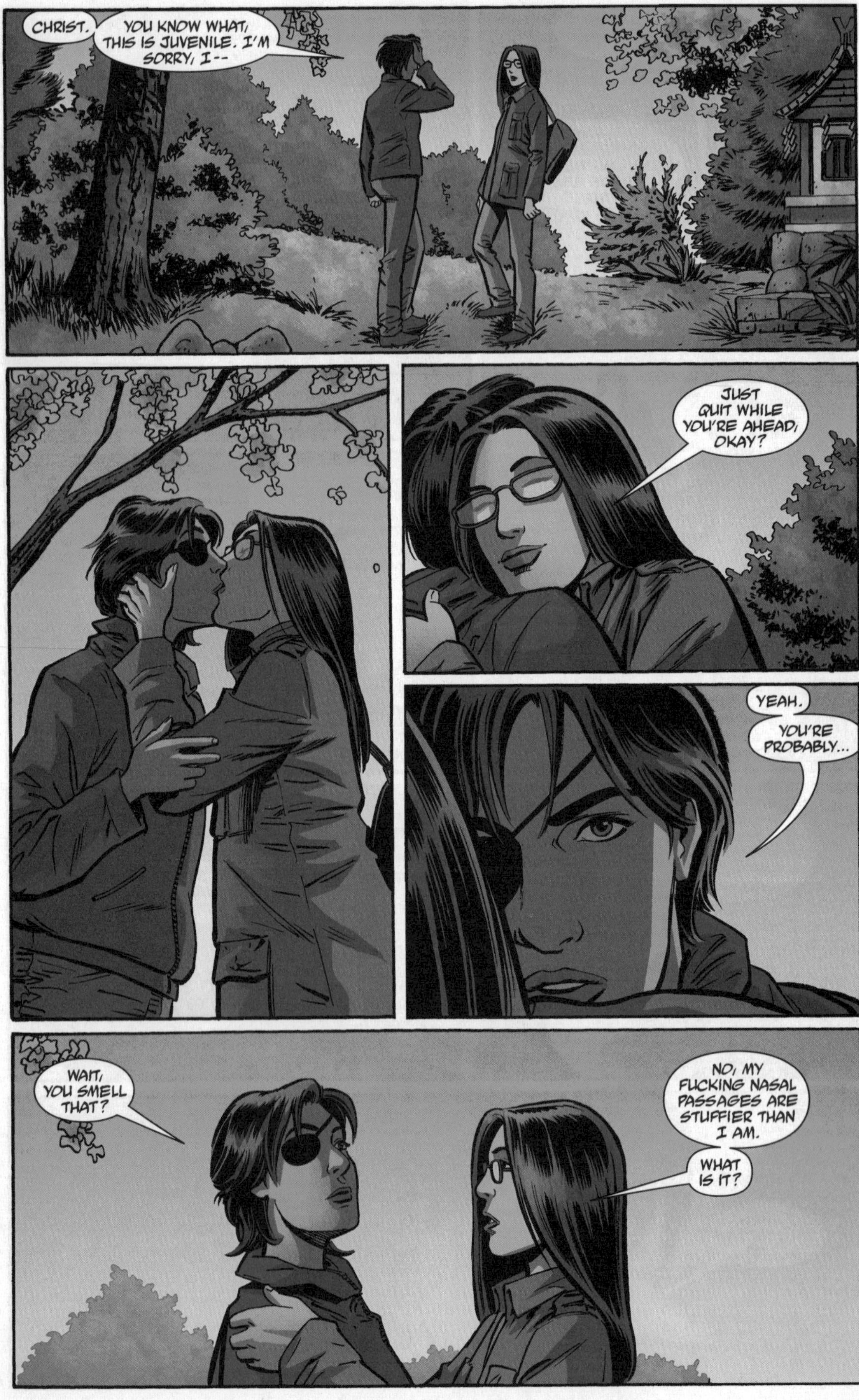
CHRIST.
YOU KNOW WHAT, THIS IS JUVENILE. I'M SORRY, I--
JUST QUIT WHILE YOU'RE AHEAD, OKAY?
YEAH.
YOU'RE PROBABLY...
WAIT, YOU SMELL THAT?
NO, MY FUCKING NASAL PASSAGES ARE STUFFIER THAN I AM.
WHAT IS IT?

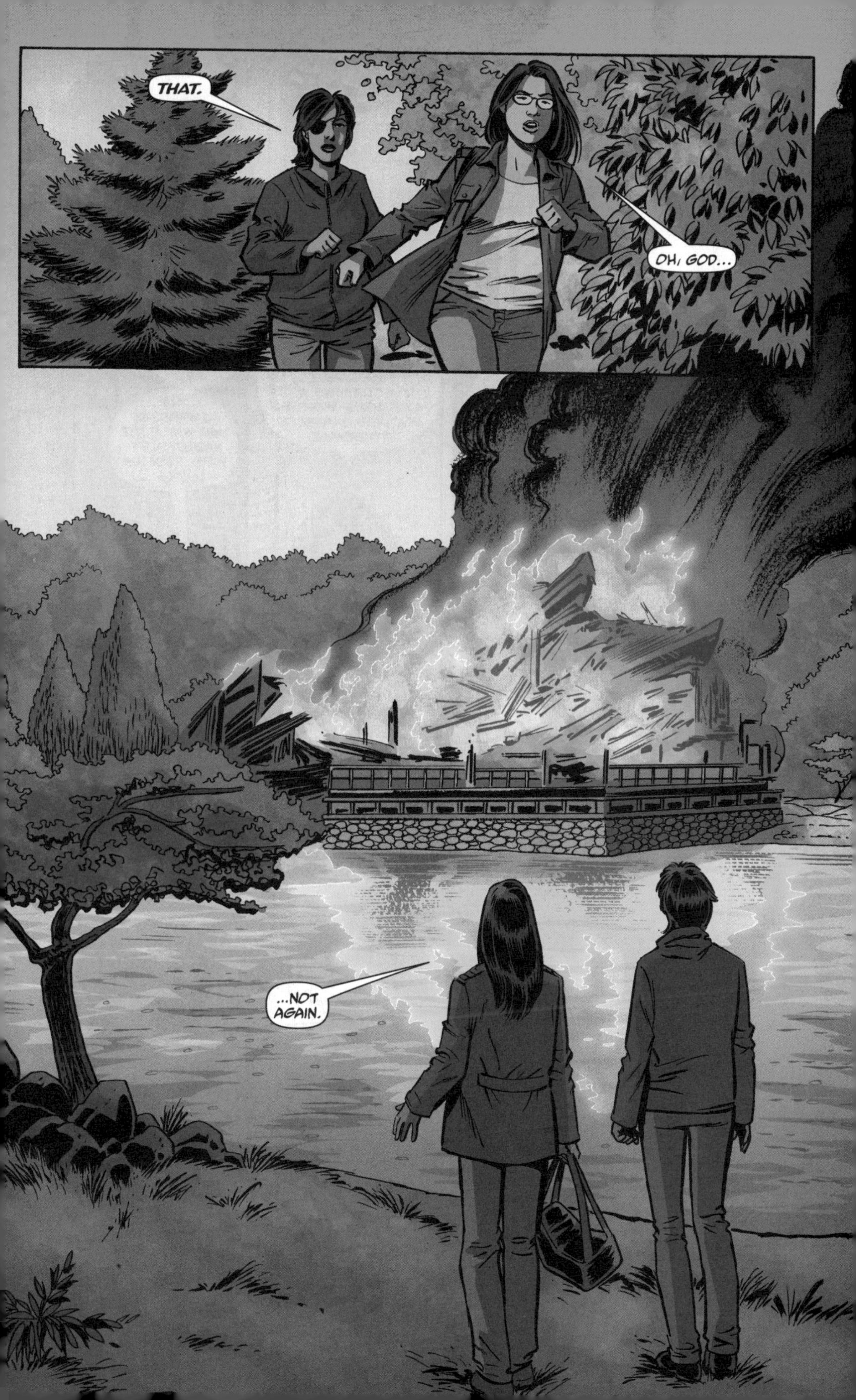
THAT.
OH, GOD...
...NOT AGAIN.

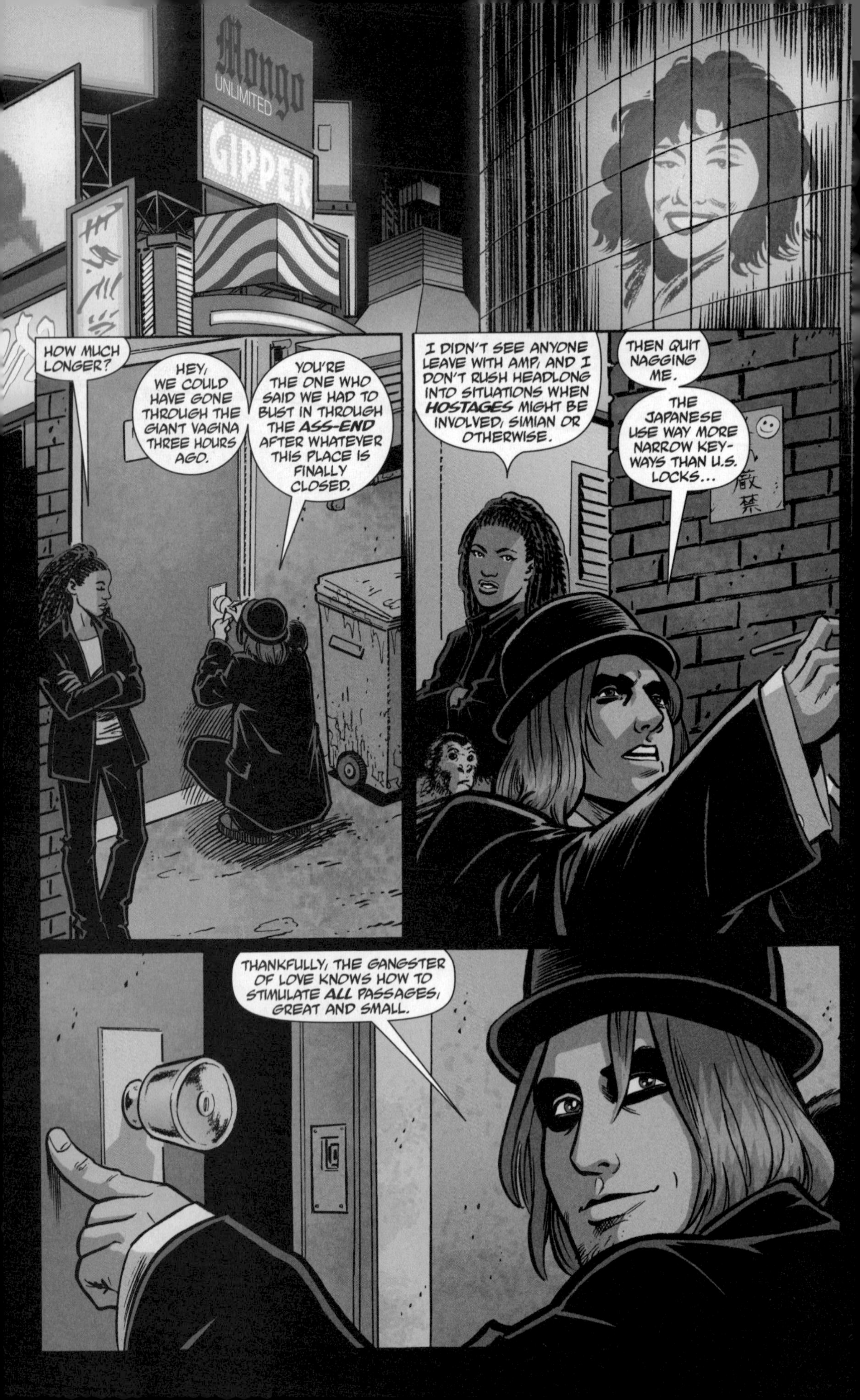

Mongo
UNLIMITED
GIPPER
HOW MUCH LONGER?
HEY, WE COULD HAVE GONE THROUGH THE GIANT VAGINA THREE HOURS AGO.
YOU'RE THE ONE WHO SAID WE HAD TO BUST IN THROUGH THE ASS-END AFTER WHATEVER THIS PLACE IS FINALLY CLOSED.
I DIDN'T SEE ANYONE LEAVE WITH AMP, AND I DON'T RUSH HEADLONG INTO SITUATIONS WHEN HOSTAGES MIGHT BE INVOLVED, SIMIAN OR OTHERWISE.
THEN QUIT NAGGING ME.
THE JAPANESE USE WAY MORE NARROW KEY-WAYS THAN U.S. LOCKS...
THANKFULLY, THE GANGSTER OF LOVE KNOWS HOW TO STIMULATE ALL PASSAGES, GREAT AND SMALL.

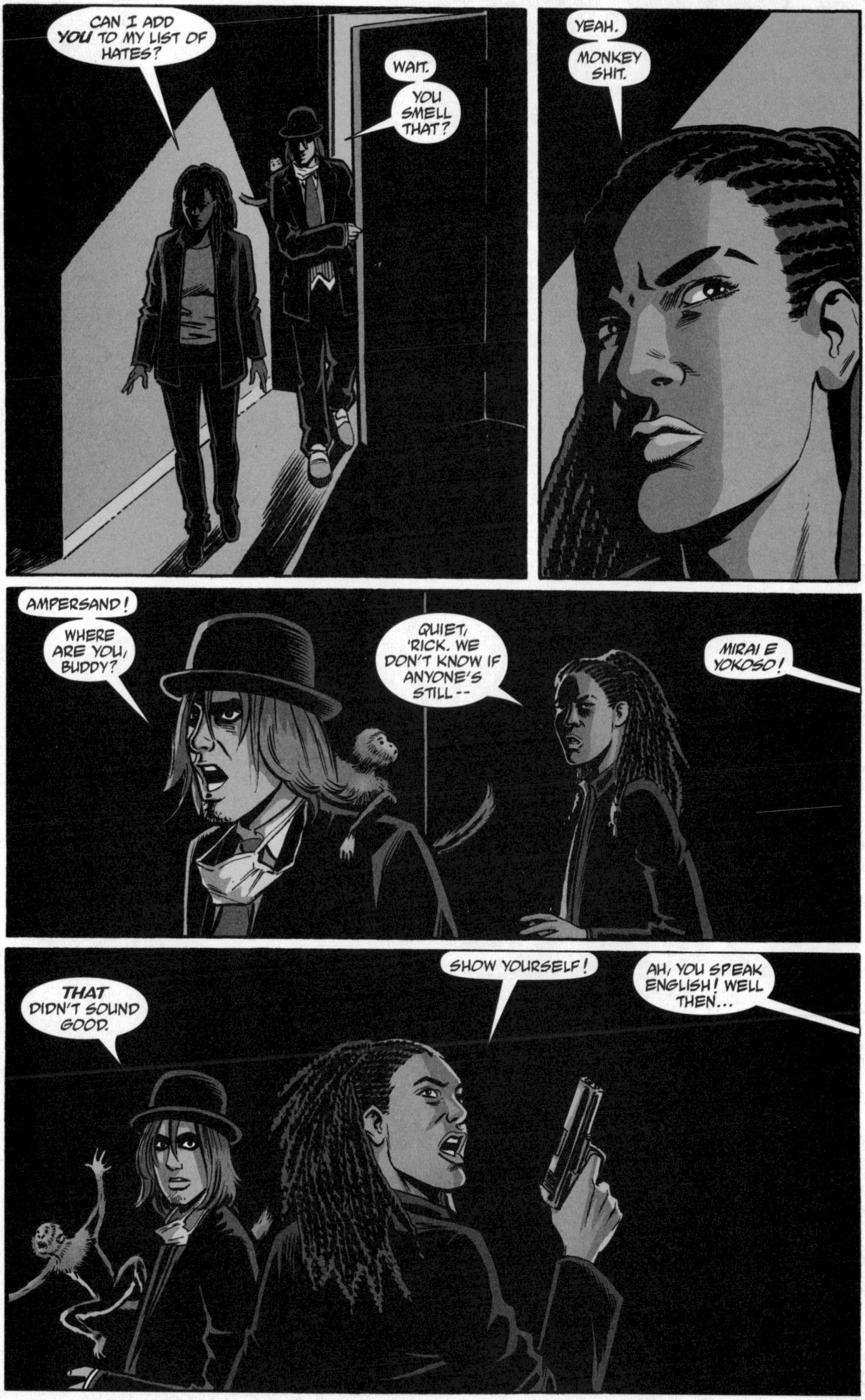
CAN I ADD YOU TO MY LIST OF HATES?
WAIT.
YOU SMELL THAT?
YEAH.
MONKEY SHIT.
AMPERSAND!
WHERE ARE YOU, BUDDY?
QUIET, 'RICK. WE DON'T KNOW IF ANYONE'S STILL --
MIRAI E YOKOSO!
THAT DIDN'T SOUND GOOD.
SHOW YOURSELF!
AH, YOU SPEAK ENGLISH! WELL THEN...

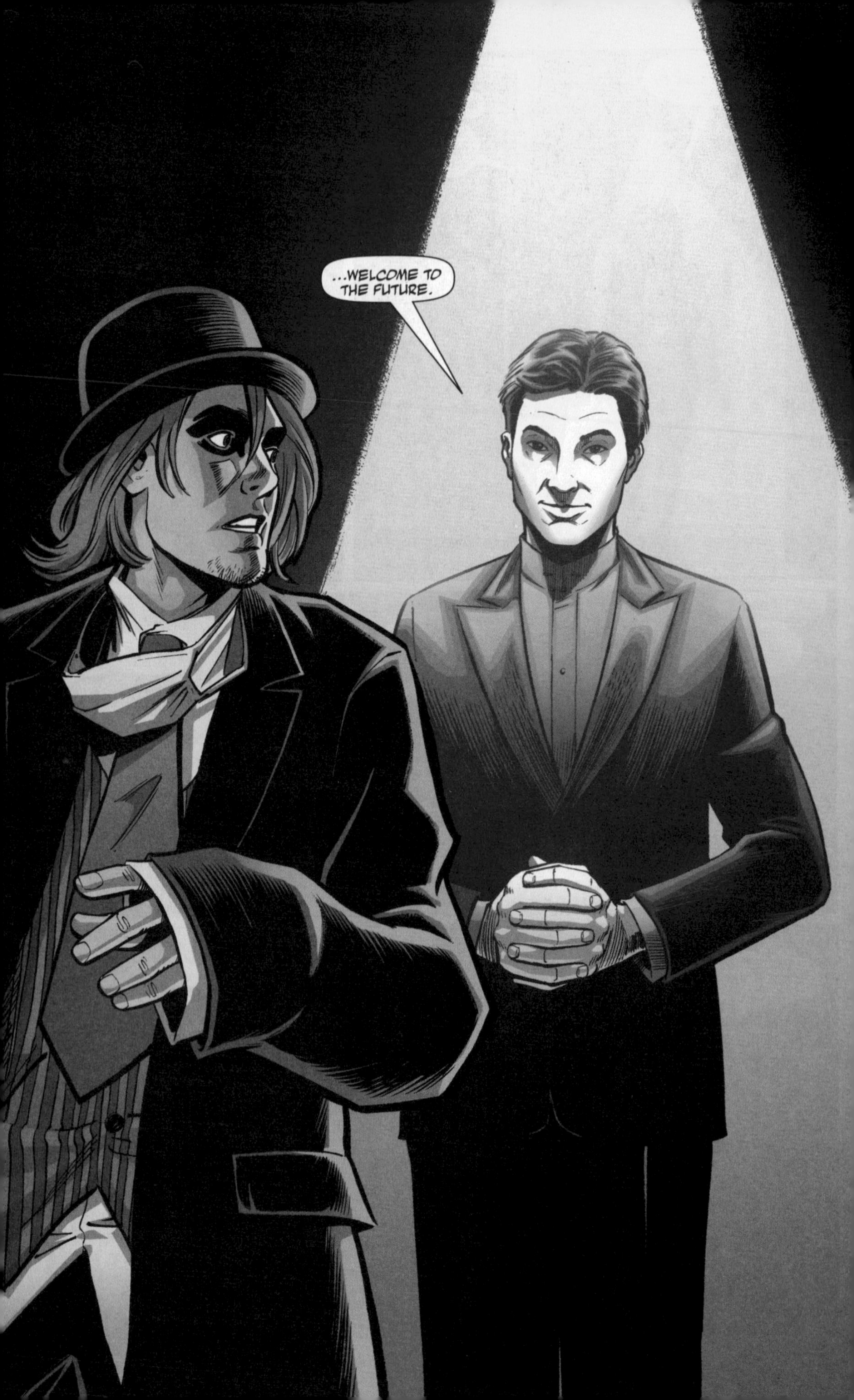
...WELCOME TO THE FUTURE.

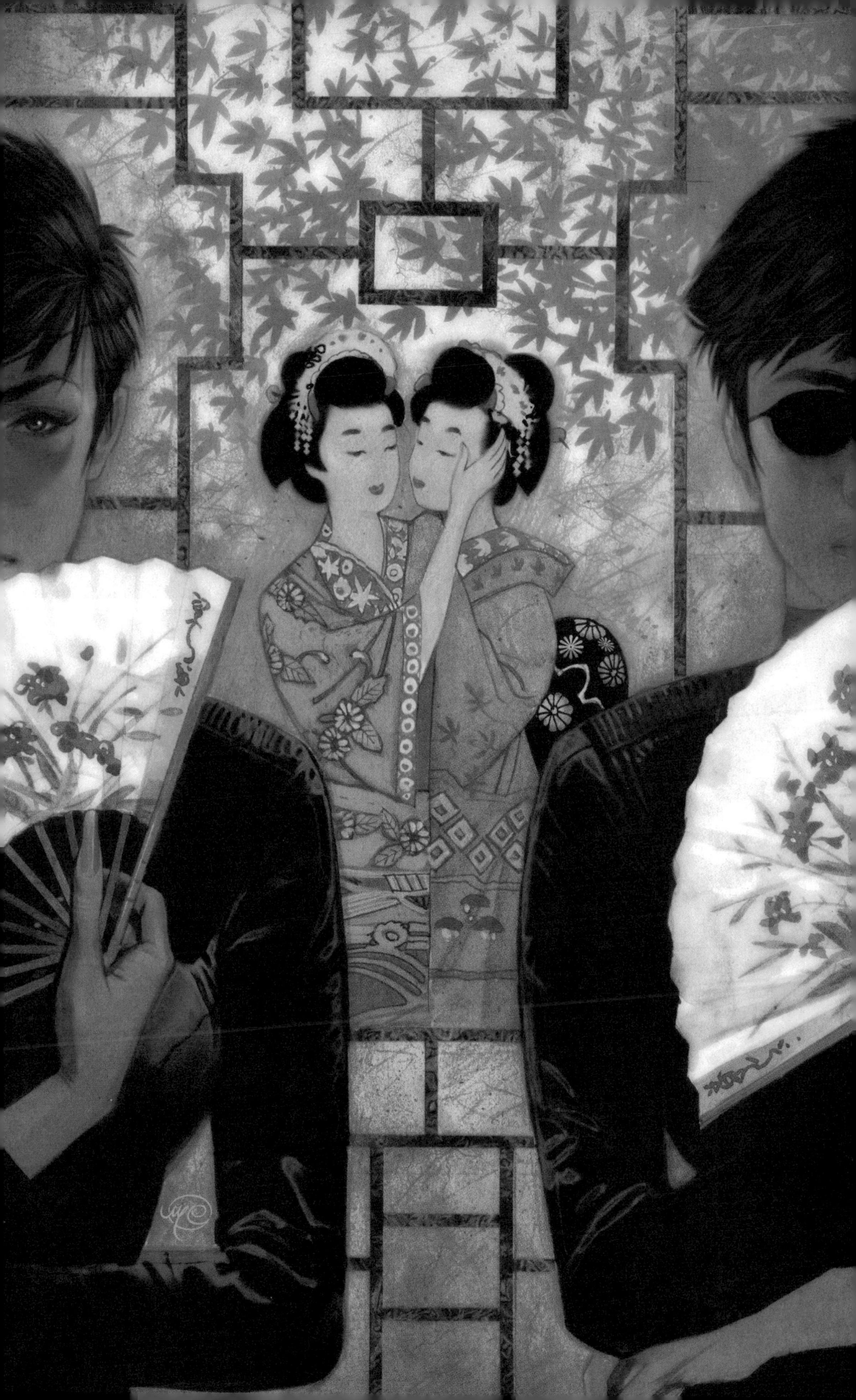

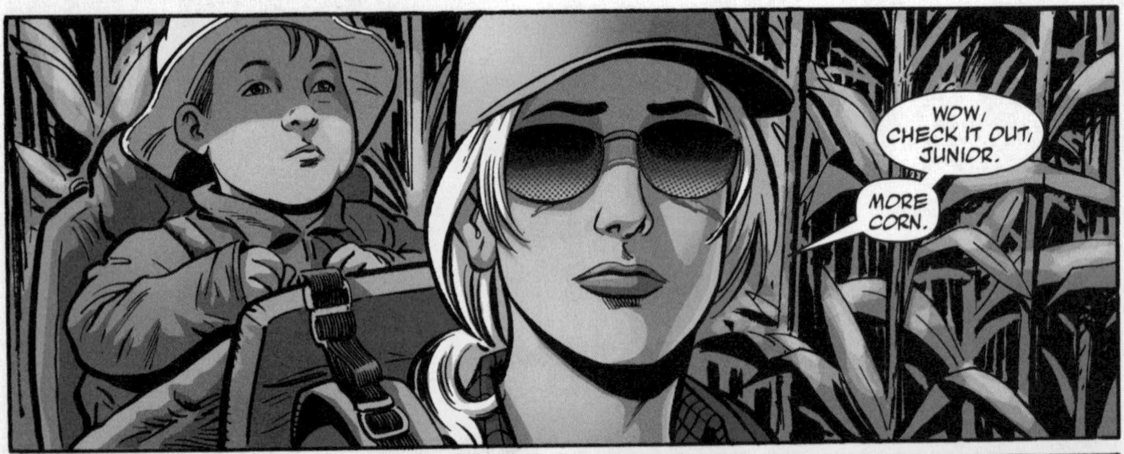
WOW, CHECK IT OUT, JUNIOR.
MORE CORN.

Oldenbrook, Kansas
Now

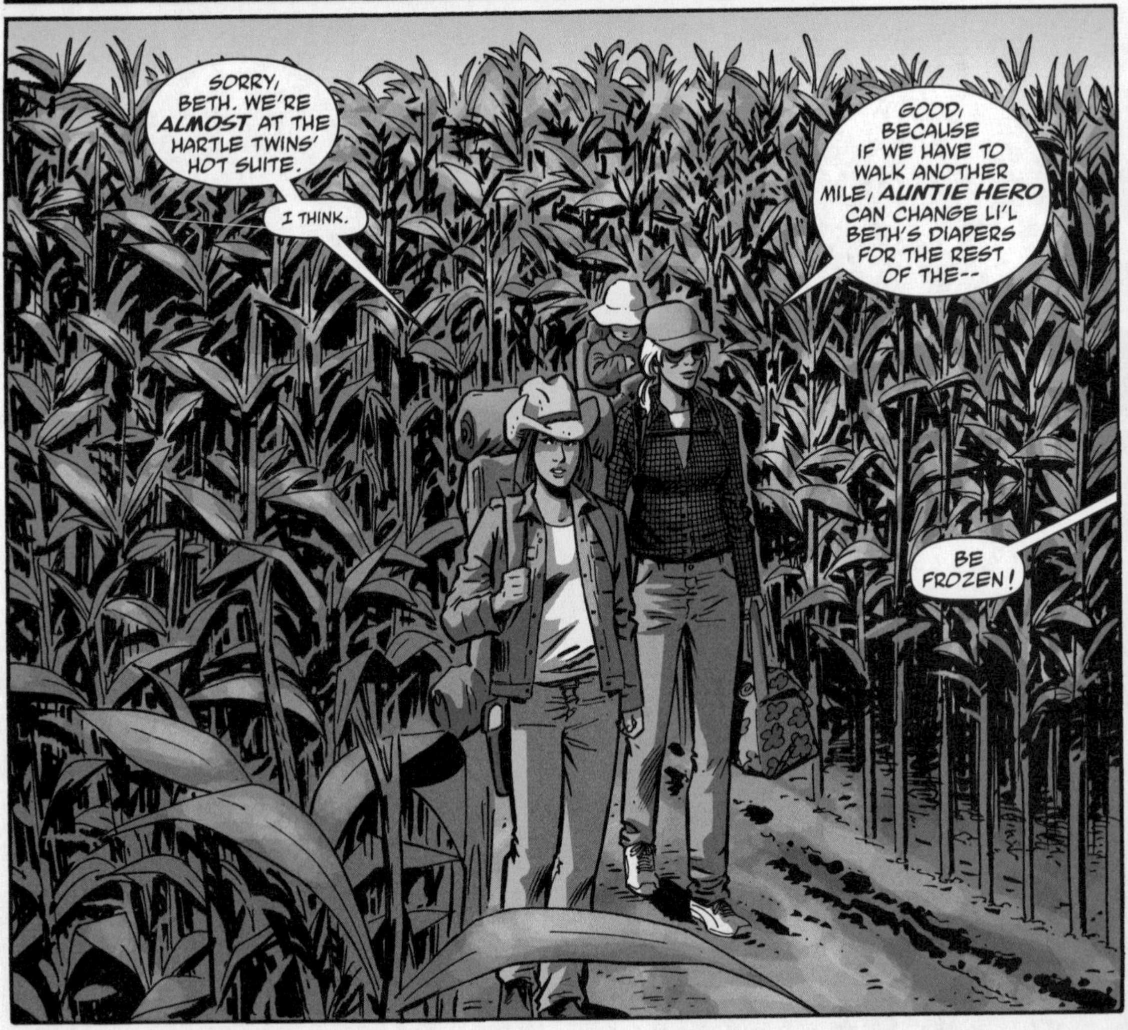
SORRY, BETH. WE'RE ALMOST AT THE HARTLE TWINS' HOT SUITE.
I THINK.
GOOD, BECAUSE IF WE HAVE TO WALK ANOTHER MILE, AUNTIE HERO CAN CHANGE LI'L BETH'S DIAPERS FOR THE REST OF THE--
BE FROZEN!

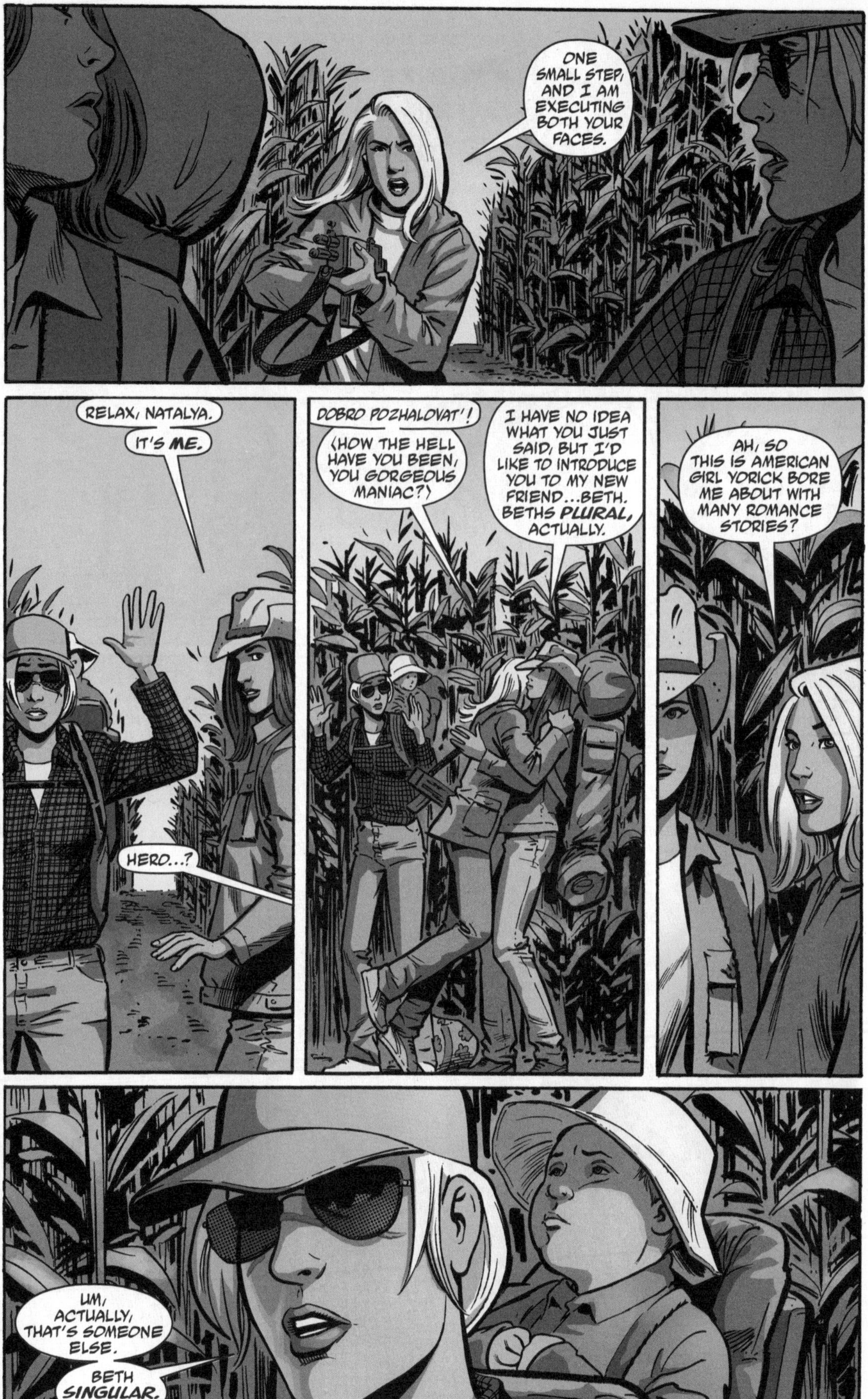
ONE SMALL STEP, AND I AM EXECUTING BOTH YOUR FACES.
RELAX, NATALYA.
IT'S ME.
HERO...?
DOBRO POZHALOVAT'!
(HOW THE HELL HAVE YOU BEEN, YOU GORGEOUS MANIAC?)
I HAVE NO IDEA WHAT YOU JUST SAID, BUT I'D LIKE TO INTRODUCE YOU TO MY NEW FRIEND...BETH. BETHS PLURAL, ACTUALLY.
AH, SO THIS IS AMERICAN GIRL YORICK BORE ME ABOUT WITH MANY ROMANCE STORIES?
UM, ACTUALLY, THAT'S SOMEONE ELSE.
BETH SINGULAR.

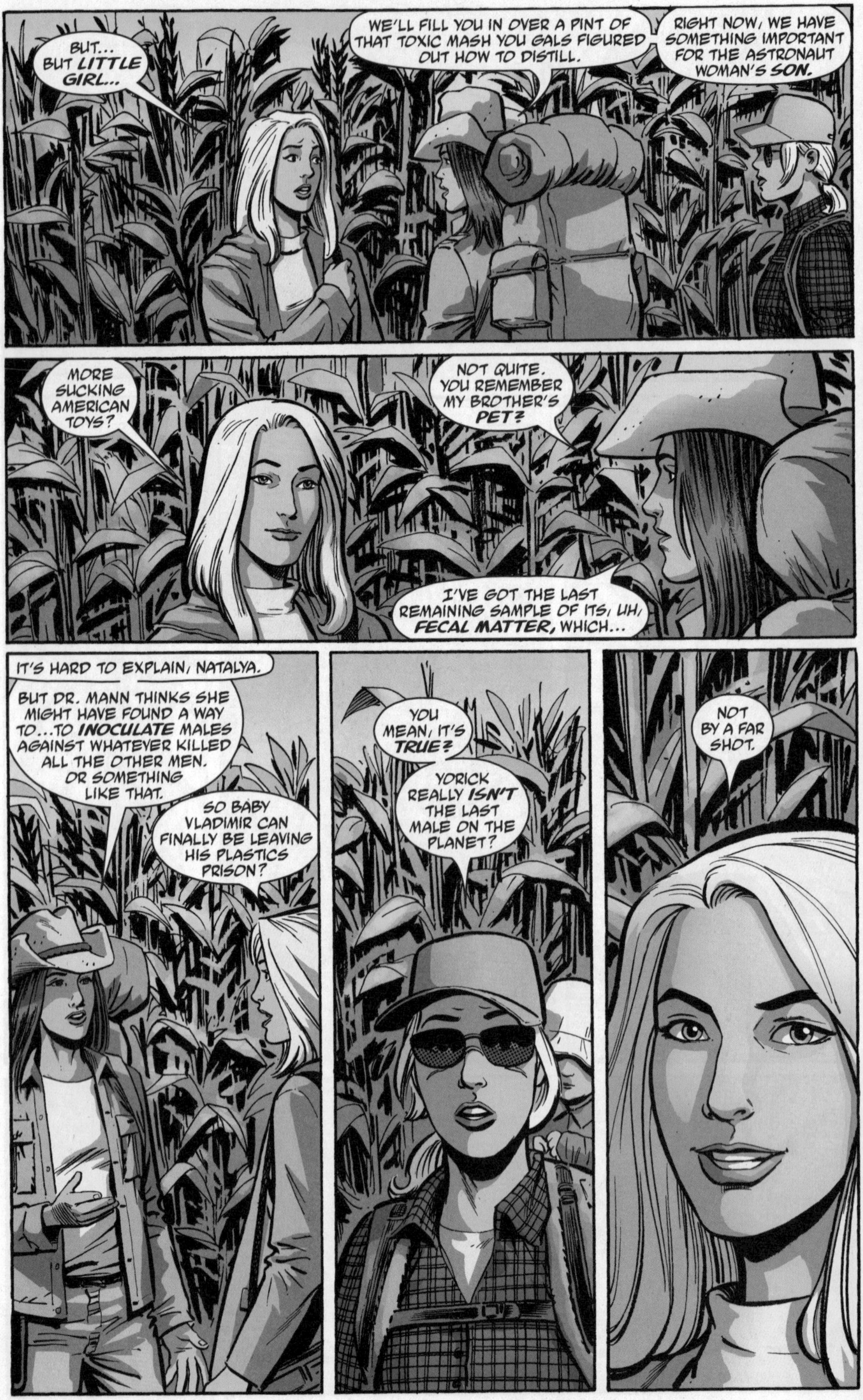
BUT... BUT LITTLE GIRL...
WE'LL FILL YOU IN OVER A PINT OF THAT TOXIC MASH YOU GALS FIGURED OUT HOW TO DISTILL.
RIGHT NOW, WE HAVE SOMETHING IMPORTANT FOR THE ASTRONAUT WOMAN'S SON.
MORE SUCKING AMERICAN TOYS?
NOT QUITE. YOU REMEMBER MY BROTHER'S PET?
I'VE GOT THE LAST REMAINING SAMPLE OF ITS, UH, FECAL MATTER, WHICH...
IT'S HARD TO EXPLAIN, NATALYA.
BUT DR. MANN THINKS SHE MIGHT HAVE FOUND A WAY TO...TO INOCULATE MALES AGAINST WHATEVER KILLED ALL THE OTHER MEN. OR SOMETHING LIKE THAT.
SO BABY VLADIMIR CAN FINALLY BE LEAVING HIS PLASTICS PRISON?
YOU MEAN, IT'S TRUE?
YORICK REALLY ISN'T THE LAST MALE ON THE PLANET?
NOT BY A FAR SHOT.

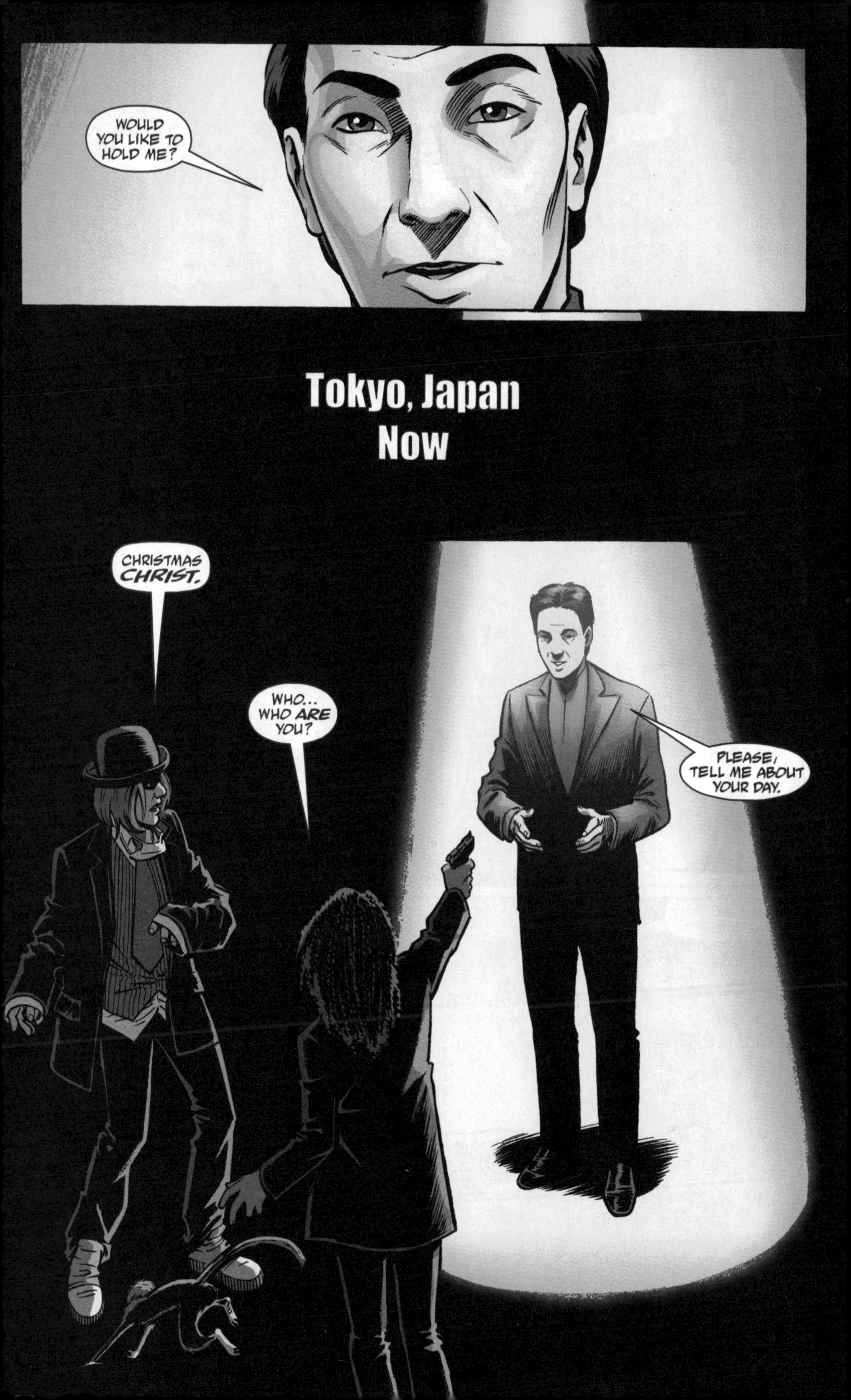
WOULD YOU LIKE TO HOLD ME?
Tokyo, Japan
Now
CHRISTMAS CHRIST.
WHO... WHO ARE YOU?
PLEASE, TELL ME ABOUT YOUR DAY.

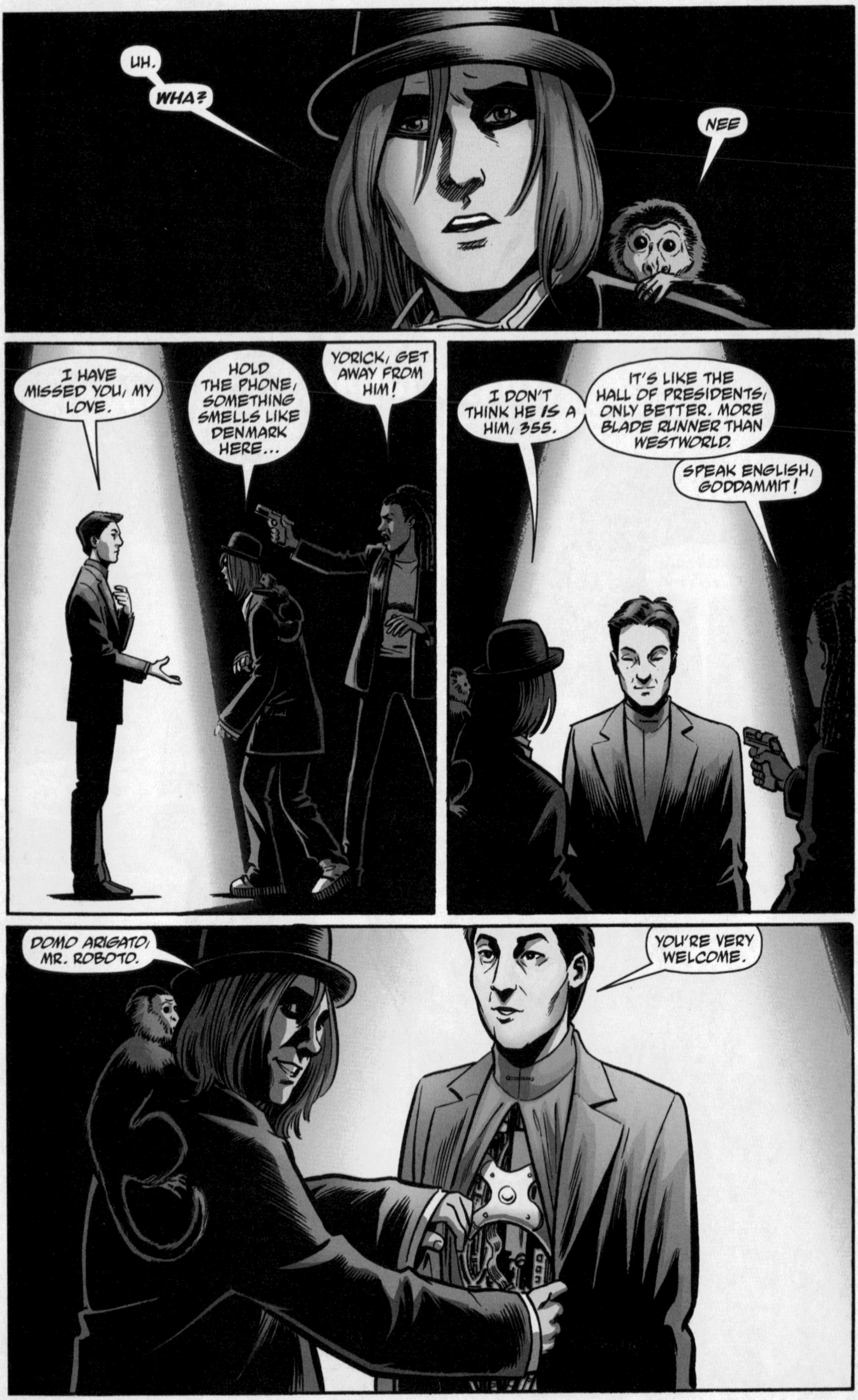
UH.
WHA?
NEE
I HAVE MISSED YOU, MY LOVE.
HOLD THE PHONE, SOMETHING SMELLS LIKE DENMARK HERE...
YORICK, GET AWAY FROM HIM!
I DON'T THINK HE IS A HIM, 355.
IT'S LIKE THE HALL OF PRESIDENTS, ONLY BETTER. MORE BLADE RUNNER THAN WESTWORLD.
SPEAK ENGLISH, GODDAMMIT!
DOMO ARIGATO, MR. ROBOTO.
YOU'RE VERY WELCOME.

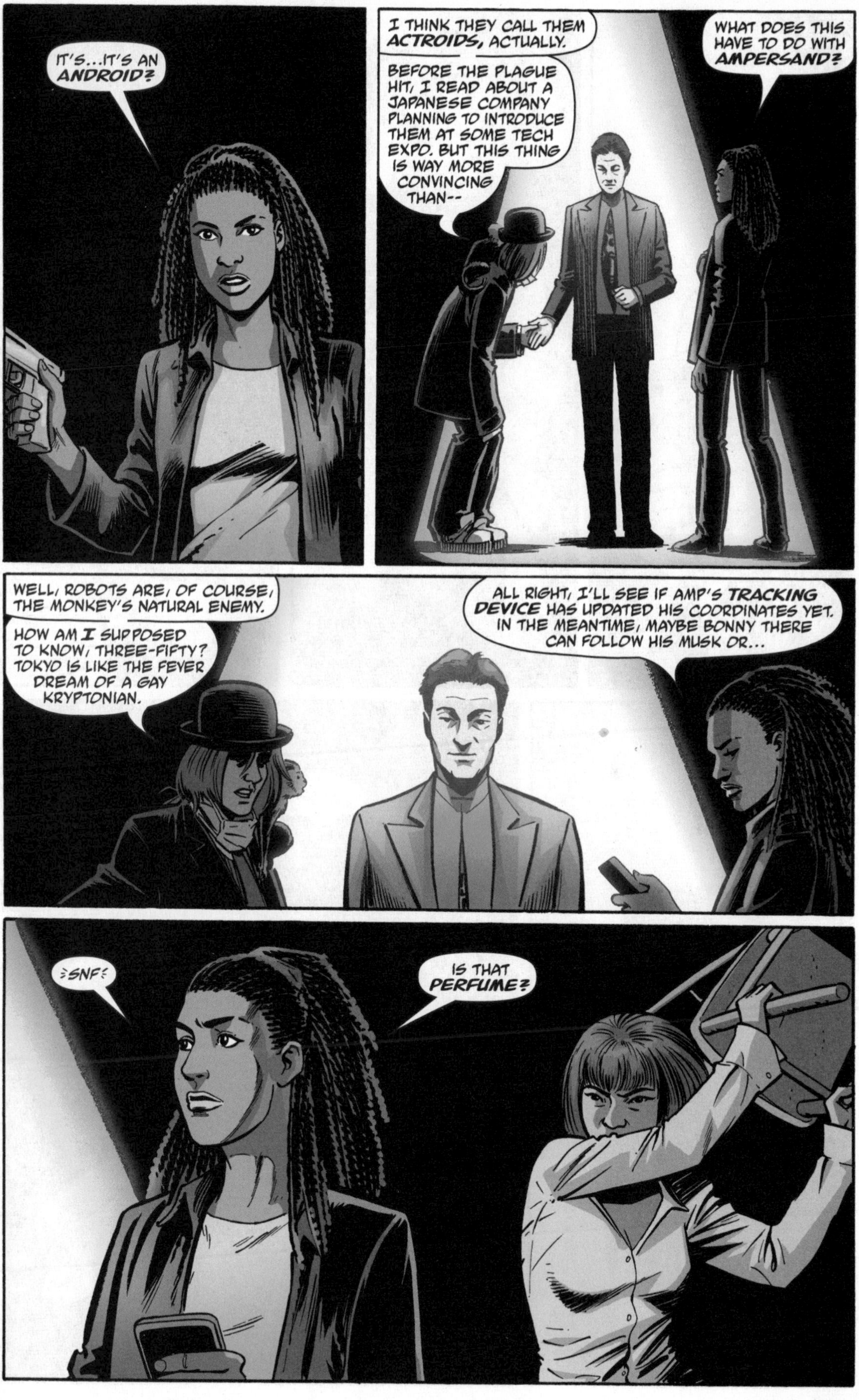
IT'S...IT'S AN ANDROID?
I THINK THEY CALL THEM ACTROIDS, ACTUALLY.
BEFORE THE PLAGUE HIT, I READ ABOUT A JAPANESE COMPANY PLANNING TO INTRODUCE THEM AT SOME TECH EXPO. BUT THIS THING IS WAY MORE CONVINCING THAN--
WHAT DOES THIS HAVE TO DO WITH AMPERSAND?
WELL, ROBOTS ARE, OF COURSE, THE MONKEY'S NATURAL ENEMY.
HOW AM I SUPPOSED TO KNOW, THREE-FIFTY? TOKYO IS LIKE THE FEVER DREAM OF A GAY KRYPTONIAN.
ALL RIGHT, I'LL SEE IF AMP'S TRACKING DEVICE HAS UPDATED HIS COORDINATES YET. IN THE MEANTIME, MAYBE BONNY THERE CAN FOLLOW HIS MUSK OR...
SNF
IS THAT PERFUME?

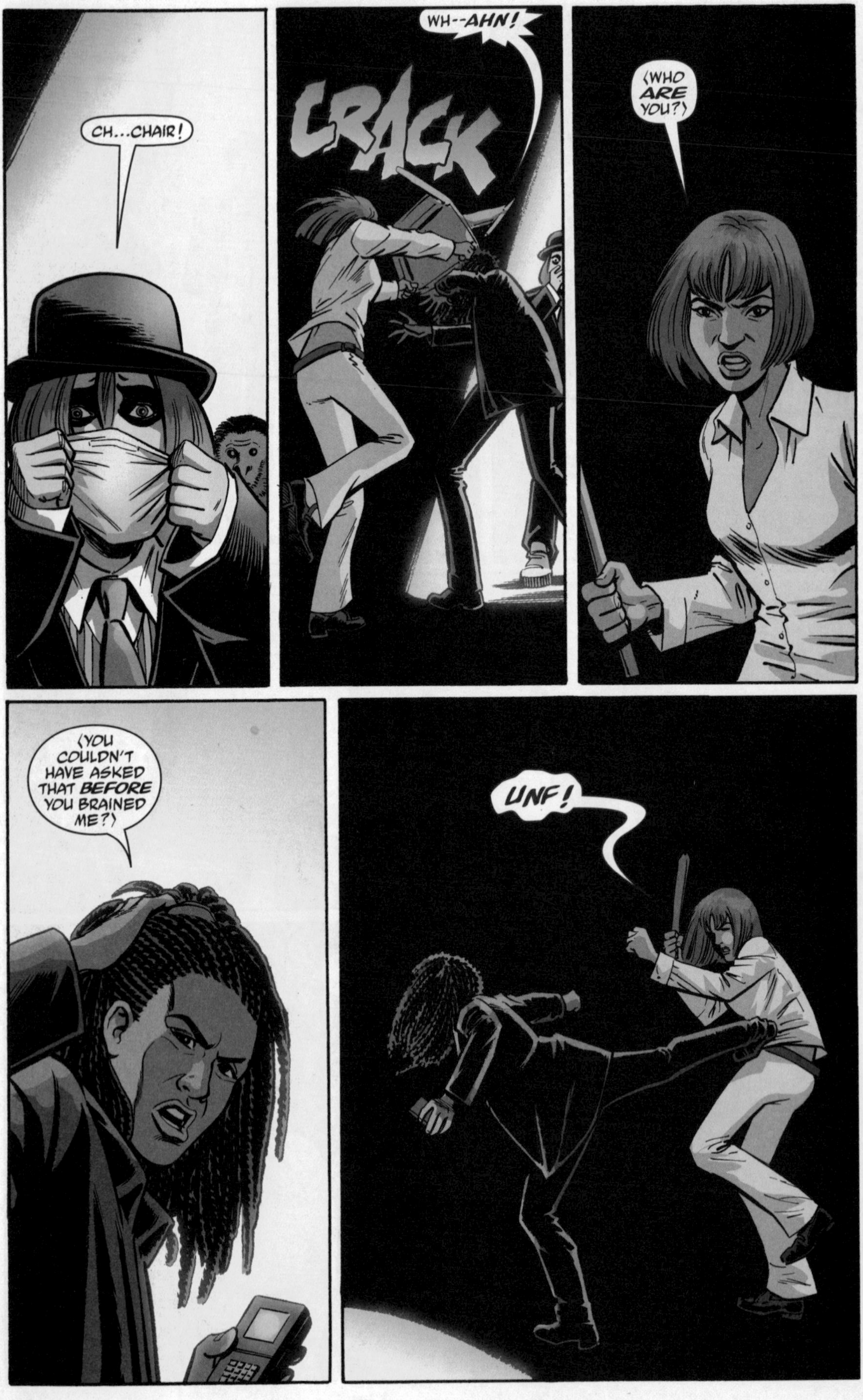
CH...CHAIR!
WH--AHN!
CRACK
⟨WHO ARE YOU?⟩
⟨YOU COULDN'T HAVE ASKED THAT BEFORE YOU BRAINED ME?⟩
UNF!

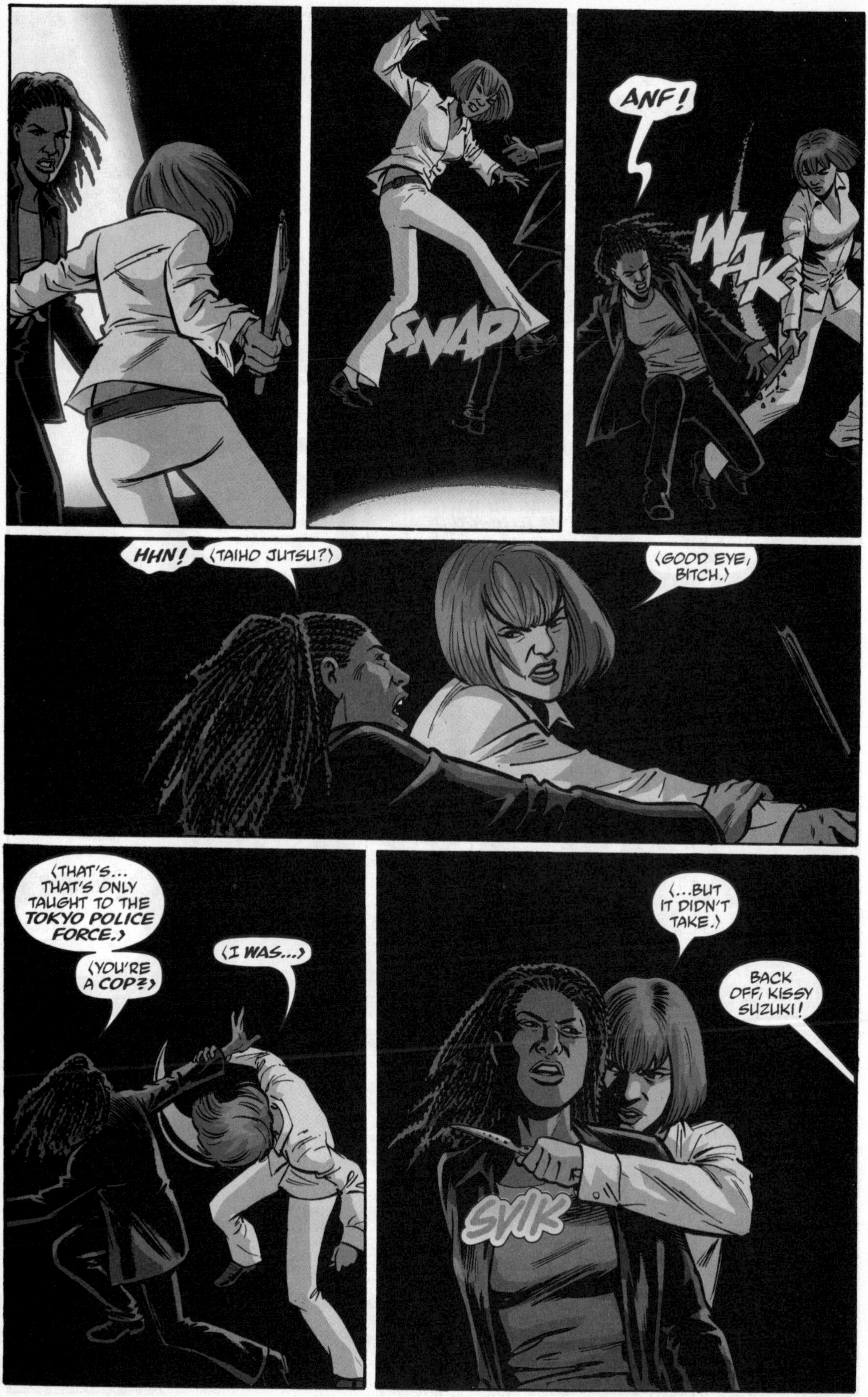
SNAP
ANF!
WAK
HHN!
‹TAIHO JUTSU?›
‹GOOD EYE, BITCH.›
‹THAT'S... THAT'S ONLY TAUGHT TO THE TOKYO POLICE FORCE.›
‹YOU'RE A COP?›
‹I WAS...›
‹...BUT IT DIDN'T TAKE.›
BACK OFF, KISSY SUZUKI!
SVIK

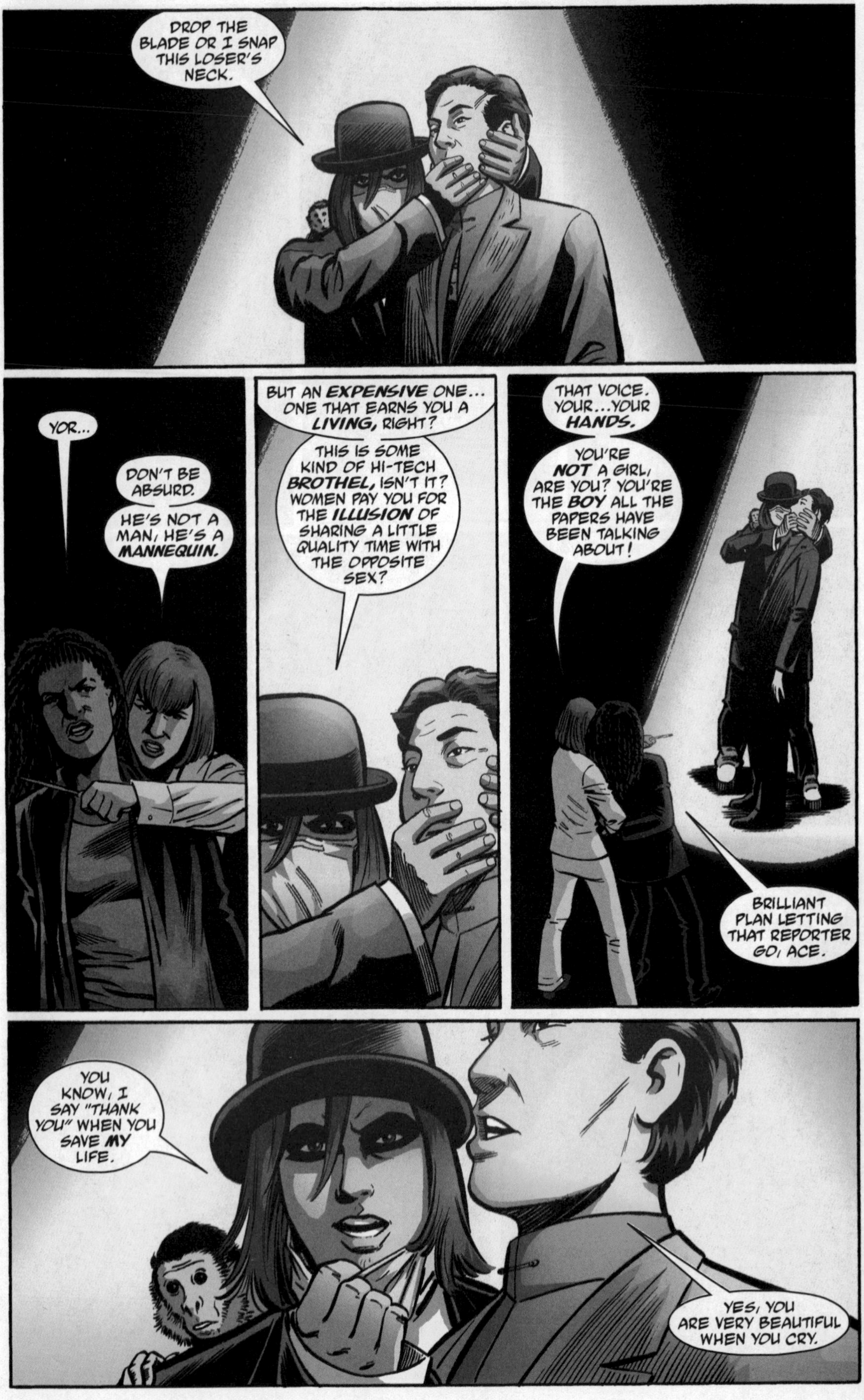

DROP THE BLADE OR I SNAP THIS LOSER'S NECK.
YOR...
DON'T BE ABSURD.
HE'S NOT A MAN, HE'S A MANNEQUIN.
BUT AN EXPENSIVE ONE... ONE THAT EARNS YOU A LIVING, RIGHT?
THIS IS SOME KIND OF HI-TECH BROTHEL, ISN'T IT? WOMEN PAY YOU FOR THE ILLUSION OF SHARING A LITTLE QUALITY TIME WITH THE OPPOSITE SEX?
THAT VOICE. YOUR...YOUR HANDS.
YOU'RE NOT A GIRL, ARE YOU? YOU'RE THE BOY ALL THE PAPERS HAVE BEEN TALKING ABOUT!
BRILLIANT PLAN LETTING THAT REPORTER GO, ACE.
YOU KNOW, I SAY "THANK YOU" WHEN YOU SAVE MY LIFE.
YES, YOU ARE VERY BEAUTIFUL WHEN YOU CRY.

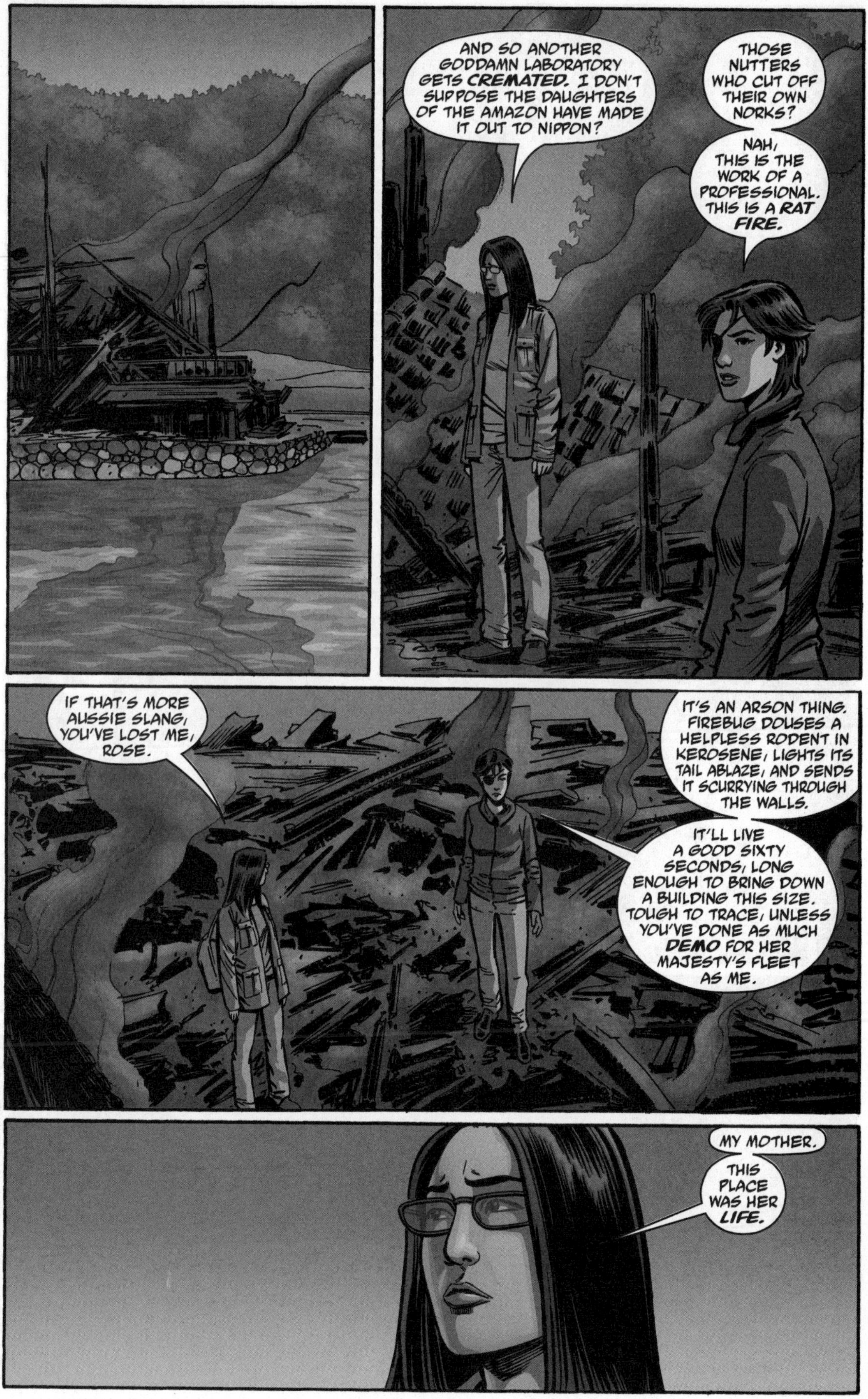
AND SO ANOTHER GODDAMN LABORATORY GETS **CREMATED.** I DON'T SUPPOSE THE DAUGHTERS OF THE AMAZON HAVE MADE IT OUT TO NIPPON?
THOSE NUTTERS WHO CUT OFF THEIR OWN NORKS?
NAH, THIS IS THE WORK OF A PROFESSIONAL. THIS IS A **RAT FIRE.**
IF THAT'S MORE AUSSIE SLANG, YOU'VE LOST ME, ROSE.
IT'S AN ARSON THING. FIREBUG DOUSES A HELPLESS RODENT IN KEROSENE, LIGHTS ITS TAIL ABLAZE, AND SENDS IT SCURRYING THROUGH THE WALLS.
IT'LL LIVE A GOOD SIXTY SECONDS, LONG ENOUGH TO BRING DOWN A BUILDING THIS SIZE. TOUGH TO TRACE, UNLESS YOU'VE DONE AS MUCH **DEMO** FOR HER MAJESTY'S FLEET AS ME.
MY MOTHER.
THIS PLACE WAS HER **LIFE.**

NO, HER *LIFE* IS HER LIFE, ALLISON.

AND THE FACT THAT SHE ISN'T A SMOLDERING *CORPSE* HERE MEANS THAT SHE'S STILL OUT THERE, ON THE RUN FROM WHO-EVER TRIED TO SMOKE HER OUT, MAYBE.

UNLESS SHE'S BEEN *KIDNAPPED* OR...OR...

NO REASON TO THINK THE WORST YET, LOVE.

IS THERE ANYWHERE SHE MIGHT HAVE GONE? A JOINT NO ONE ELSE WOULD KNOW TO CHECK?

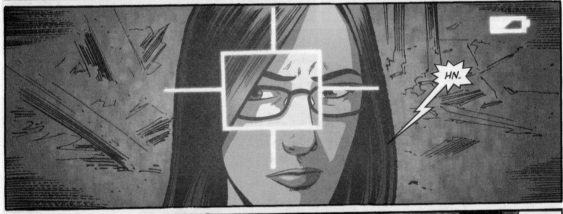

HN.

THAT A GIRL.

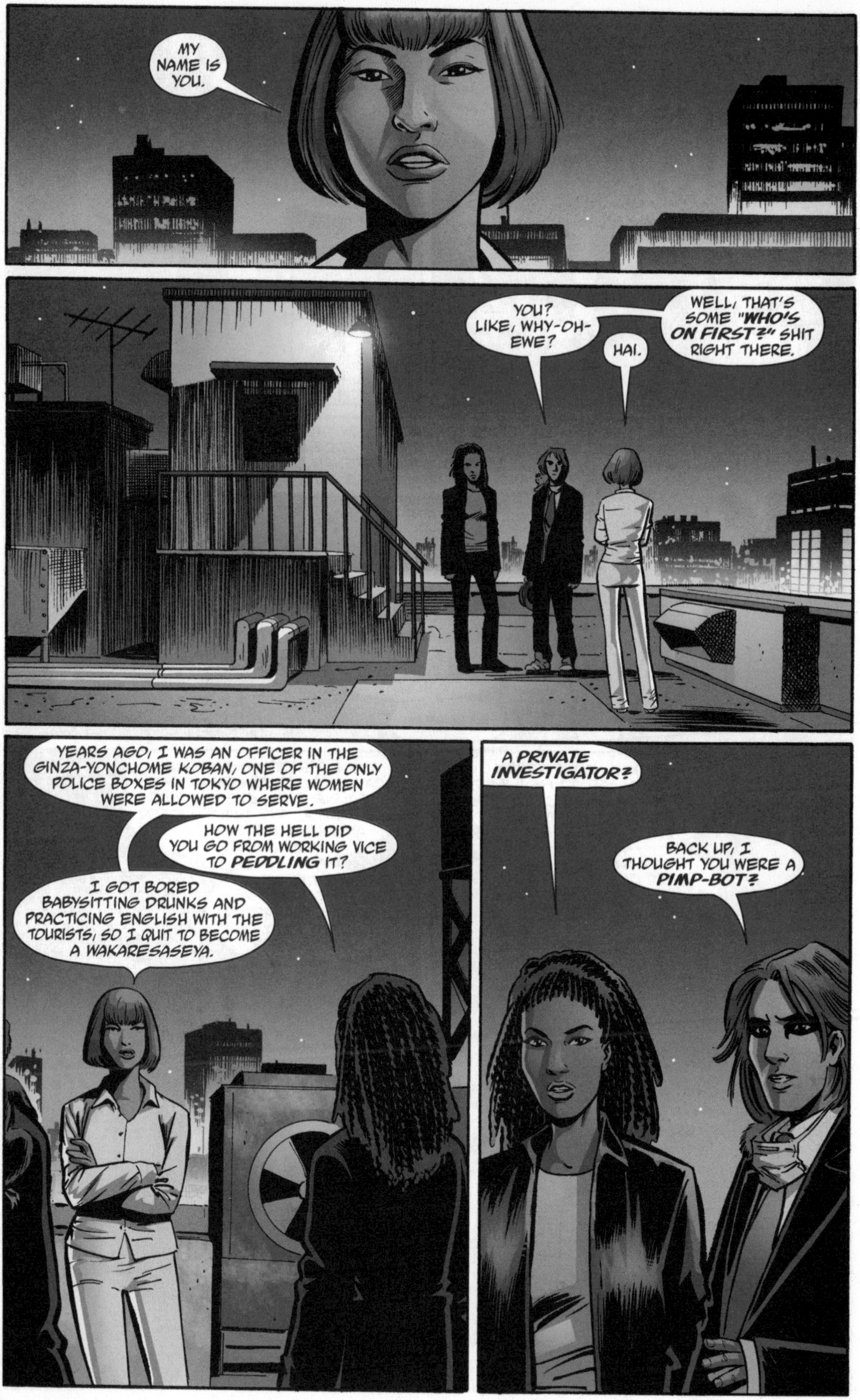

MY NAME IS YOU.
YOU? LIKE, WHY-OH-EWE?
HAI.
WELL, THAT'S SOME "WHO'S ON FIRST?" SHIT RIGHT THERE.
YEARS AGO, I WAS AN OFFICER IN THE GINZA-YONCHOME KOBAN, ONE OF THE ONLY POLICE BOXES IN TOKYO WHERE WOMEN WERE ALLOWED TO SERVE.
HOW THE HELL DID YOU GO FROM WORKING VICE TO PEDDLING IT?
I GOT BORED BABYSITTING DRUNKS AND PRACTICING ENGLISH WITH THE TOURISTS, SO I QUIT TO BECOME A WAKARESASEYA.
A PRIVATE INVESTIGATOR?
BACK UP, I THOUGHT YOU WERE A PIMP-BOT?

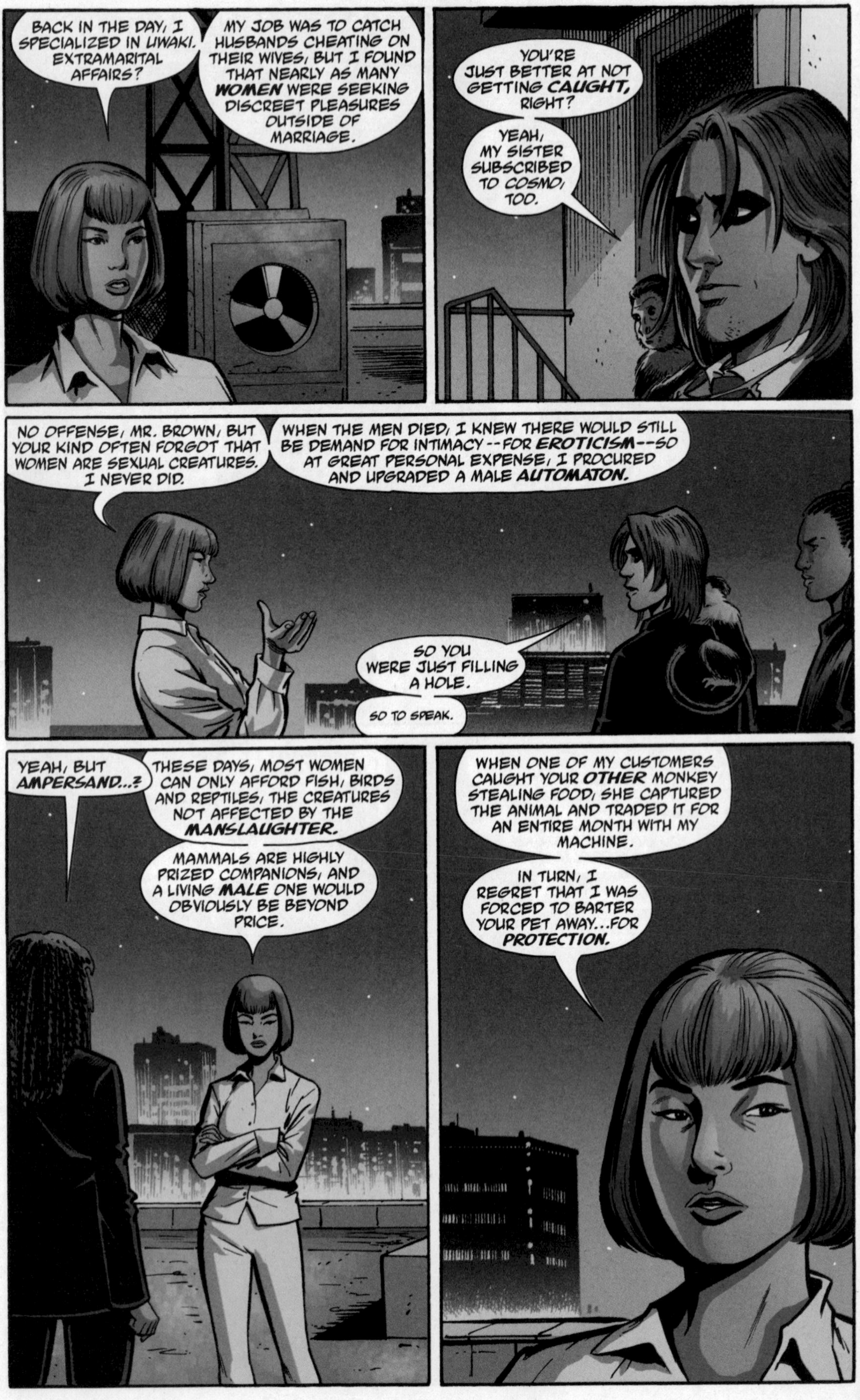
BACK IN THE DAY, I SPECIALIZED IN UWAKI. EXTRAMARITAL AFFAIRS?
MY JOB WAS TO CATCH HUSBANDS CHEATING ON THEIR WIVES, BUT I FOUND THAT NEARLY AS MANY WOMEN WERE SEEKING DISCREET PLEASURES OUTSIDE OF MARRIAGE.
YOU'RE JUST BETTER AT NOT GETTING CAUGHT, RIGHT?
YEAH, MY SISTER SUBSCRIBED TO COSMO, TOO.
NO OFFENSE, MR. BROWN, BUT YOUR KIND OFTEN FORGOT THAT WOMEN ARE SEXUAL CREATURES. I NEVER DID.
WHEN THE MEN DIED, I KNEW THERE WOULD STILL BE DEMAND FOR INTIMACY--FOR EROTICISM--SO AT GREAT PERSONAL EXPENSE, I PROCURED AND UPGRADED A MALE AUTOMATON.
SO YOU WERE JUST FILLING A HOLE.
SO TO SPEAK.
YEAH, BUT AMPERSAND...?
THESE DAYS, MOST WOMEN CAN ONLY AFFORD FISH, BIRDS AND REPTILES, THE CREATURES NOT AFFECTED BY THE MANSLAUGHTER.
MAMMALS ARE HIGHLY PRIZED COMPANIONS, AND A LIVING MALE ONE WOULD OBVIOUSLY BE BEYOND PRICE.
WHEN ONE OF MY CUSTOMERS CAUGHT YOUR OTHER MONKEY STEALING FOOD, SHE CAPTURED THE ANIMAL AND TRADED IT FOR AN ENTIRE MONTH WITH MY MACHINE.
IN TURN, I REGRET THAT I WAS FORCED TO BARTER YOUR PET AWAY...FOR PROTECTION.

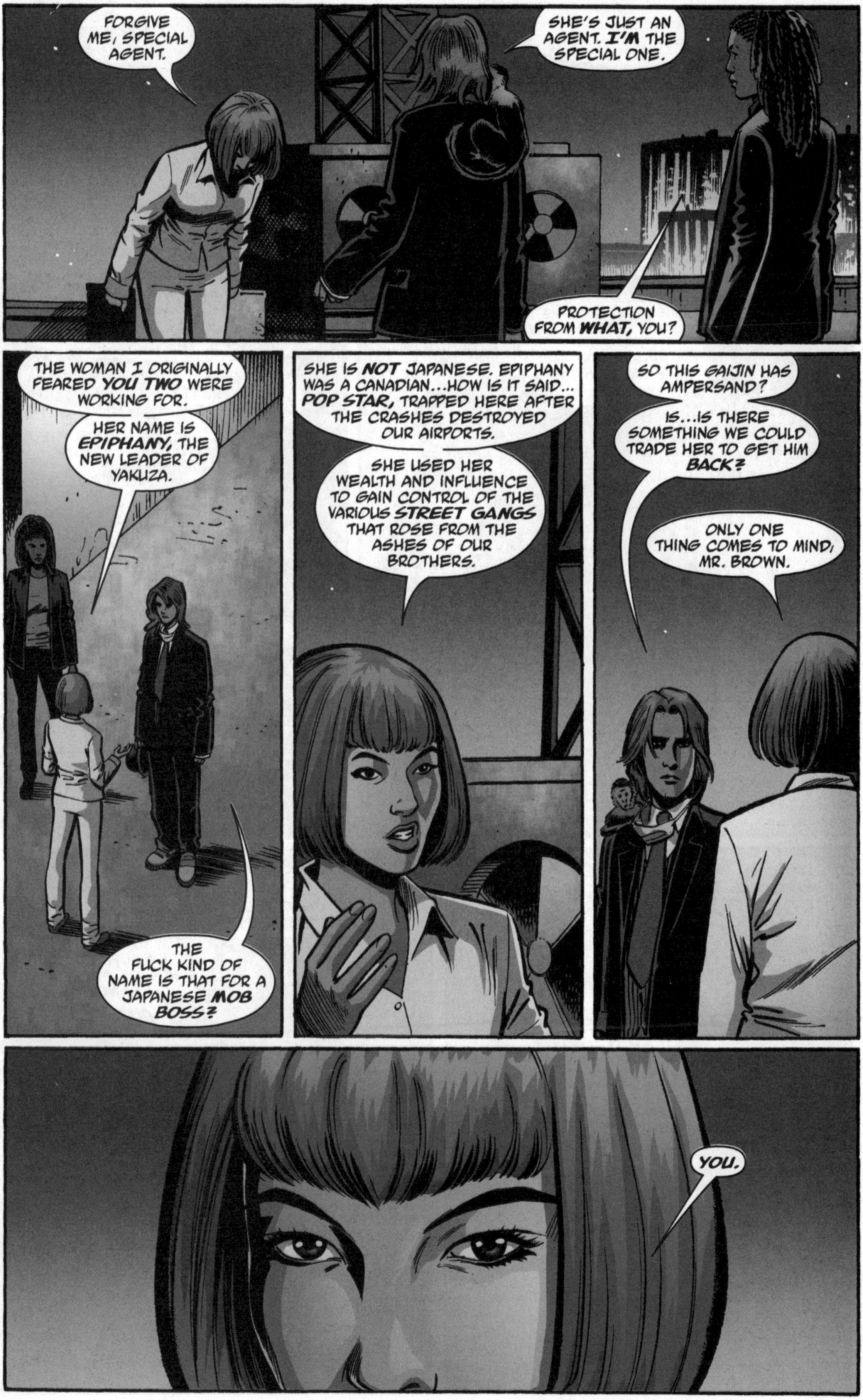

FORGIVE ME, SPECIAL AGENT.
SHE'S JUST AN AGENT. I'M THE SPECIAL ONE.
PROTECTION FROM WHAT, YOU?
THE WOMAN I ORIGINALLY FEARED YOU TWO WERE WORKING FOR.
HER NAME IS EPIPHANY, THE NEW LEADER OF YAKUZA.
THE FUCK KIND OF NAME IS THAT FOR A JAPANESE MOB BOSS?
SHE IS NOT JAPANESE. EPIPHANY WAS A CANADIAN...HOW IS IT SAID... POP STAR, TRAPPED HERE AFTER THE CRASHES DESTROYED OUR AIRPORTS.
SHE USED HER WEALTH AND INFLUENCE TO GAIN CONTROL OF THE VARIOUS STREET GANGS THAT ROSE FROM THE ASHES OF OUR BROTHERS.
SO THIS GAIJIN HAS AMPERSAND?
IS...IS THERE SOMETHING WE COULD TRADE HER TO GET HIM BACK?
ONLY ONE THING COMES TO MIND, MR. BROWN.
YOU.

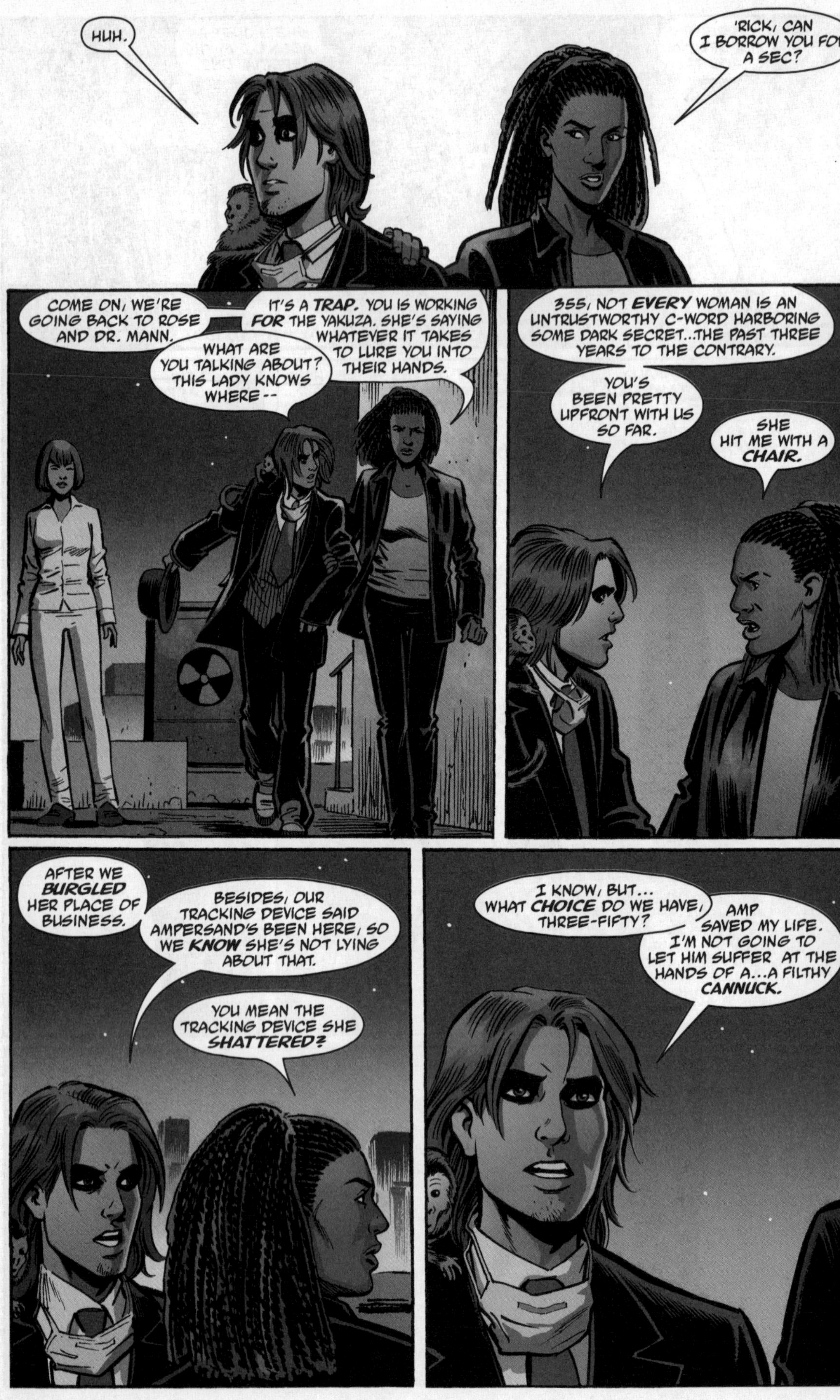
HUH.
'RICK, CAN I BORROW YOU FOR A SEC?
COME ON, WE'RE GOING BACK TO ROSE AND DR. MANN.
WHAT ARE YOU TALKING ABOUT? THIS LADY KNOWS WHERE--
IT'S A TRAP. YOU IS WORKING FOR THE YAKUZA. SHE'S SAYING WHATEVER IT TAKES TO LURE YOU INTO THEIR HANDS.
355, NOT EVERY WOMAN IS AN UNTRUSTWORTHY C-WORD HARBORING SOME DARK SECRET...THE PAST THREE YEARS TO THE CONTRARY.
YOU'S BEEN PRETTY UPFRONT WITH US SO FAR.
SHE HIT ME WITH A CHAIR.
AFTER WE BURGLED HER PLACE OF BUSINESS.
BESIDES, OUR TRACKING DEVICE SAID AMPERSAND'S BEEN HERE, SO WE KNOW SHE'S NOT LYING ABOUT THAT.
YOU MEAN THE TRACKING DEVICE SHE SHATTERED?
I KNOW, BUT... WHAT CHOICE DO WE HAVE, THREE-FIFTY?
AMP SAVED MY LIFE. I'M NOT GOING TO LET HIM SUFFER AT THE HANDS OF A...A FILTHY CANNUCK.

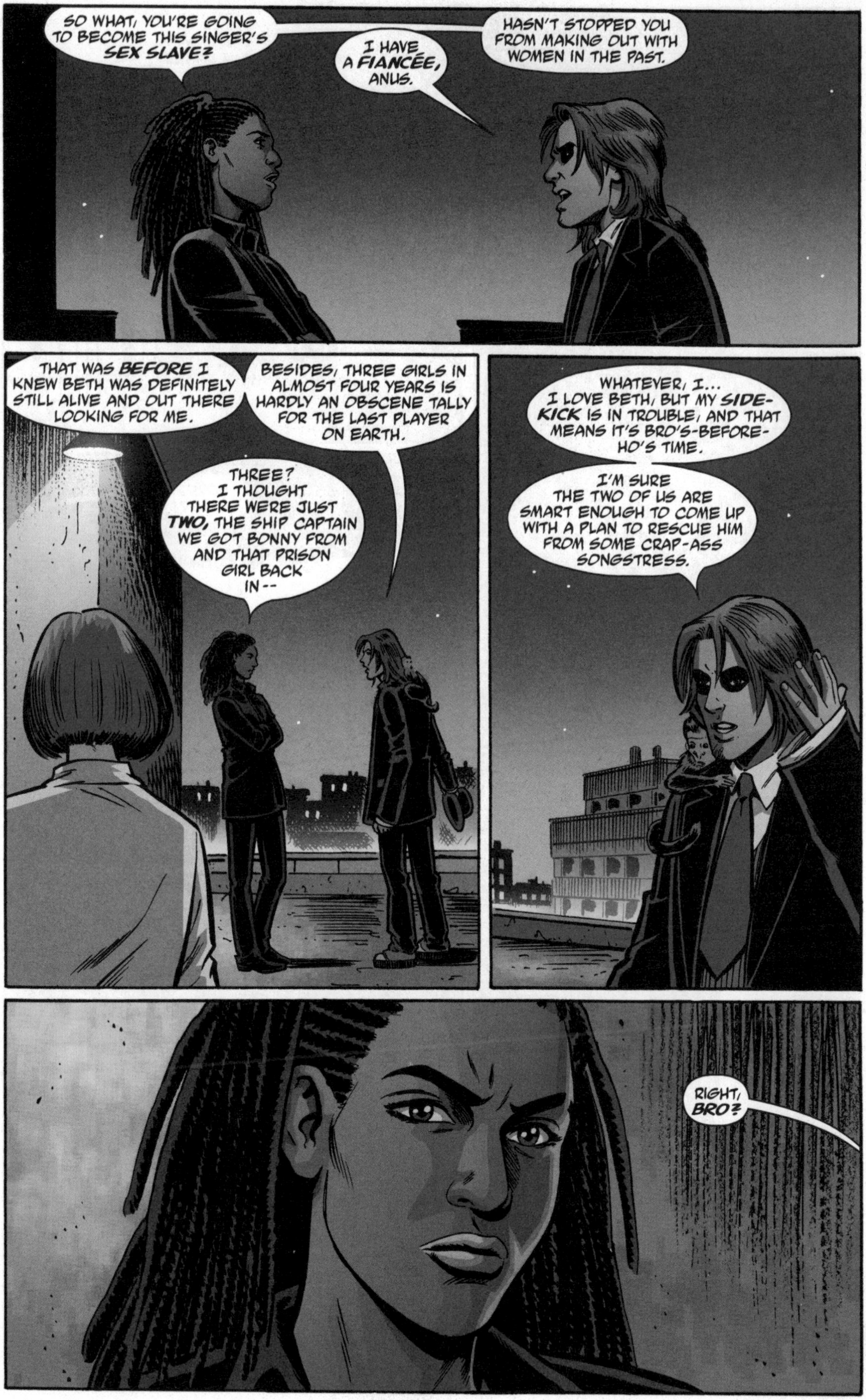
SO WHAT, YOU'RE GOING TO BECOME THIS SINGER'S **SEX SLAVE?**
I HAVE A **FIANCÉE,** ANUS.
HASN'T STOPPED YOU FROM MAKING OUT WITH WOMEN IN THE PAST.
THAT WAS **BEFORE** I KNEW BETH WAS DEFINITELY STILL ALIVE AND OUT THERE LOOKING FOR ME.
BESIDES, THREE GIRLS IN ALMOST FOUR YEARS IS HARDLY AN OBSCENE TALLY FOR THE LAST PLAYER ON EARTH.
THREE? I THOUGHT THERE WERE JUST **TWO,** THE SHIP CAPTAIN WE GOT BONNY FROM AND THAT PRISON GIRL BACK IN--
WHATEVER, I... I LOVE BETH, BUT MY **SIDE-KICK** IS IN TROUBLE, AND THAT MEANS IT'S BRO'S-BEFORE-HO'S TIME.
I'M SURE THE TWO OF US ARE SMART ENOUGH TO COME UP WITH A PLAN TO RESCUE HIM FROM SOME CRAP-ASS SONGSTRESS.
RIGHT, **BRO?**

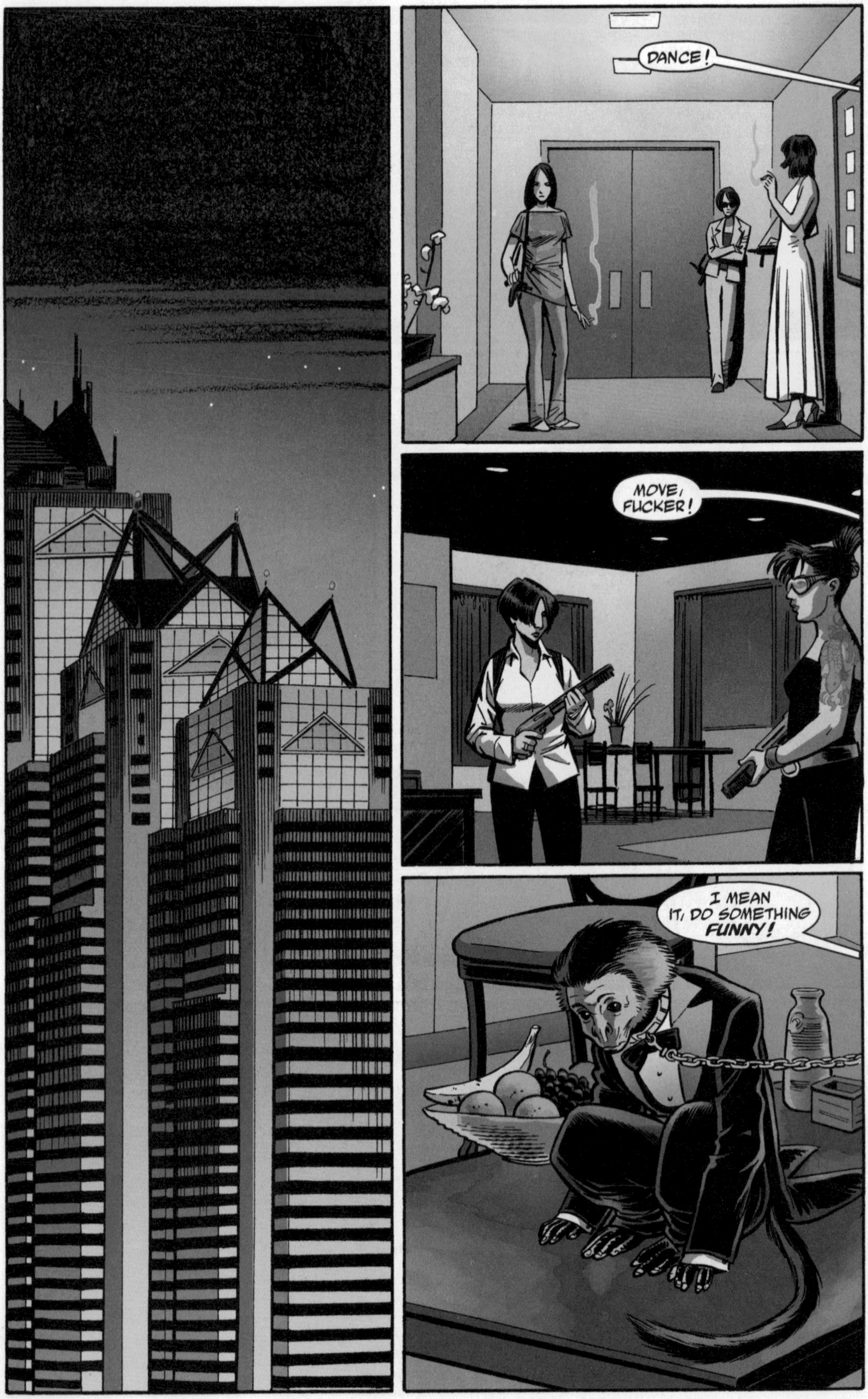
DANCE!
MOVE, FUCKER!
I MEAN IT, DO SOMETHING FUNNY!

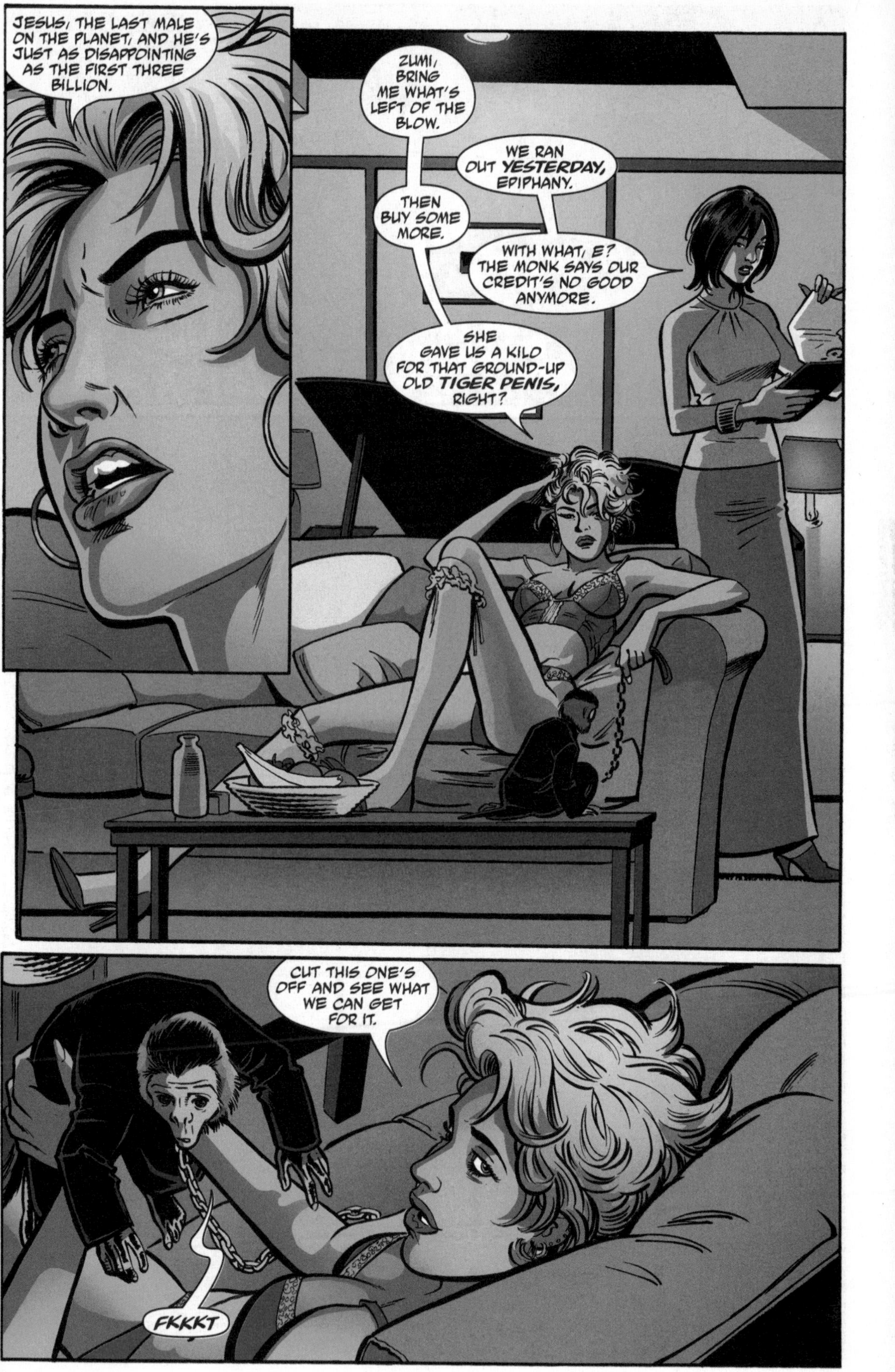
JESUS, THE LAST MALE ON THE PLANET, AND HE'S JUST AS DISAPPOINTING AS THE FIRST THREE BILLION.
ZUMI, BRING ME WHAT'S LEFT OF THE BLOW.
WE RAN OUT YESTERDAY, EPIPHANY.
THEN BUY SOME MORE.
WITH WHAT, E? THE MONK SAYS OUR CREDIT'S NO GOOD ANYMORE.
SHE GAVE US A KILO FOR THAT GROUND-UP OLD TIGER PENIS, RIGHT?
CUT THIS ONE'S OFF AND SEE WHAT WE CAN GET FOR IT.
FKKKT

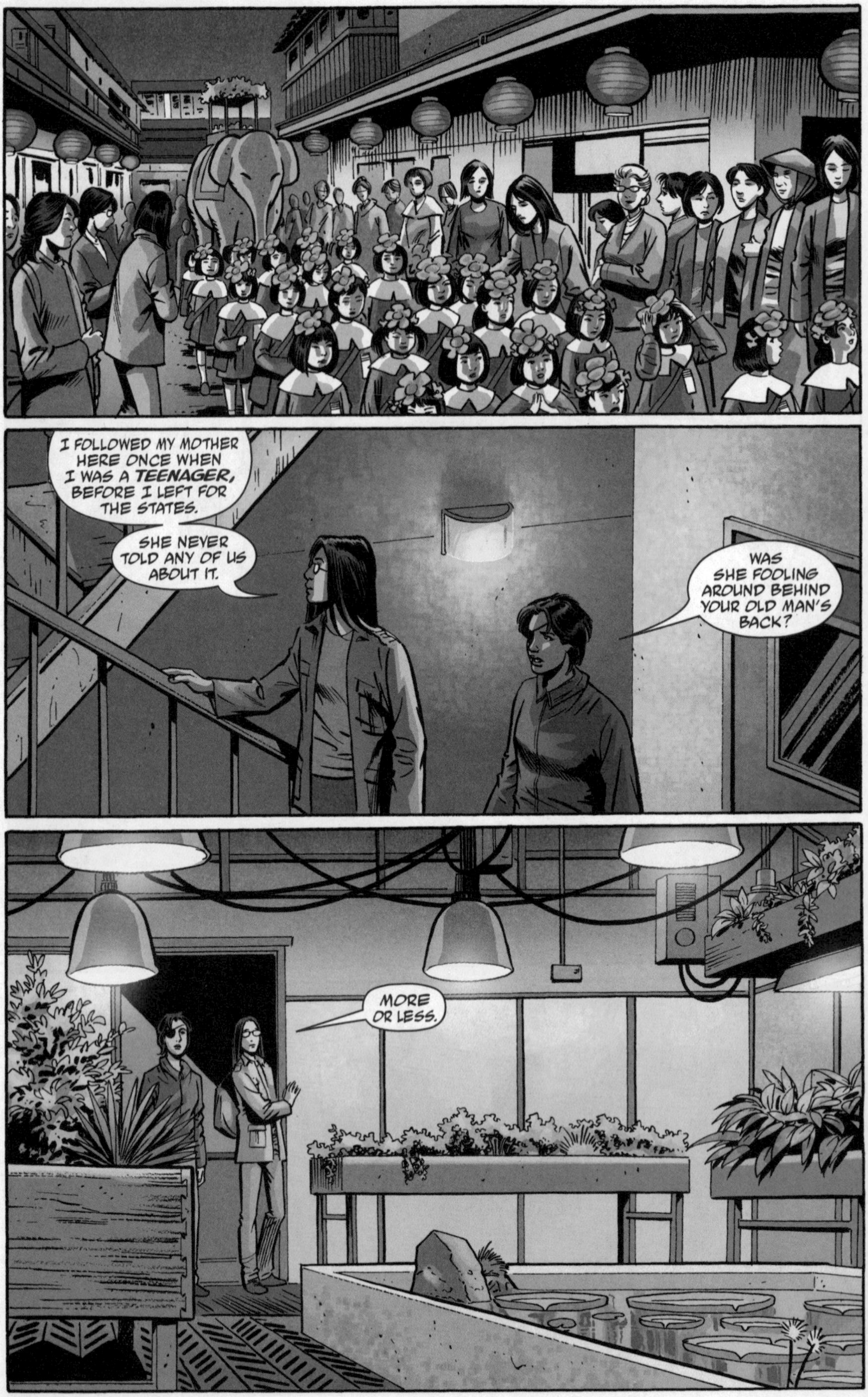
I FOLLOWED MY MOTHER HERE ONCE WHEN I WAS A **TEENAGER,** BEFORE I LEFT FOR THE STATES.
SHE NEVER TOLD ANY OF US ABOUT IT.
WAS SHE FOOLING AROUND BEHIND YOUR OLD MAN'S BACK?
MORE OR LESS.

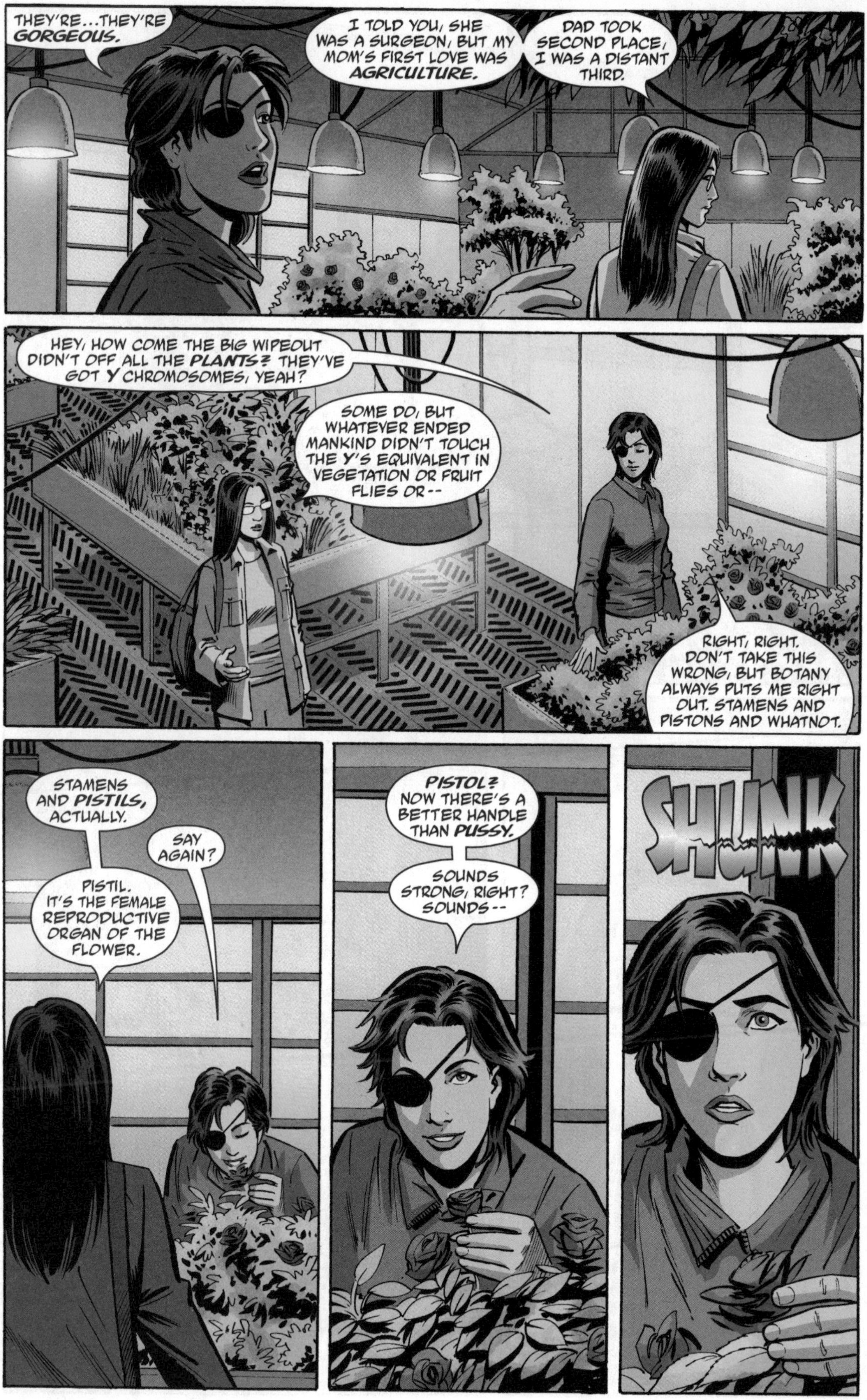
THEY'RE...THEY'RE GORGEOUS.
I TOLD YOU, SHE WAS A SURGEON, BUT MY MOM'S FIRST LOVE WAS AGRICULTURE.
DAD TOOK SECOND PLACE, I WAS A DISTANT THIRD.
HEY, HOW COME THE BIG WIPEOUT DIDN'T OFF ALL THE PLANTS? THEY'VE GOT Y CHROMOSOMES, YEAH?
SOME DO, BUT WHATEVER ENDED MANKIND DIDN'T TOUCH THE Y'S EQUIVALENT IN VEGETATION OR FRUIT FLIES OR--
RIGHT, RIGHT. DON'T TAKE THIS WRONG, BUT BOTANY ALWAYS PUTS ME RIGHT OUT. STAMENS AND PISTONS AND WHATNOT.
STAMENS AND PISTILS, ACTUALLY.
SAY AGAIN?
PISTIL. IT'S THE FEMALE REPRODUCTIVE ORGAN OF THE FLOWER.
PISTOL? NOW THERE'S A BETTER HANDLE THAN PUSSY.
SOUNDS STRONG, RIGHT? SOUNDS--
SHUNK

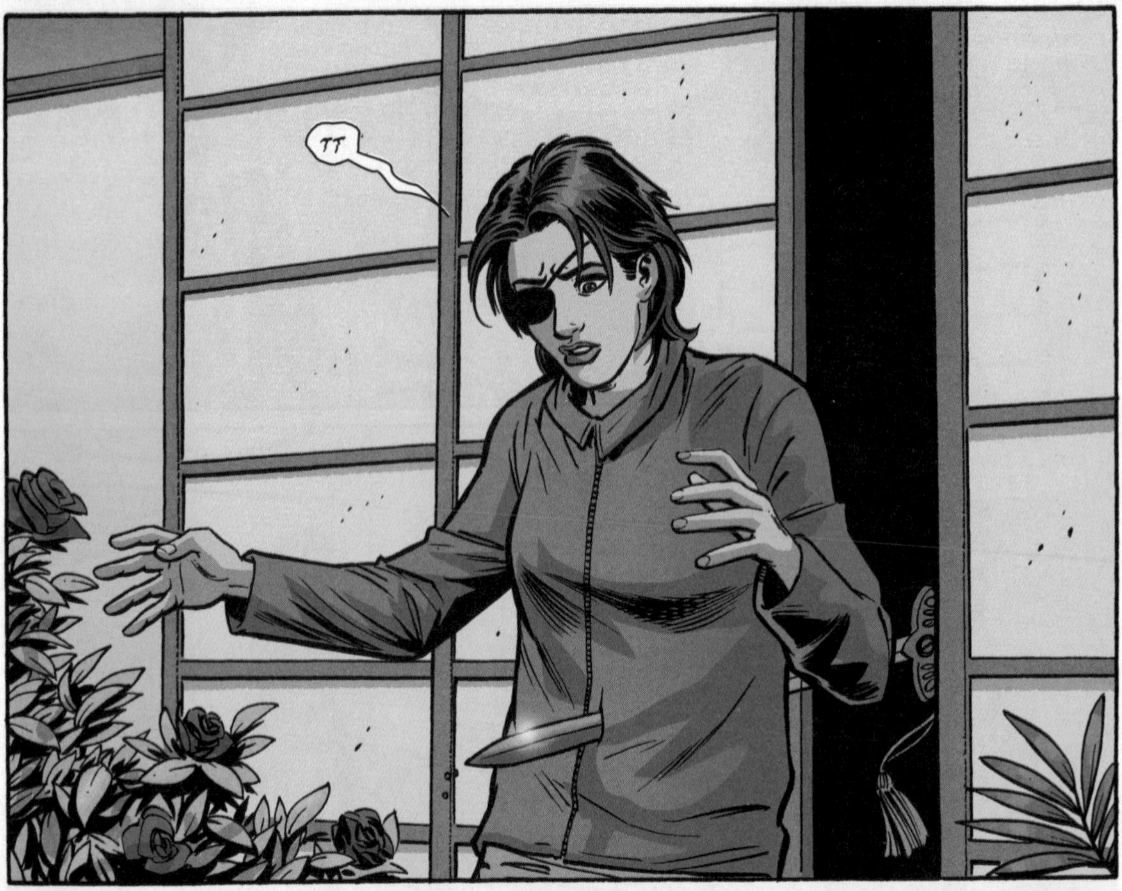
TT

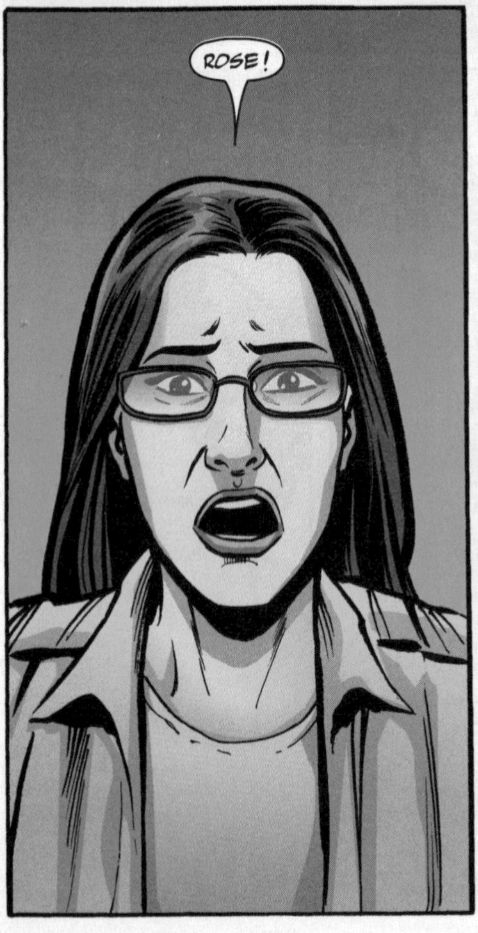
ROSE!

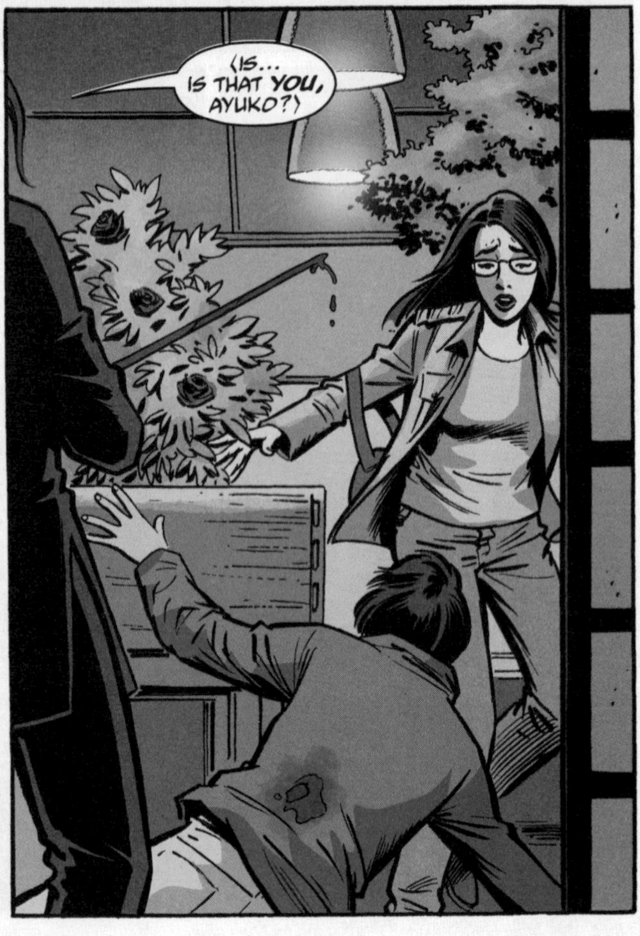
⟨IS...
IS THAT YOU, AYUKO?⟩

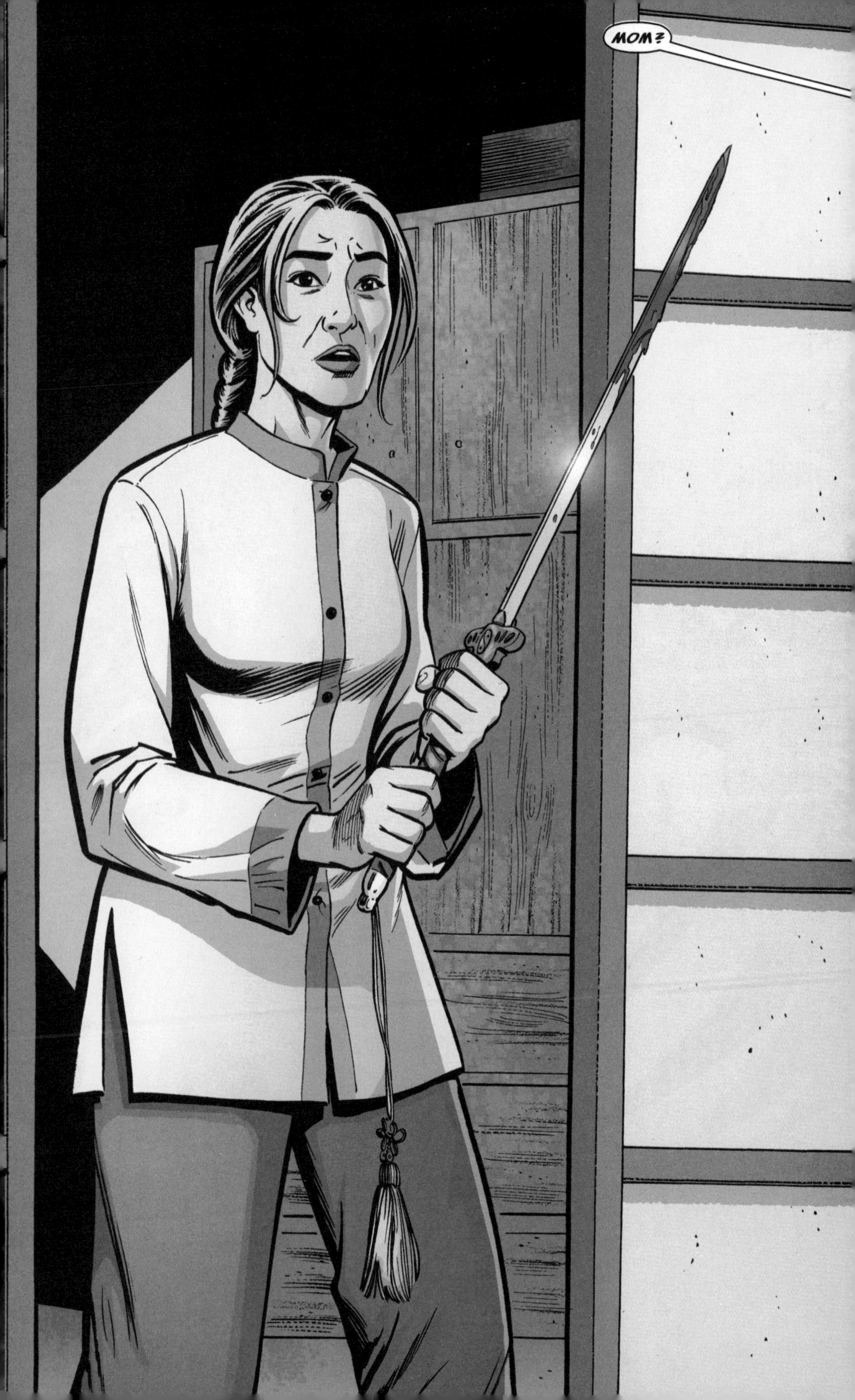
MOM?

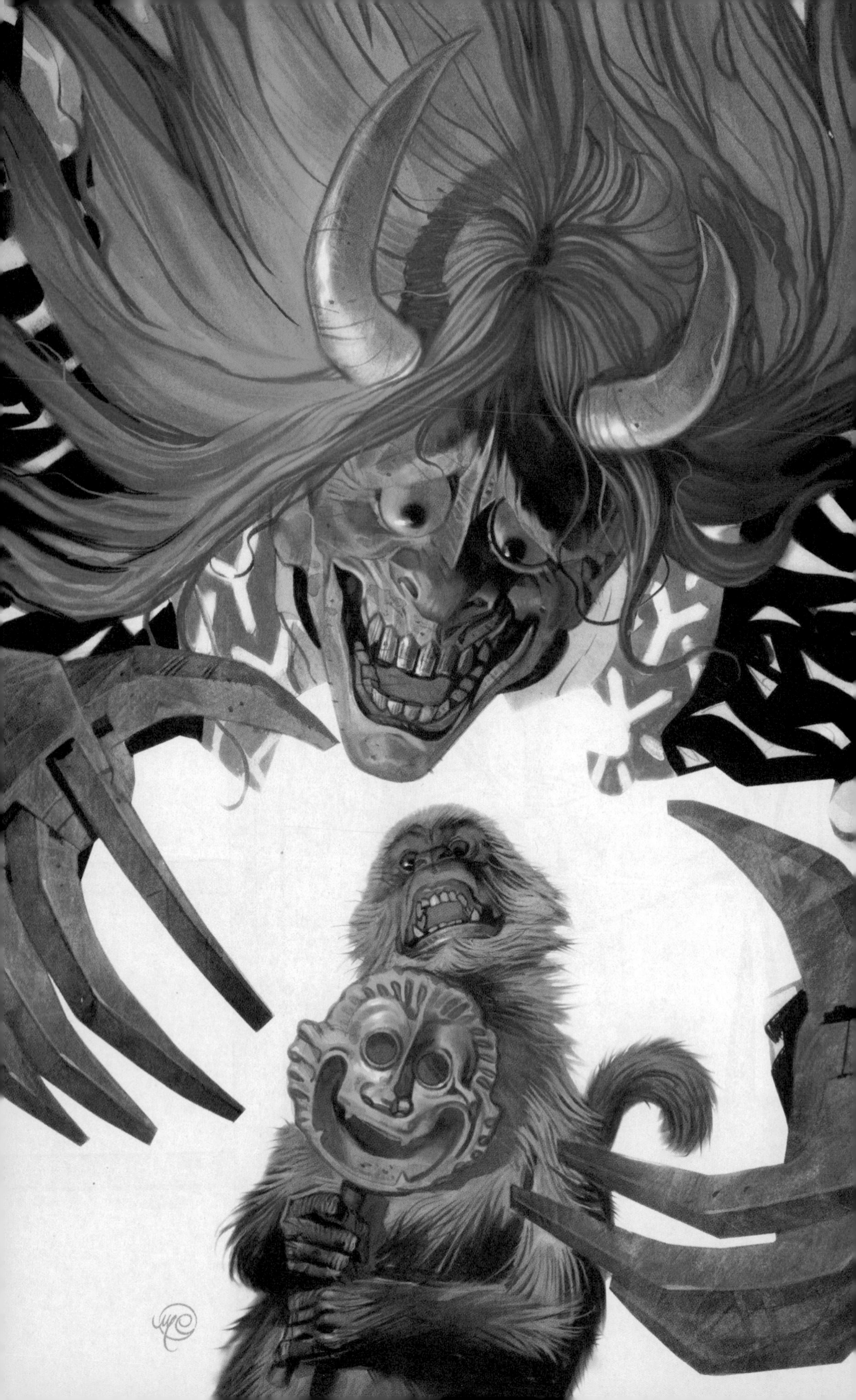

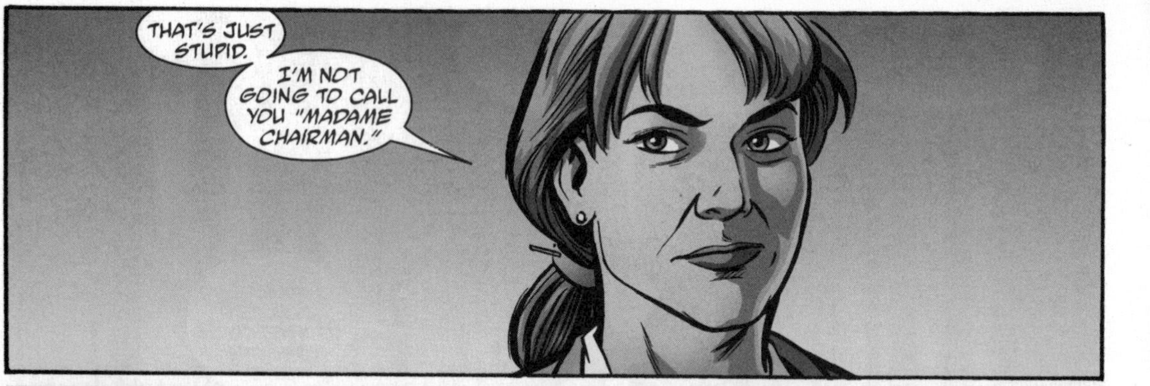
THAT'S JUST STUPID.
I'M NOT GOING TO CALL YOU "MADAME CHAIRMAN."

**Washington, D.C.
Months Ago**

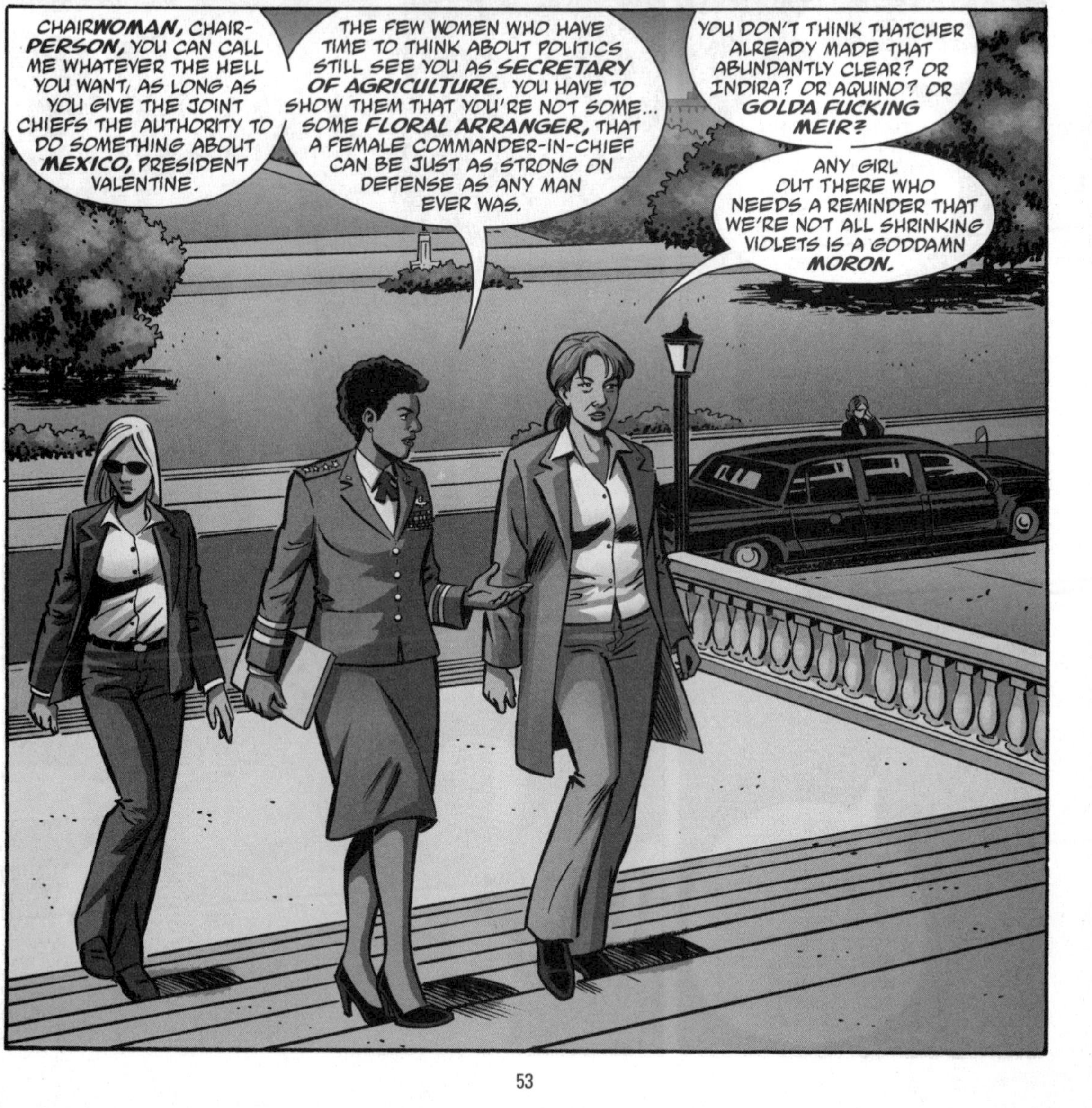
CHAIRWOMAN, CHAIRPERSON, YOU CAN CALL ME WHATEVER THE HELL YOU WANT, AS LONG AS YOU GIVE THE JOINT CHIEFS THE AUTHORITY TO DO SOMETHING ABOUT MEXICO, PRESIDENT VALENTINE.
THE FEW WOMEN WHO HAVE TIME TO THINK ABOUT POLITICS STILL SEE YOU AS SECRETARY OF AGRICULTURE. YOU HAVE TO SHOW THEM THAT YOU'RE NOT SOME... SOME FLORAL ARRANGER, THAT A FEMALE COMMANDER-IN-CHIEF CAN BE JUST AS STRONG ON DEFENSE AS ANY MAN EVER WAS.
YOU DON'T THINK THATCHER ALREADY MADE THAT ABUNDANTLY CLEAR? OR INDIRA? OR AQUINO? OR GOLDA FUCKING MEIR?
ANY GIRL OUT THERE WHO NEEDS A REMINDER THAT WE'RE NOT ALL SHRINKING VIOLETS IS A GODDAMN MORON.

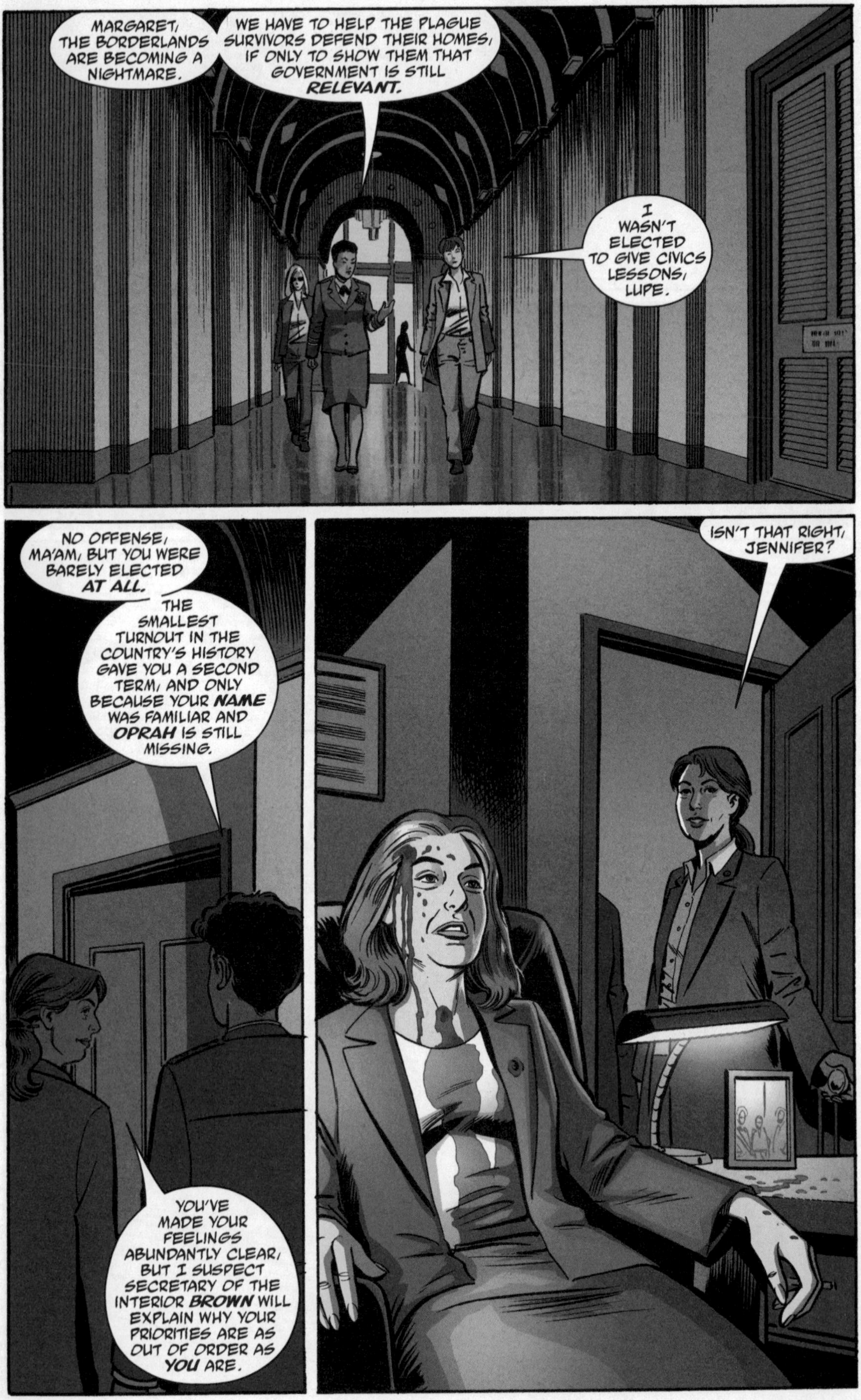
MARGARET, THE BORDERLANDS ARE BECOMING A NIGHTMARE.
WE HAVE TO HELP THE PLAGUE SURVIVORS DEFEND THEIR HOMES, IF ONLY TO SHOW THEM THAT GOVERNMENT IS STILL RELEVANT.
I WASN'T ELECTED TO GIVE CIVICS LESSONS, LUPE.
NO OFFENSE, MA'AM, BUT YOU WERE BARELY ELECTED AT ALL.
THE SMALLEST TURNOUT IN THE COUNTRY'S HISTORY GAVE YOU A SECOND TERM, AND ONLY BECAUSE YOUR NAME WAS FAMILIAR AND OPRAH IS STILL MISSING.
YOU'VE MADE YOUR FEELINGS ABUNDANTLY CLEAR, BUT I SUSPECT SECRETARY OF THE INTERIOR BROWN WILL EXPLAIN WHY YOUR PRIORITIES ARE AS OUT OF ORDER AS YOU ARE.
ISN'T THAT RIGHT, JENNIFER?

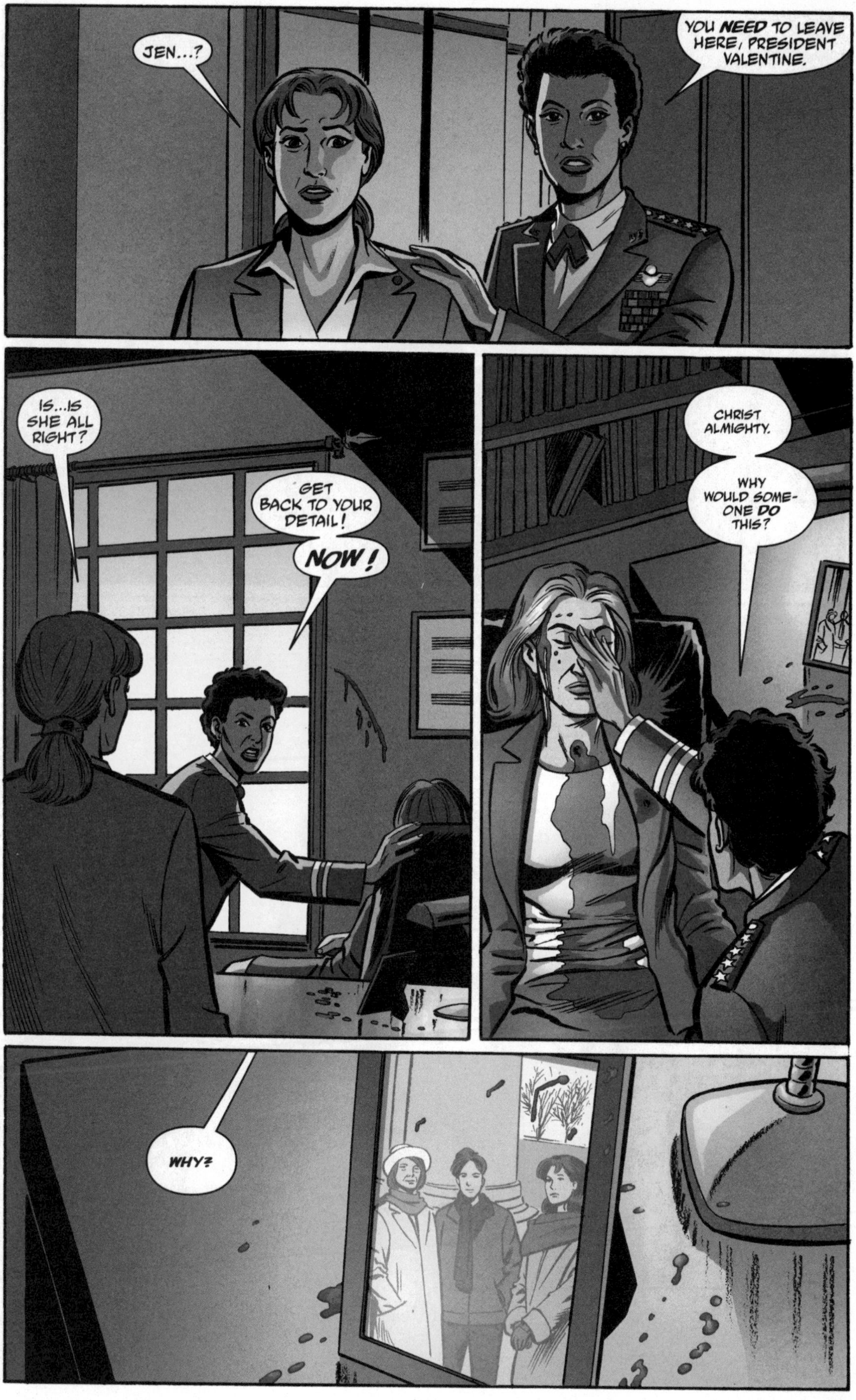
JEN...?
YOU NEED TO LEAVE HERE, PRESIDENT VALENTINE.
IS...IS SHE ALL RIGHT?
GET BACK TO YOUR DETAIL!
NOW!
CHRIST ALMIGHTY.
WHY WOULD SOME-ONE DO THIS?
WHY?

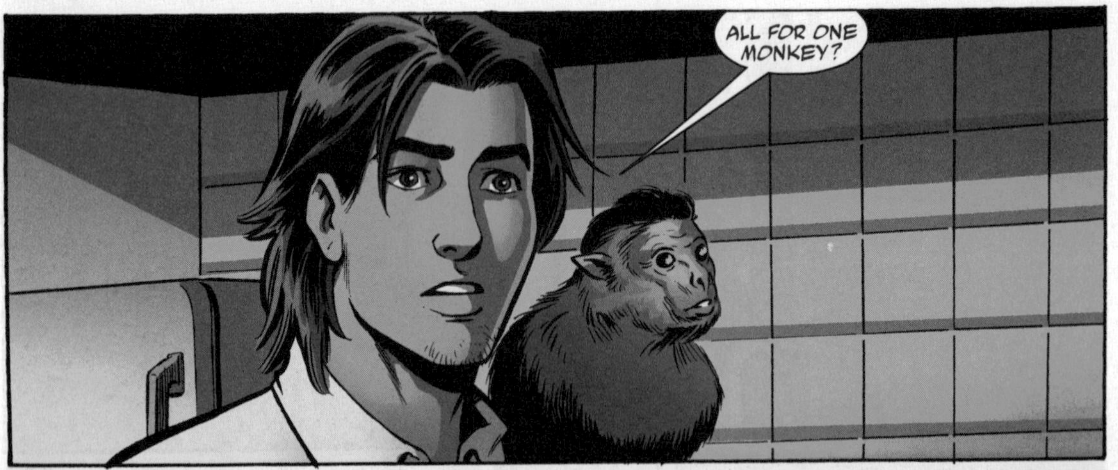
ALL FOR ONE MONKEY?

Tokyo, Japan
Now

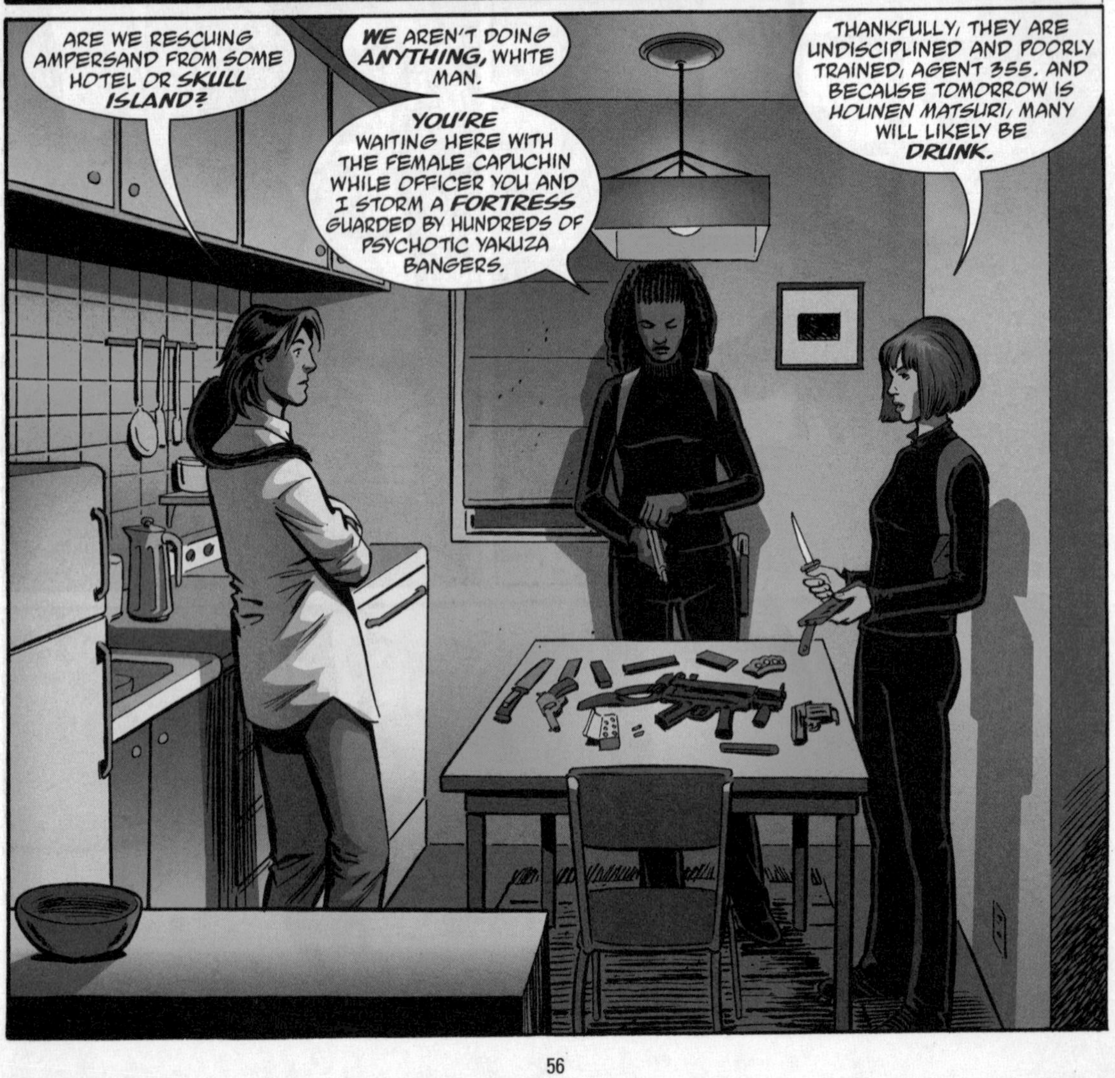
ARE WE RESCUING AMPERSAND FROM SOME HOTEL OR SKULL ISLAND?
WE AREN'T DOING ANYTHING, WHITE MAN.
YOU'RE WAITING HERE WITH THE FEMALE CAPUCHIN WHILE OFFICER YOU AND I STORM A FORTRESS GUARDED BY HUNDREDS OF PSYCHOTIC YAKUZA BANGERS.
THANKFULLY, THEY ARE UNDISCIPLINED AND POORLY TRAINED, AGENT 355. AND BECAUSE TOMORROW IS HOUNEN MATSURI, MANY WILL LIKELY BE DRUNK.

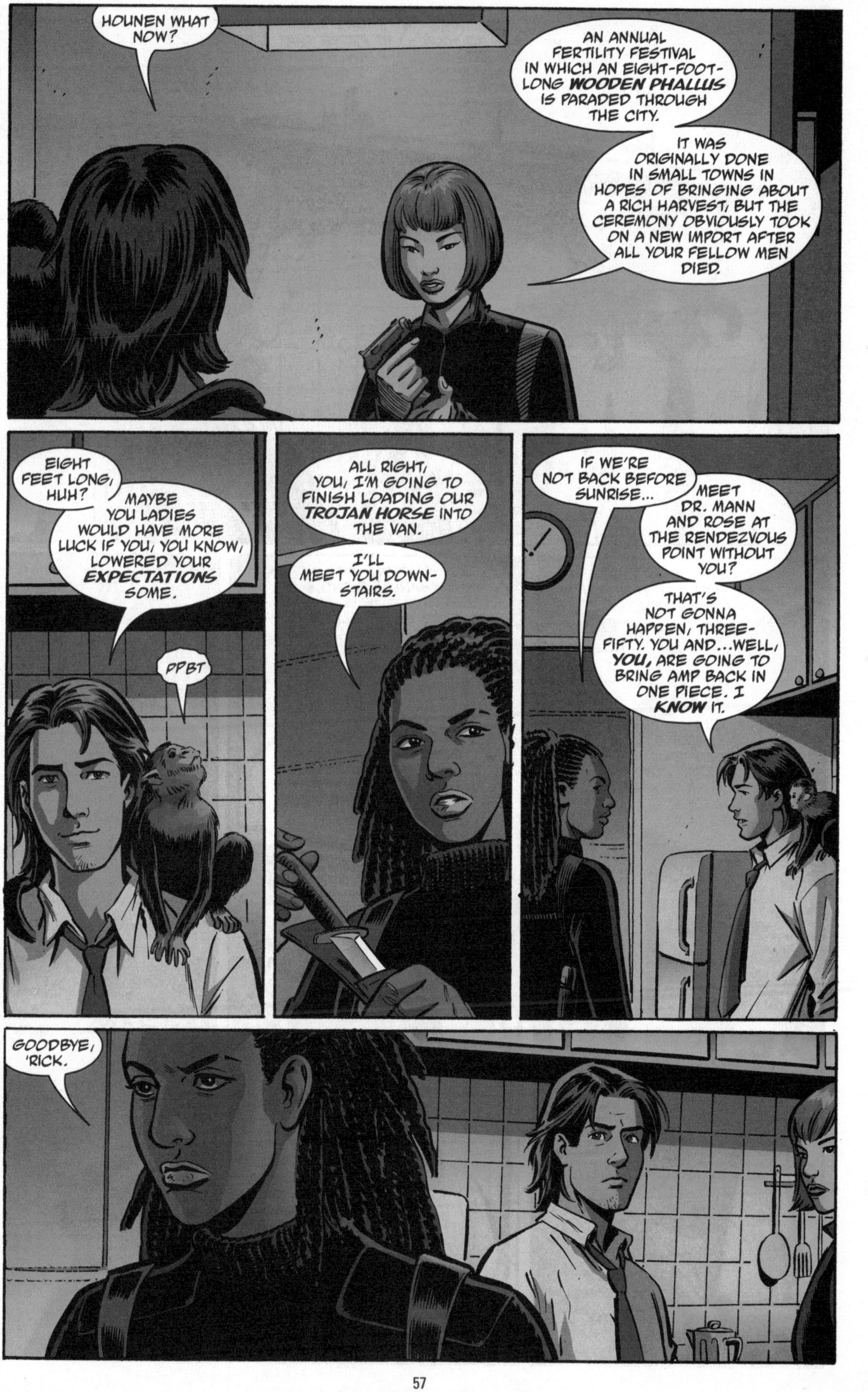
HOUNEN WHAT NOW?
AN ANNUAL FERTILITY FESTIVAL IN WHICH AN EIGHT-FOOT-LONG **WOODEN PHALLUS** IS PARADED THROUGH THE CITY.
IT WAS ORIGINALLY DONE IN SMALL TOWNS IN HOPES OF BRINGING ABOUT A RICH HARVEST, BUT THE CEREMONY OBVIOUSLY TOOK ON A NEW IMPORT AFTER ALL YOUR FELLOW MEN DIED.
EIGHT FEET LONG, HUH?
MAYBE YOU LADIES WOULD HAVE MORE LUCK IF YOU, YOU KNOW, LOWERED YOUR **EXPECTATIONS** SOME.
PPBT
ALL RIGHT, YOU, I'M GOING TO FINISH LOADING OUR **TROJAN HORSE** INTO THE VAN.
I'LL MEET YOU DOWN-STAIRS.
IF WE'RE NOT BACK BEFORE SUNRISE...
MEET DR. MANN AND ROSE AT THE RENDEZVOUS POINT WITHOUT YOU?
THAT'S NOT GONNA HAPPEN, THREE-FIFTY. YOU AND...WELL, **YOU,** ARE GOING TO BRING AMP BACK IN ONE PIECE. I **KNOW** IT.
GOODBYE, 'RICK.

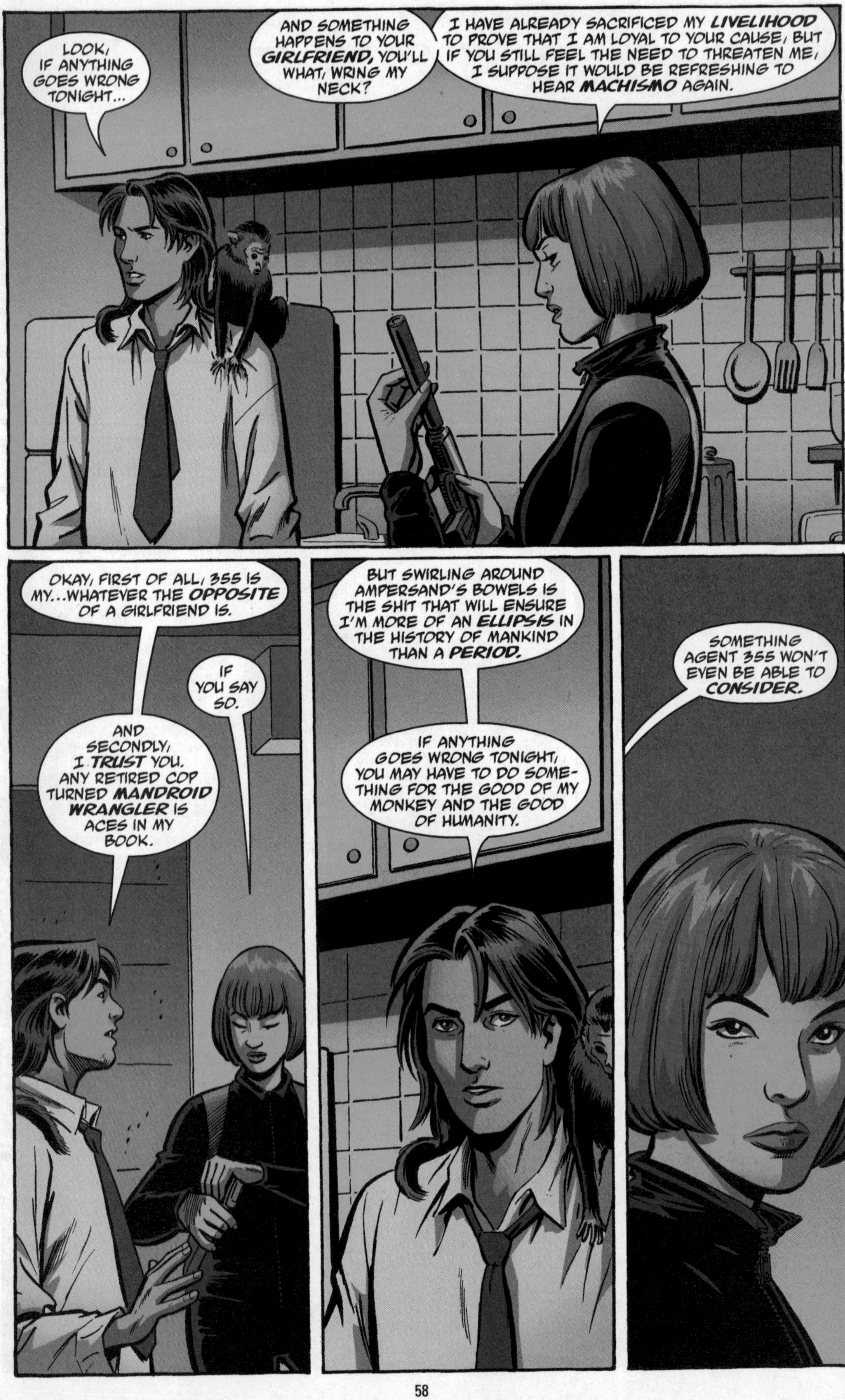
LOOK, IF ANYTHING GOES WRONG TONIGHT...
AND SOMETHING HAPPENS TO YOUR GIRLFRIEND, YOU'LL WHAT, WRING MY NECK?
I HAVE ALREADY SACRIFICED MY LIVELIHOOD TO PROVE THAT I AM LOYAL TO YOUR CAUSE, BUT IF YOU STILL FEEL THE NEED TO THREATEN ME, I SUPPOSE IT WOULD BE REFRESHING TO HEAR MACHISMO AGAIN.
OKAY, FIRST OF ALL, 355 IS MY...WHATEVER THE OPPOSITE OF A GIRLFRIEND IS.
IF YOU SAY SO.
AND SECONDLY, I TRUST YOU. ANY RETIRED COP TURNED MANDROID WRANGLER IS ACES IN MY BOOK.
BUT SWIRLING AROUND AMPERSAND'S BOWELS IS THE SHIT THAT WILL ENSURE I'M MORE OF AN ELLIPSIS IN THE HISTORY OF MANKIND THAN A PERIOD.
IF ANYTHING GOES WRONG TONIGHT, YOU MAY HAVE TO DO SOME-THING FOR THE GOOD OF MY MONKEY AND THE GOOD OF HUMANITY.
SOMETHING AGENT 355 WON'T EVEN BE ABLE TO CONSIDER.

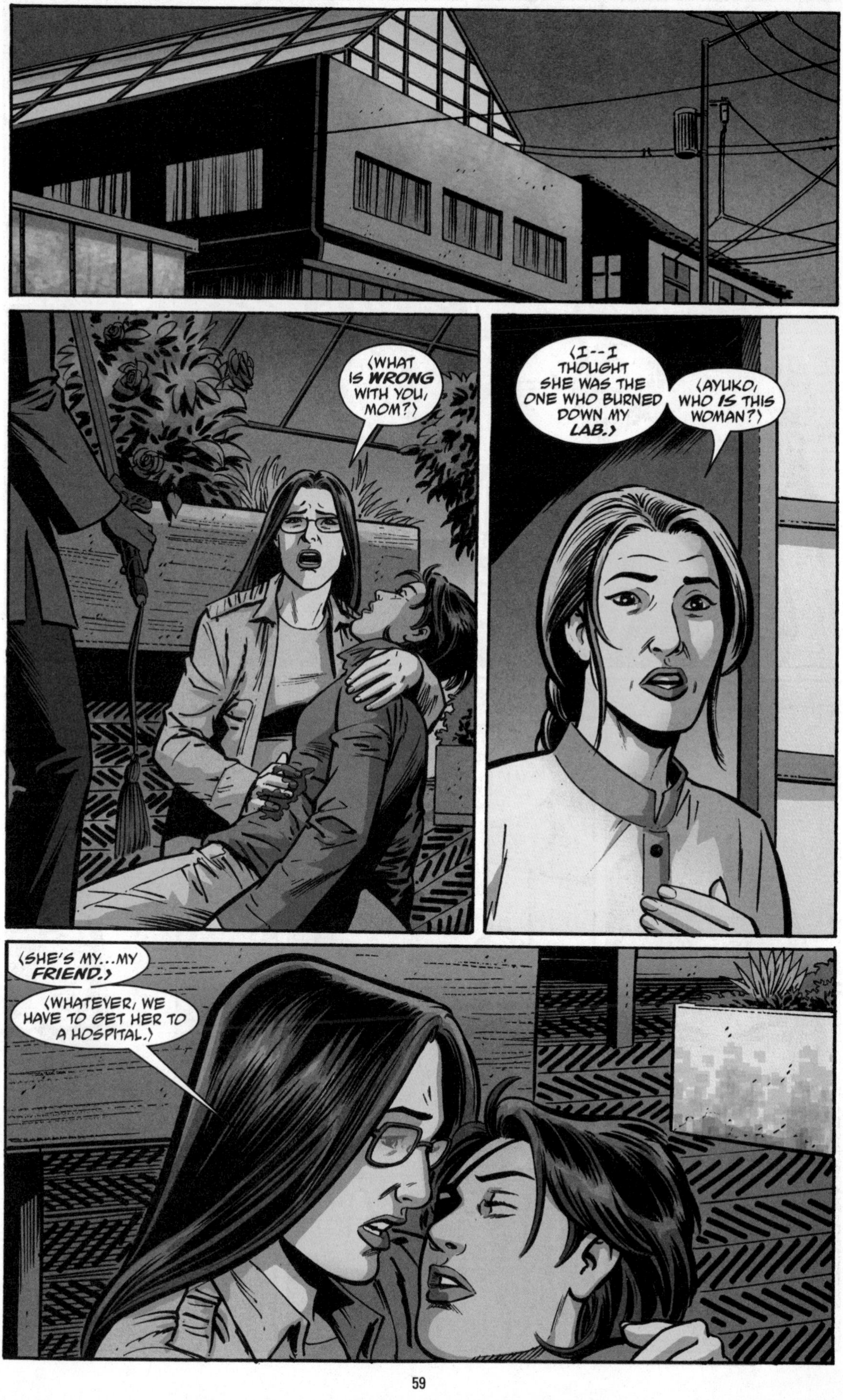
⟨WHAT IS WRONG WITH YOU, MOM?⟩
⟨I--I THOUGHT SHE WAS THE ONE WHO BURNED DOWN MY LAB.⟩
⟨AYUKO, WHO IS THIS WOMAN?⟩
⟨SHE'S MY...MY FRIEND.⟩
⟨WHATEVER, WE HAVE TO GET HER TO A HOSPITAL.⟩

⟨DON'T BE IDIOTIC, OUR HOSPITALS ARE ALL STAFFED BY GLORIFIED **CANDY STRIPERS**.⟩

⟨IF I WASN'T THE GREATEST SURGEON ALIVE **BEFORE** THE GENDERCIDE, I CERTAINLY AM **NOW**. WE'LL TAKE CARE OF THE WOMAN HERE, AYUKO.⟩

STOP CALLING ME THAT, GODDAMMIT! MY NAME IS **ALLISON MANN**.

⟨WHETHER YOU LIKE IT OR NOT, YOU ARE STILL A **MATSUMORI**. WE BOTH ARE.⟩

⟨AND YOU WILL SPEAK TO ME IN JAPANESE OR CHINESE, BUT IF YOU INSIST ON ENGLISH, THIS OPERATION IS GOING TO GO VERY, VERY SLOWLY. AM I UNDERSTOOD?⟩

SHI.

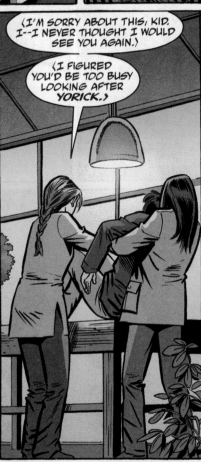

⟨I'M SORRY ABOUT THIS, KID. I--I NEVER THOUGHT I WOULD SEE YOU AGAIN.⟩

⟨I FIGURED YOU'D BE TOO BUSY LOOKING AFTER **YORICK**.⟩

...

WHAT DID YOU SAY?

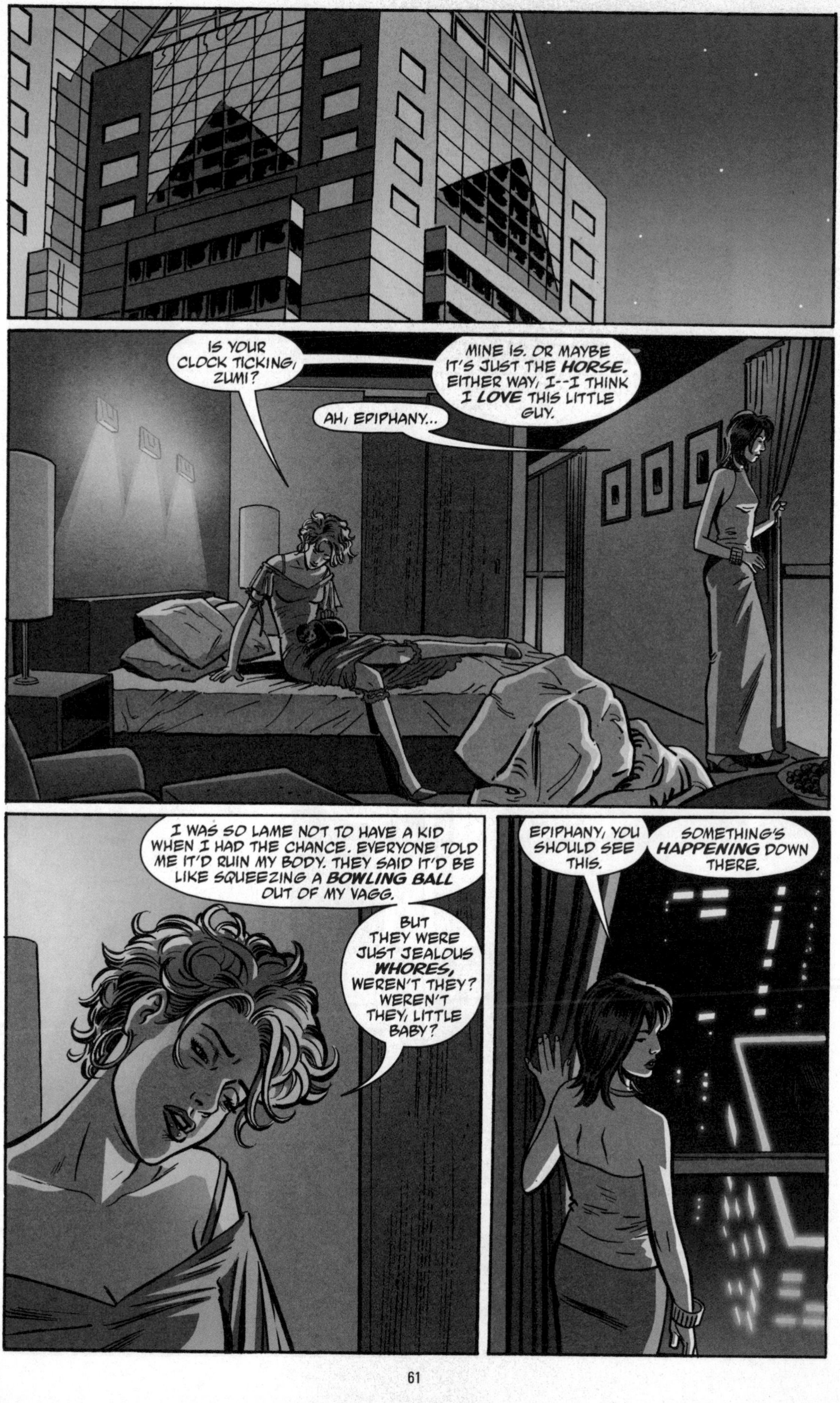
IS YOUR CLOCK TICKING, ZUMI?
MINE IS. OR MAYBE IT'S JUST THE **HORSE.** EITHER WAY, I--I THINK **I LOVE** THIS LITTLE GUY.
AH, EPIPHANY...
I WAS SO LAME NOT TO HAVE A KID WHEN I HAD THE CHANCE. EVERYONE TOLD ME IT'D RUIN MY BODY. THEY SAID IT'D BE LIKE SQUEEZING A **BOWLING BALL** OUT OF MY VAGG.
BUT THEY WERE JUST JEALOUS **WHORES,** WEREN'T THEY? WEREN'T THEY, LITTLE BABY?
EPIPHANY, YOU SHOULD SEE THIS.
SOMETHING'S **HAPPENING** DOWN THERE.

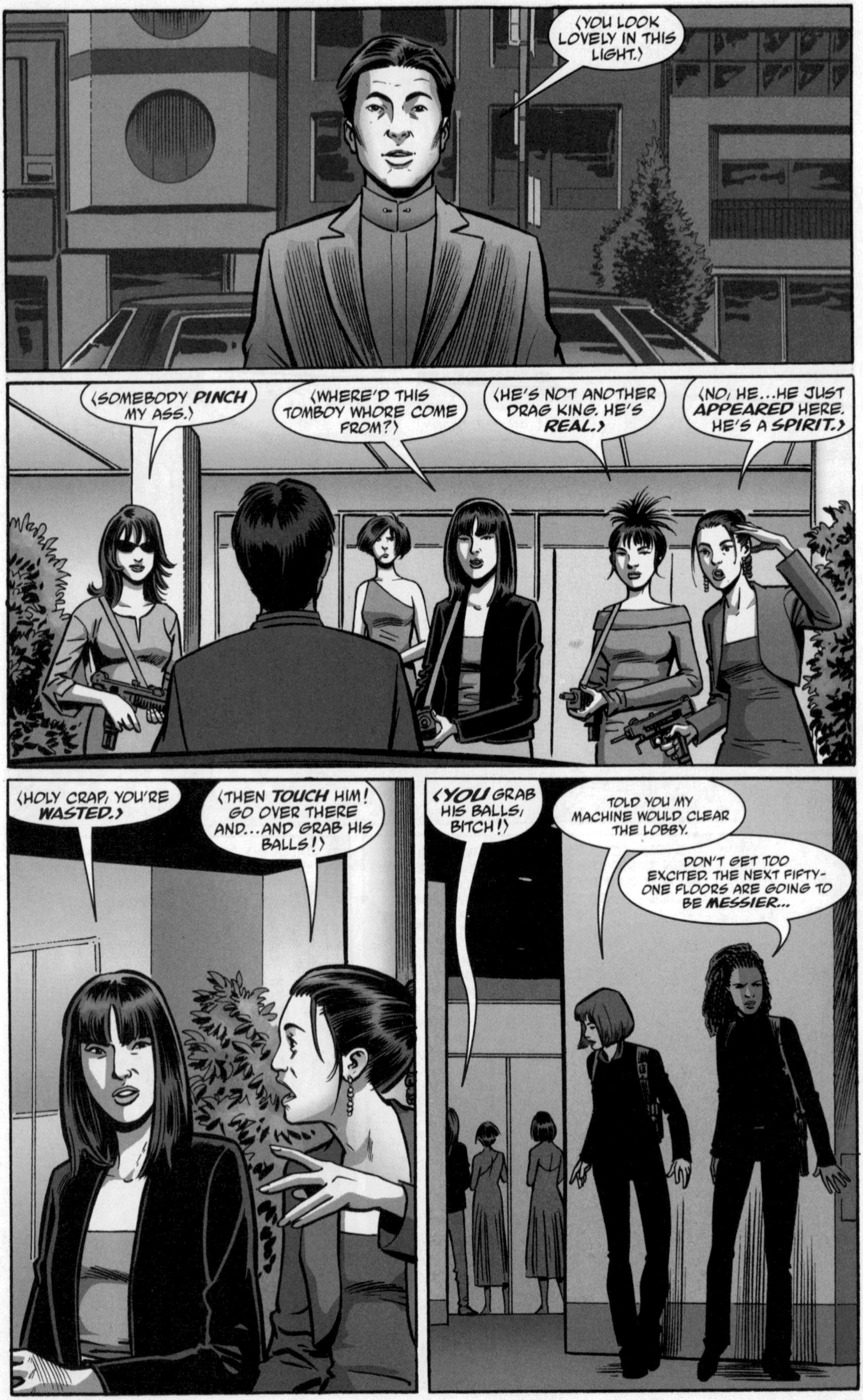
‹YOU LOOK LOVELY IN THIS LIGHT.›
‹SOMEBODY PINCH MY ASS.›
‹WHERE'D THIS TOMBOY WHORE COME FROM?›
‹HE'S NOT ANOTHER DRAG KING. HE'S REAL.›
‹NO, HE...HE JUST APPEARED HERE. HE'S A SPIRIT.›
‹HOLY CRAP, YOU'RE WASTED.›
‹THEN TOUCH HIM! GO OVER THERE AND...AND GRAB HIS BALLS!›
‹YOU GRAB HIS BALLS, BITCH!›
TOLD YOU MY MACHINE WOULD CLEAR THE LOBBY.
DON'T GET TOO EXCITED. THE NEXT FIFTY-ONE FLOORS ARE GOING TO BE MESSIER...

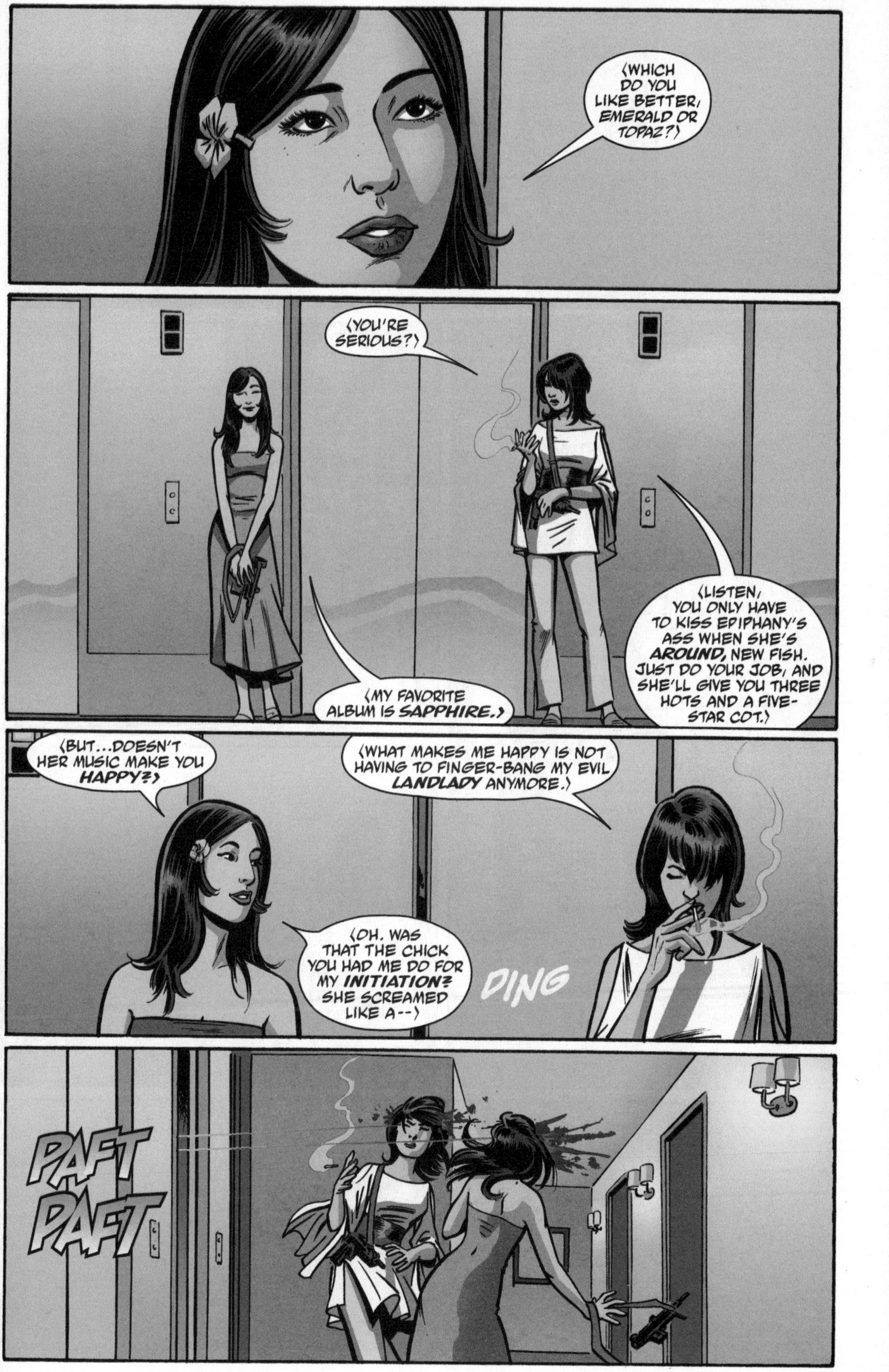
⟨WHICH DO YOU LIKE BETTER, EMERALD OR TOPAZ?⟩
⟨YOU'RE SERIOUS?⟩
⟨MY FAVORITE ALBUM IS **SAPPHIRE.**⟩
⟨LISTEN, YOU ONLY HAVE TO KISS EPIPHANY'S ASS WHEN SHE'S **AROUND,** NEW FISH. JUST DO YOUR JOB, AND SHE'LL GIVE YOU THREE HOTS AND A FIVE-STAR COT.⟩
⟨BUT...DOESN'T HER MUSIC MAKE YOU **HAPPY?**⟩
⟨WHAT MAKES ME HAPPY IS NOT HAVING TO FINGER-BANG MY EVIL **LANDLADY** ANYMORE.⟩
⟨OH. WAS THAT THE CHICK YOU HAD ME DO FOR MY **INITIATION?** SHE SCREAMED LIKE A--⟩
DING
PAFT PAFT

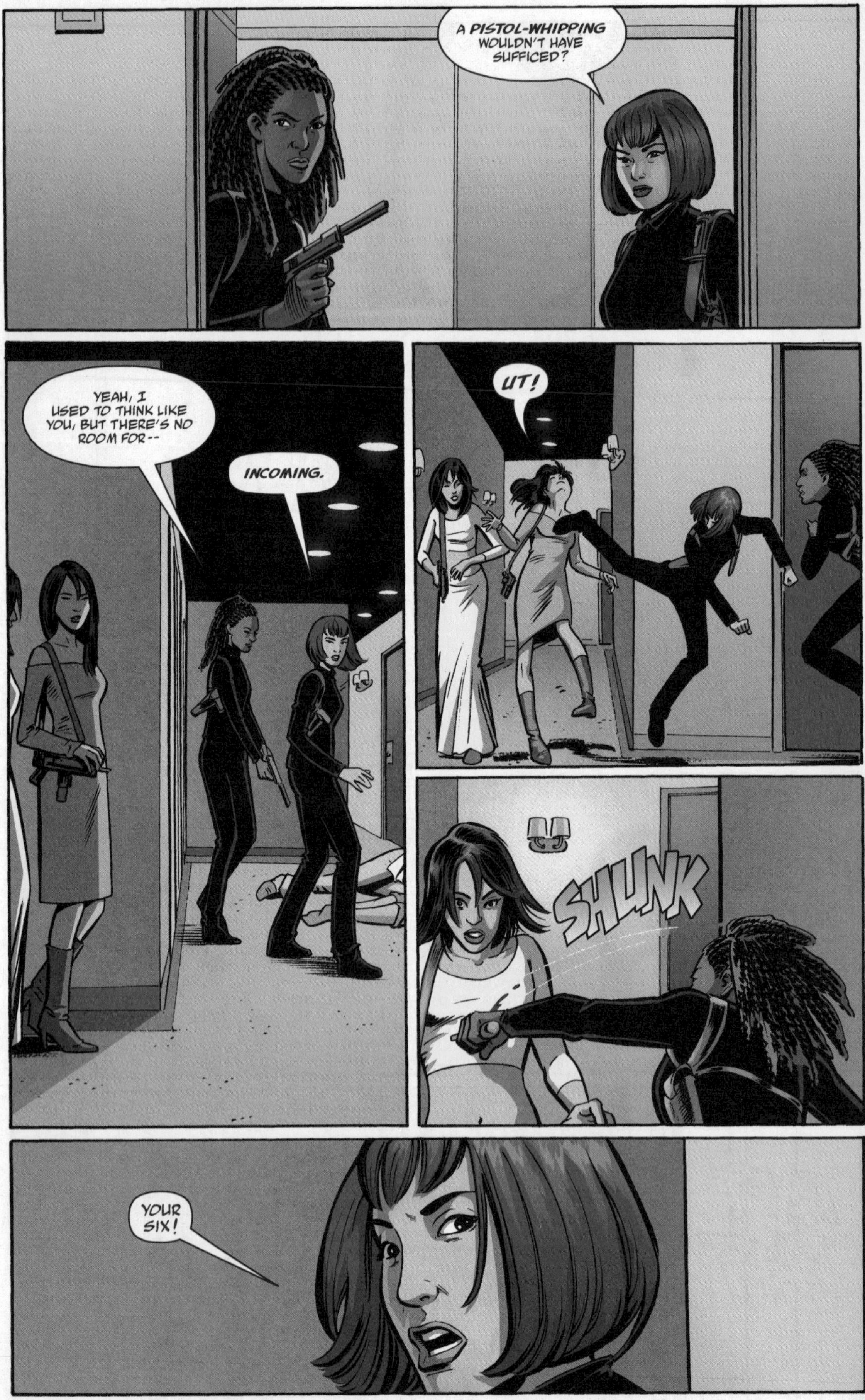
A PISTOL-WHIPPING WOULDN'T HAVE SUFFICED?
YEAH, I USED TO THINK LIKE YOU, BUT THERE'S NO ROOM FOR--
INCOMING.
UT!
SHUNK
YOUR SIX!

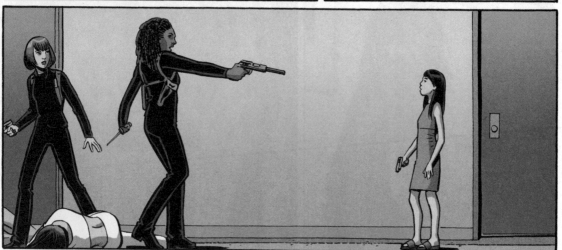

SON OF A...

EPIPHANYYYYYYYYY!

KLICK KLICK

65

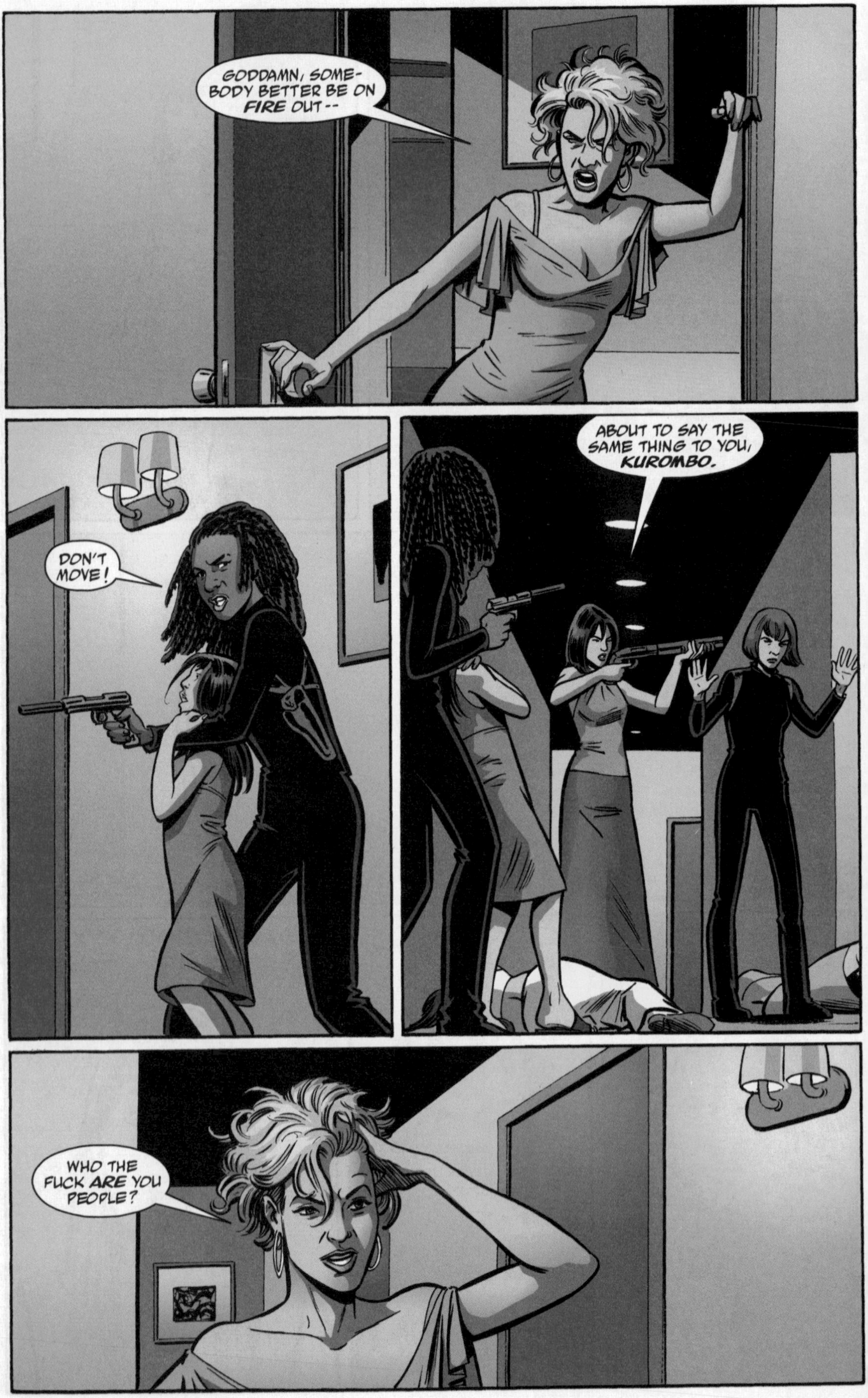
GODDAMN, SOME-BODY BETTER BE ON FIRE OUT--
DON'T MOVE!
ABOUT TO SAY THE SAME THING TO YOU, KUROMBO.
WHO THE FUCK ARE YOU PEOPLE?

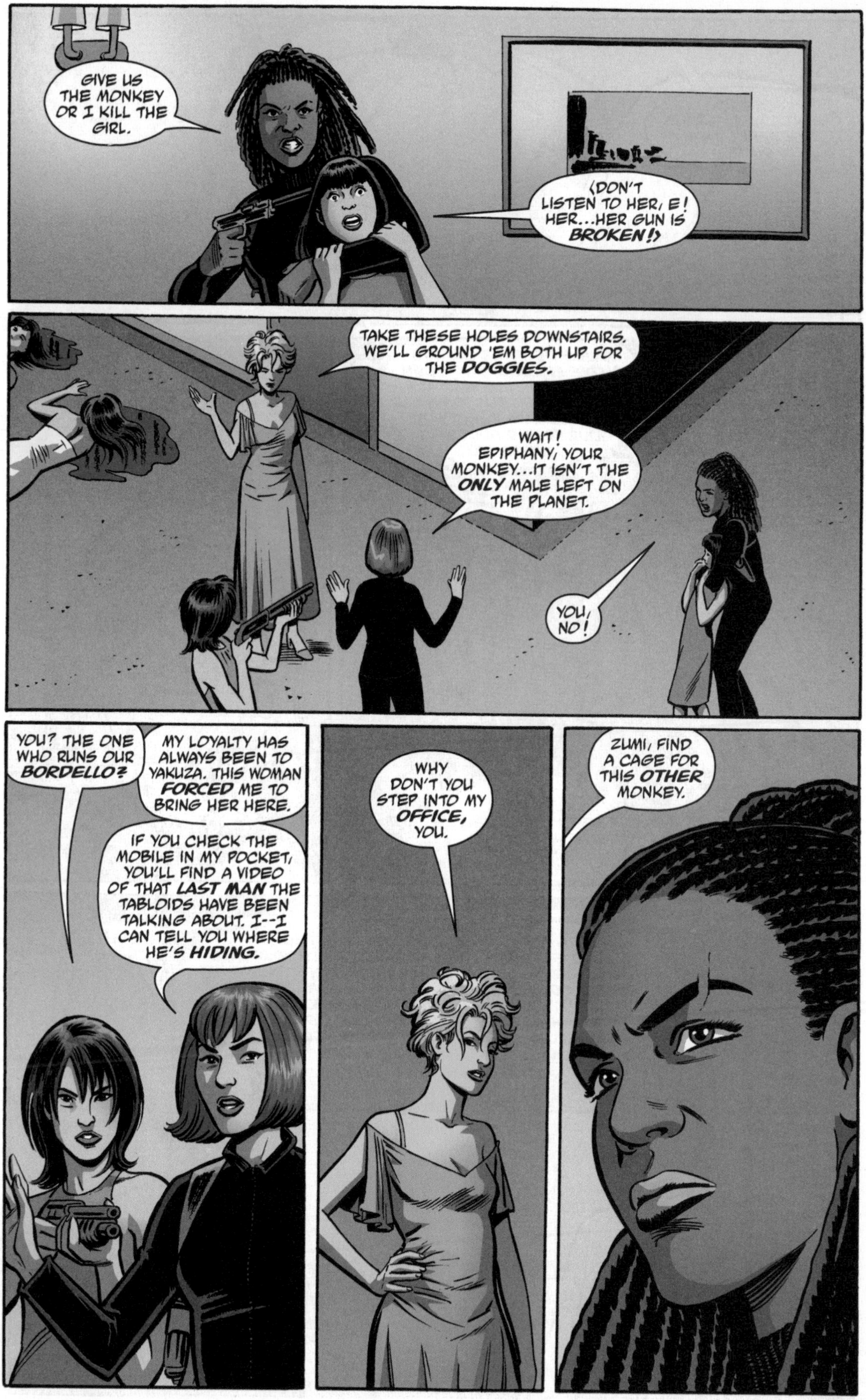
GIVE US THE MONKEY OR I KILL THE GIRL.
‹DON'T LISTEN TO HER, E! HER...HER GUN IS BROKEN!›
TAKE THESE HOLES DOWNSTAIRS. WE'LL GROUND 'EM BOTH UP FOR THE DOGGIES.
WAIT! EPIPHANY, YOUR MONKEY...IT ISN'T THE ONLY MALE LEFT ON THE PLANET.
YOU, NO!
YOU? THE ONE WHO RUNS OUR BORDELLO?
MY LOYALTY HAS ALWAYS BEEN TO YAKUZA. THIS WOMAN FORCED ME TO BRING HER HERE.
IF YOU CHECK THE MOBILE IN MY POCKET, YOU'LL FIND A VIDEO OF THAT LAST MAN THE TABLOIDS HAVE BEEN TALKING ABOUT. I--I CAN TELL YOU WHERE HE'S HIDING.
WHY DON'T YOU STEP INTO MY OFFICE, YOU.
ZUMI, FIND A CAGE FOR THIS OTHER MONKEY.

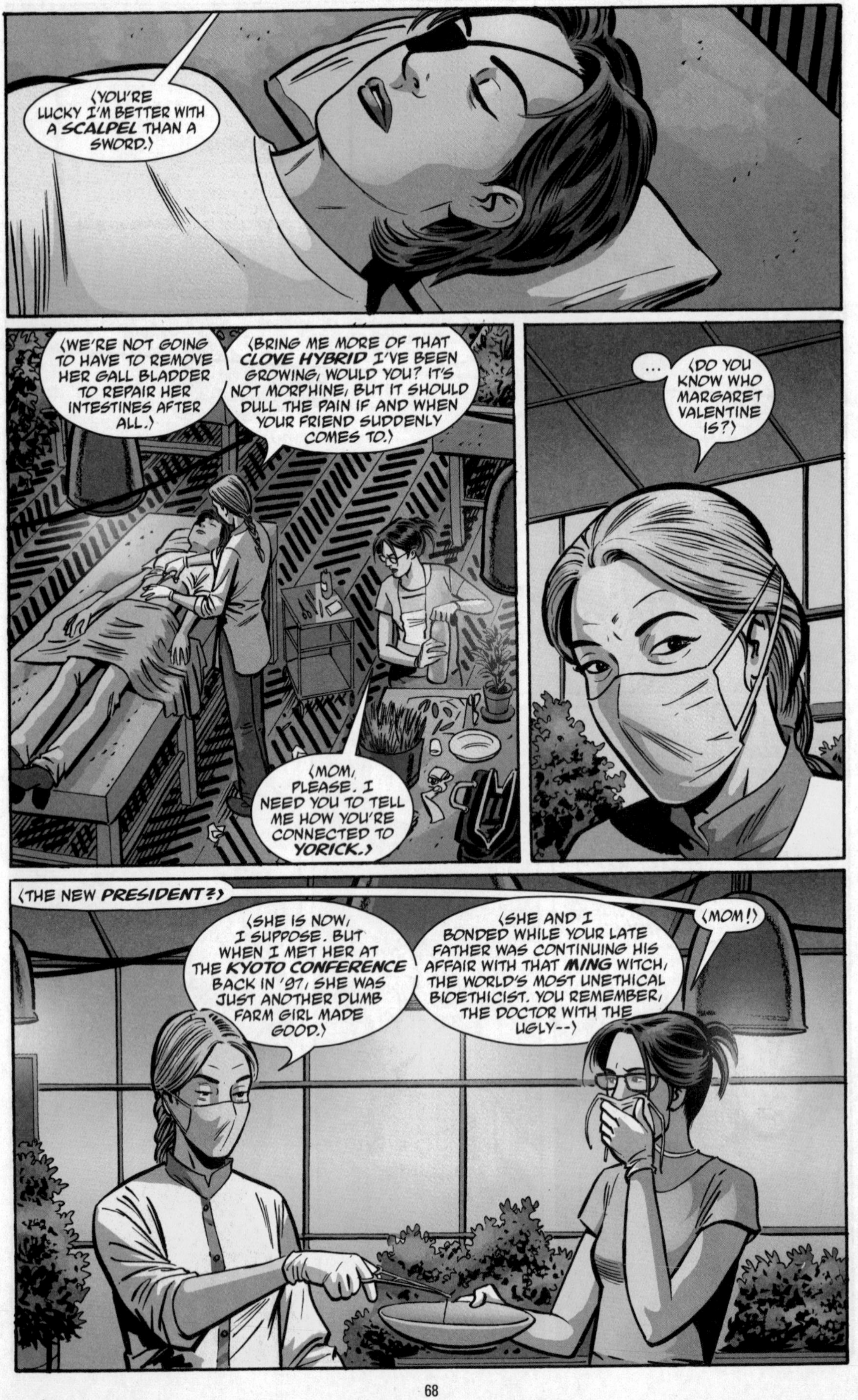

⟨YOU'RE LUCKY I'M BETTER WITH A SCALPEL THAN A SWORD.⟩
⟨WE'RE NOT GOING TO HAVE TO REMOVE HER GALL BLADDER TO REPAIR HER INTESTINES AFTER ALL.⟩
⟨BRING ME MORE OF THAT CLOVE HYBRID I'VE BEEN GROWING, WOULD YOU? IT'S NOT MORPHINE, BUT IT SHOULD DULL THE PAIN IF AND WHEN YOUR FRIEND SUDDENLY COMES TO.⟩
⟨MOM, PLEASE. I NEED YOU TO TELL ME HOW YOU'RE CONNECTED TO YORICK.⟩
...
⟨DO YOU KNOW WHO MARGARET VALENTINE IS?⟩
⟨THE NEW PRESIDENT?⟩
⟨SHE IS NOW, I SUPPOSE. BUT WHEN I MET HER AT THE KYOTO CONFERENCE BACK IN '97, SHE WAS JUST ANOTHER DUMB FARM GIRL MADE GOOD.⟩
⟨SHE AND I BONDED WHILE YOUR LATE FATHER WAS CONTINUING HIS AFFAIR WITH THAT MING WITCH, THE WORLD'S MOST UNETHICAL BIOETHICIST. YOU REMEMBER, THE DOCTOR WITH THE UGLY--⟩
⟨MOM!⟩

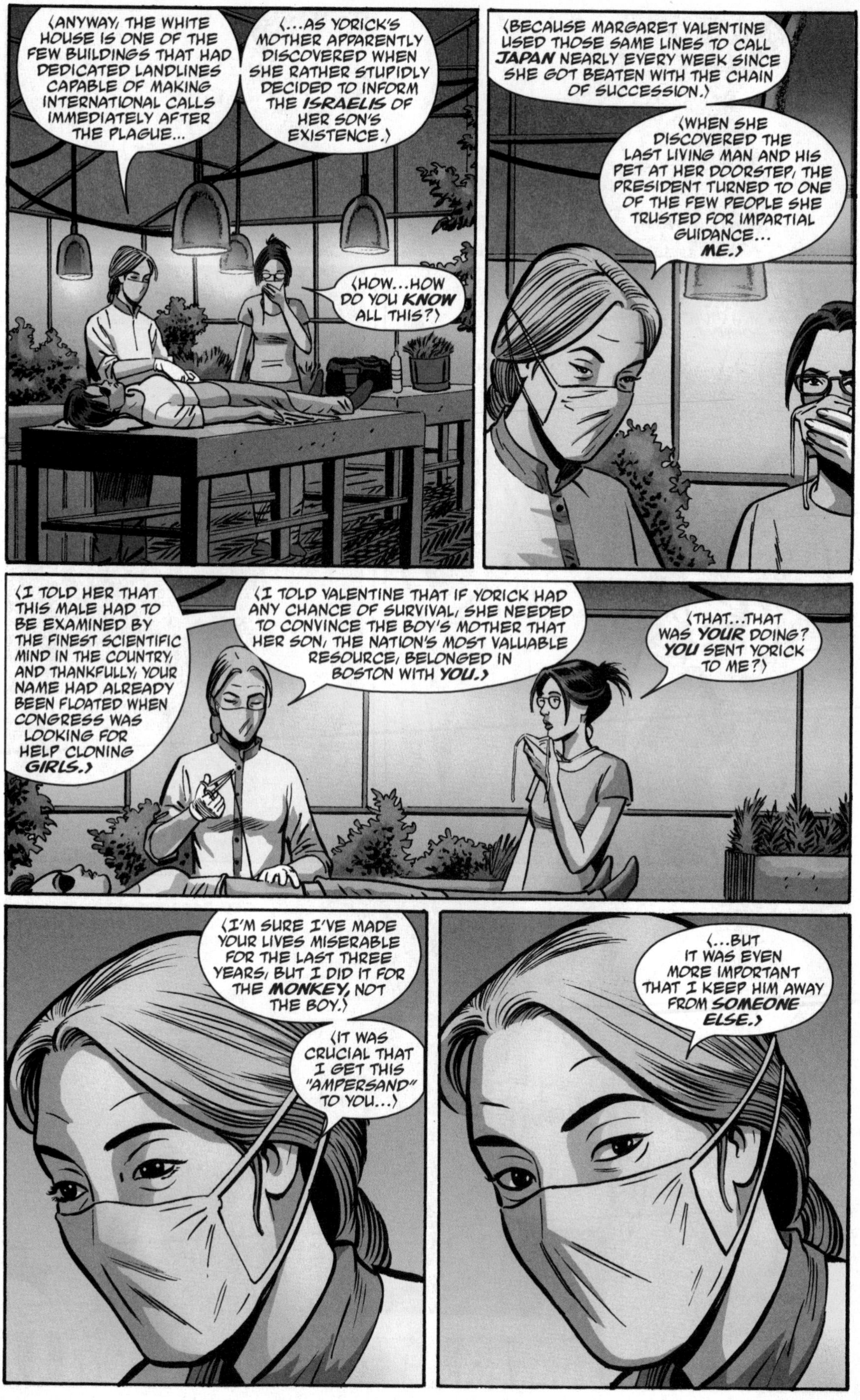
‹ANYWAY, THE WHITE HOUSE IS ONE OF THE FEW BUILDINGS THAT HAD DEDICATED LANDLINES CAPABLE OF MAKING INTERNATIONAL CALLS IMMEDIATELY AFTER THE PLAGUE...
‹...AS YORICK'S MOTHER APPARENTLY DISCOVERED WHEN SHE RATHER STUPIDLY DECIDED TO INFORM THE ISRAELIS OF HER SON'S EXISTENCE.›
‹HOW...HOW DO YOU KNOW ALL THIS?›
‹BECAUSE MARGARET VALENTINE USED THOSE SAME LINES TO CALL JAPAN NEARLY EVERY WEEK SINCE SHE GOT BEATEN WITH THE CHAIN OF SUCCESSION.›
‹WHEN SHE DISCOVERED THE LAST LIVING MAN AND HIS PET AT HER DOORSTEP, THE PRESIDENT TURNED TO ONE OF THE FEW PEOPLE SHE TRUSTED FOR IMPARTIAL GUIDANCE... ME.›
‹I TOLD HER THAT THIS MALE HAD TO BE EXAMINED BY THE FINEST SCIENTIFIC MIND IN THE COUNTRY, AND THANKFULLY, YOUR NAME HAD ALREADY BEEN FLOATED WHEN CONGRESS WAS LOOKING FOR HELP CLONING GIRLS.›
‹I TOLD VALENTINE THAT IF YORICK HAD ANY CHANCE OF SURVIVAL, SHE NEEDED TO CONVINCE THE BOY'S MOTHER THAT HER SON, THE NATION'S MOST VALUABLE RESOURCE, BELONGED IN BOSTON WITH YOU.›
‹THAT...THAT WAS YOUR DOING? YOU SENT YORICK TO ME?›
‹I'M SURE I'VE MADE YOUR LIVES MISERABLE FOR THE LAST THREE YEARS, BUT I DID IT FOR THE MONKEY, NOT THE BOY.›
‹IT WAS CRUCIAL THAT I GET THIS "AMPERSAND" TO YOU...›
‹...BUT IT WAS EVEN MORE IMPORTANT THAT I KEEP HIM AWAY FROM SOMEONE ELSE.›

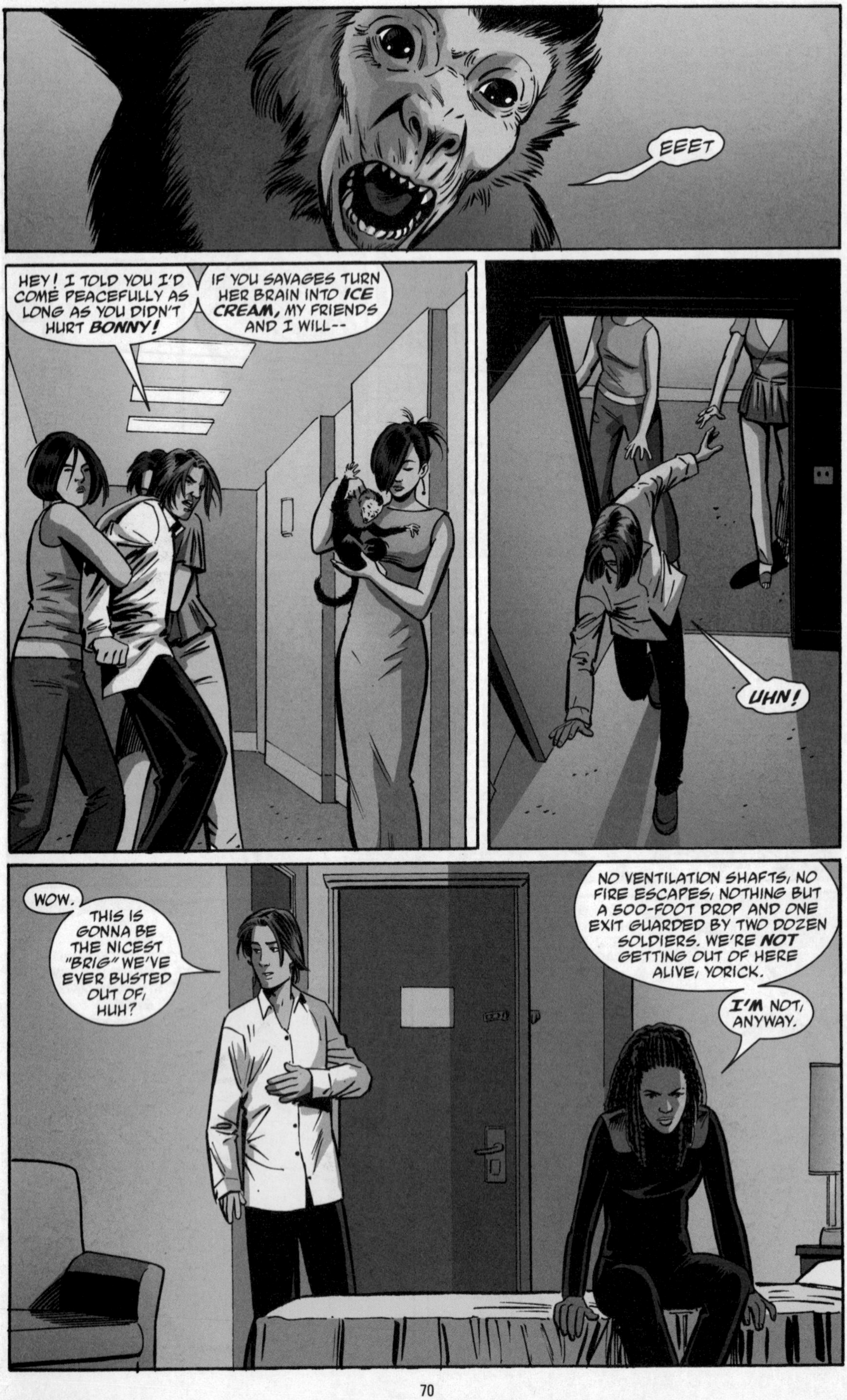
EEEt
HEY! I TOLD YOU I'D COME PEACEFULLY AS LONG AS YOU DIDN'T HURT BONNY!
IF YOU SAVAGES TURN HER BRAIN INTO ICE CREAM, MY FRIENDS AND I WILL--
UHN!
WOW.
THIS IS GONNA BE THE NICEST "BRIG" WE'VE EVER BUSTED OUT OF, HUH?
NO VENTILATION SHAFTS, NO FIRE ESCAPES, NOTHING BUT A 500-FOOT DROP AND ONE EXIT GUARDED BY TWO DOZEN SOLDIERS. WE'RE NOT GETTING OUT OF HERE ALIVE, YORICK.
I'M NOT, ANYWAY.

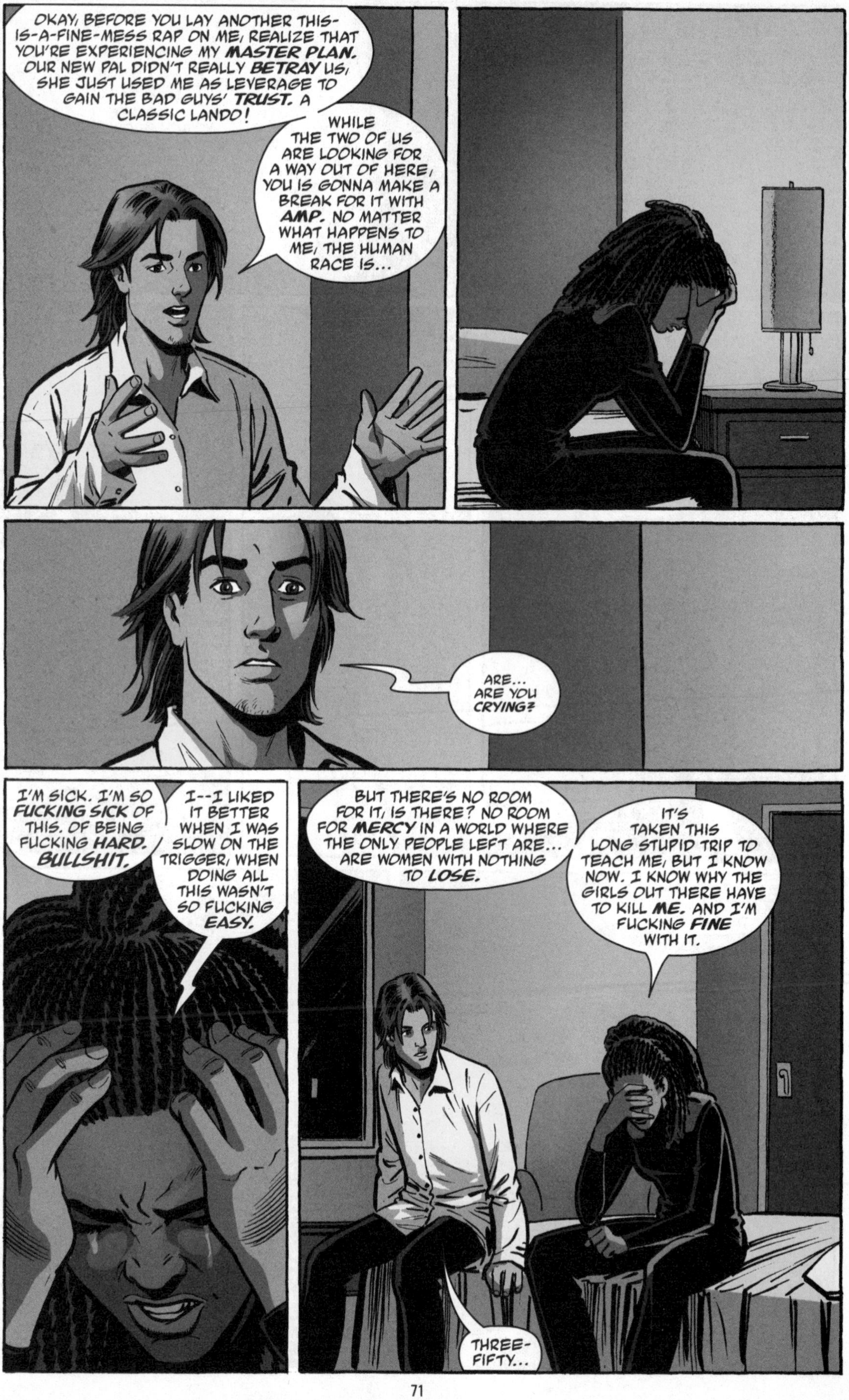
OKAY, BEFORE YOU LAY ANOTHER THIS-IS-A-FINE-MESS RAP ON ME, REALIZE THAT YOU'RE EXPERIENCING MY MASTER PLAN. OUR NEW PAL DIDN'T REALLY BETRAY US, SHE JUST USED ME AS LEVERAGE TO GAIN THE BAD GUYS' TRUST. A CLASSIC LANDO!
WHILE THE TWO OF US ARE LOOKING FOR A WAY OUT OF HERE, YOU IS GONNA MAKE A BREAK FOR IT WITH AMP. NO MATTER WHAT HAPPENS TO ME, THE HUMAN RACE IS...
ARE... ARE YOU CRYING?
I'M SICK. I'M SO FUCKING SICK OF THIS. OF BEING FUCKING HARD. BULLSHIT.
I--I LIKED IT BETTER WHEN I WAS SLOW ON THE TRIGGER, WHEN DOING ALL THIS WASN'T SO FUCKING EASY.
BUT THERE'S NO ROOM FOR IT, IS THERE? NO ROOM FOR MERCY IN A WORLD WHERE THE ONLY PEOPLE LEFT ARE... ARE WOMEN WITH NOTHING TO LOSE.
IT'S TAKEN THIS LONG STUPID TRIP TO TEACH ME, BUT I KNOW NOW. I KNOW WHY THE GIRLS OUT THERE HAVE TO KILL ME. AND I'M FUCKING FINE WITH IT.
THREE-FIFTY...

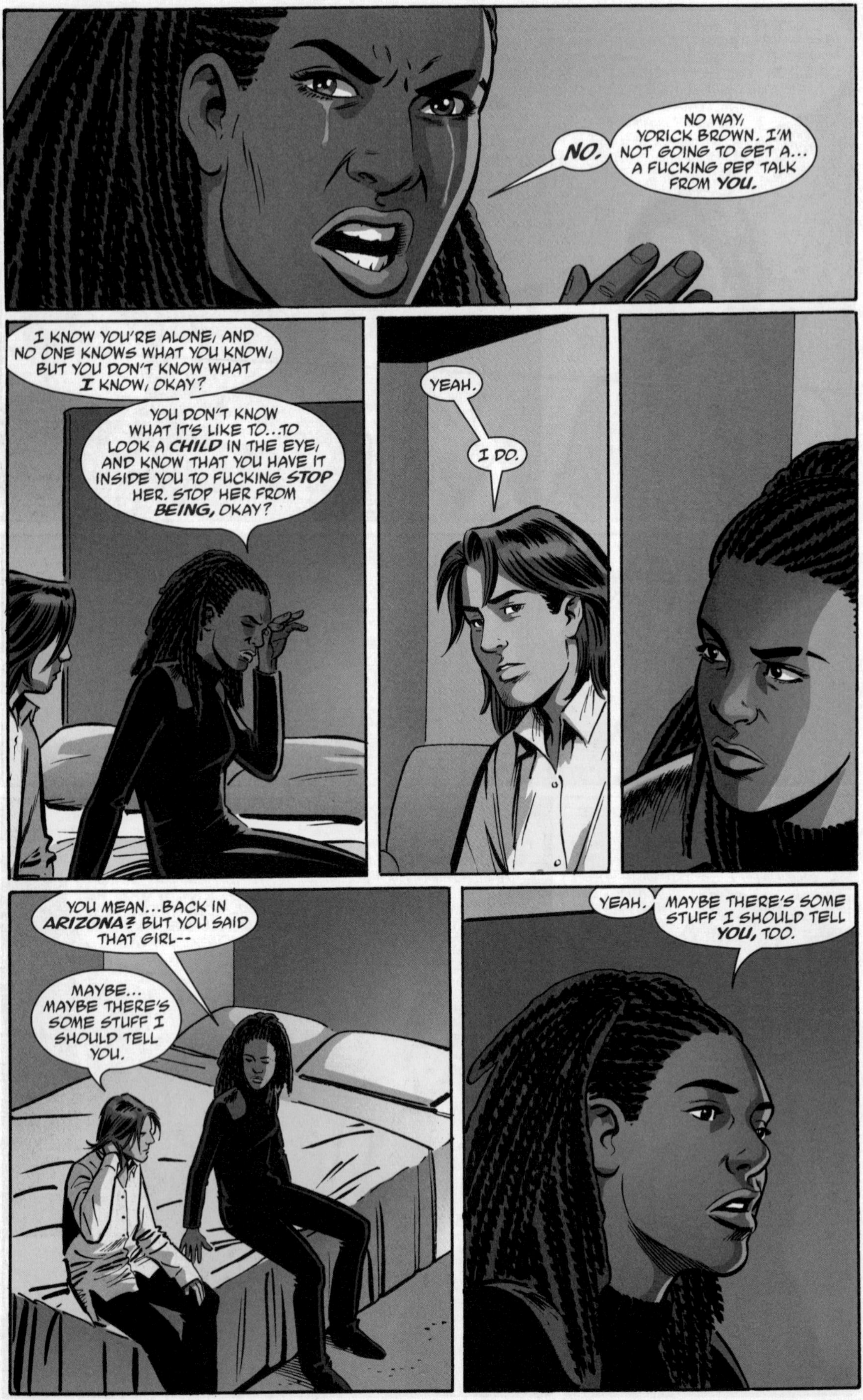
NO.
NO WAY, YORICK BROWN. I'M NOT GOING TO GET A... A FUCKING PEP TALK FROM YOU.
I KNOW YOU'RE ALONE, AND NO ONE KNOWS WHAT YOU KNOW, BUT YOU DON'T KNOW WHAT I KNOW, OKAY?
YOU DON'T KNOW WHAT IT'S LIKE TO...TO LOOK A CHILD IN THE EYE, AND KNOW THAT YOU HAVE IT INSIDE YOU TO FUCKING STOP HER. STOP HER FROM BEING, OKAY?
YEAH.
I DO.
YOU MEAN...BACK IN ARIZONA? BUT YOU SAID THAT GIRL--
MAYBE... MAYBE THERE'S SOME STUFF I SHOULD TELL YOU.
YEAH.
MAYBE THERE'S SOME STUFF I SHOULD TELL YOU, TOO.

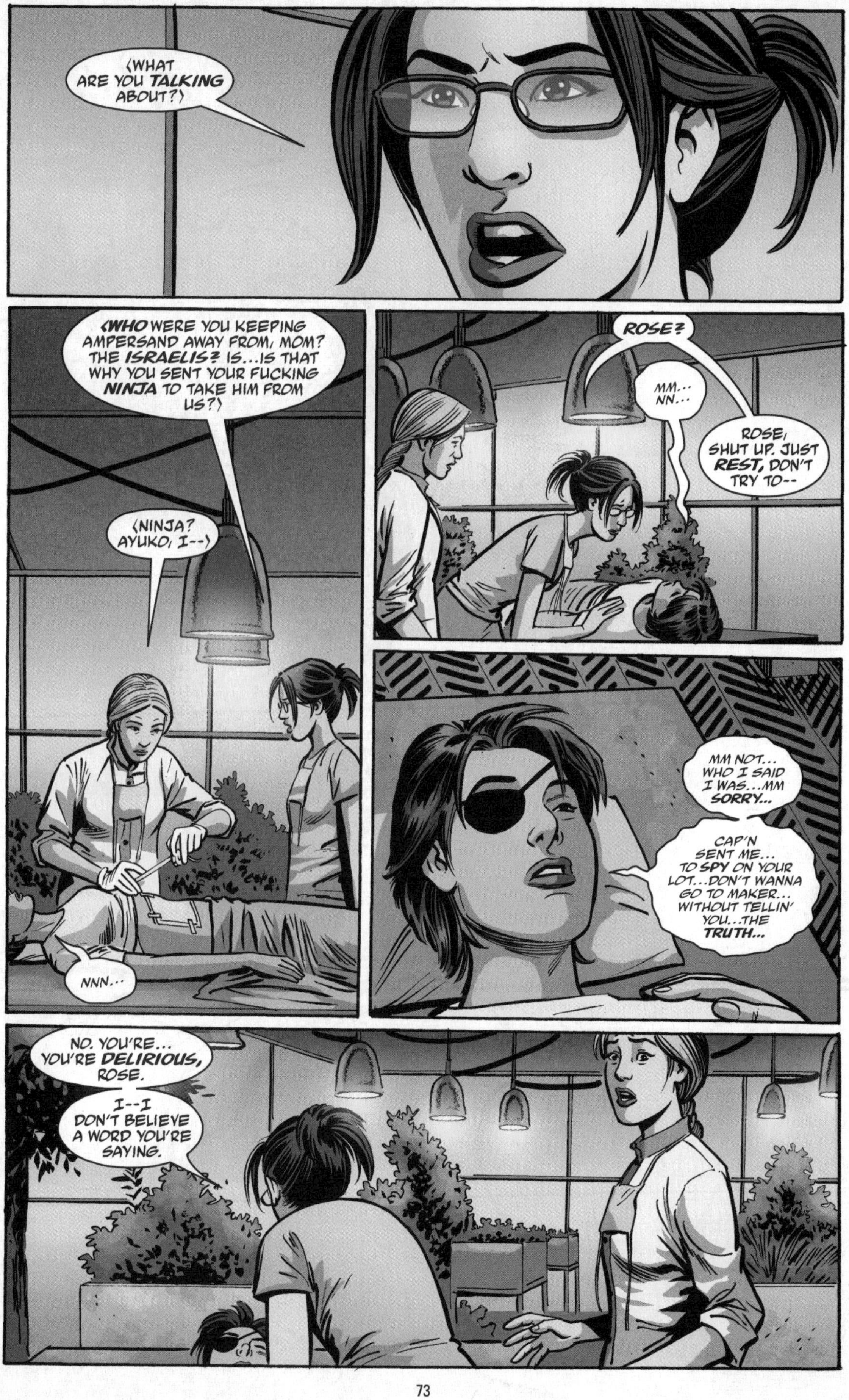

‹WHAT ARE YOU TALKING ABOUT?›
‹WHO WERE YOU KEEPING AMPERSAND AWAY FROM, MOM? THE ISRAELIS? IS...IS THAT WHY YOU SENT YOUR FUCKING NINJA TO TAKE HIM FROM US?›
‹NINJA? AYUKO, I--›
NNN...
ROSE?
MM... NN...
ROSE, SHUT UP. JUST REST, DON'T TRY TO--
MM NOT... WHO I SAID I WAS...MM SORRY...
CAP'N SENT ME... TO SPY ON YOUR LOT...DON'T WANNA GO TO MAKER... WITHOUT TELLIN' YOU...THE TRUTH...
NO. YOU'RE... YOU'RE DELIRIOUS, ROSE.
I--I DON'T BELIEVE A WORD YOU'RE SAYING.

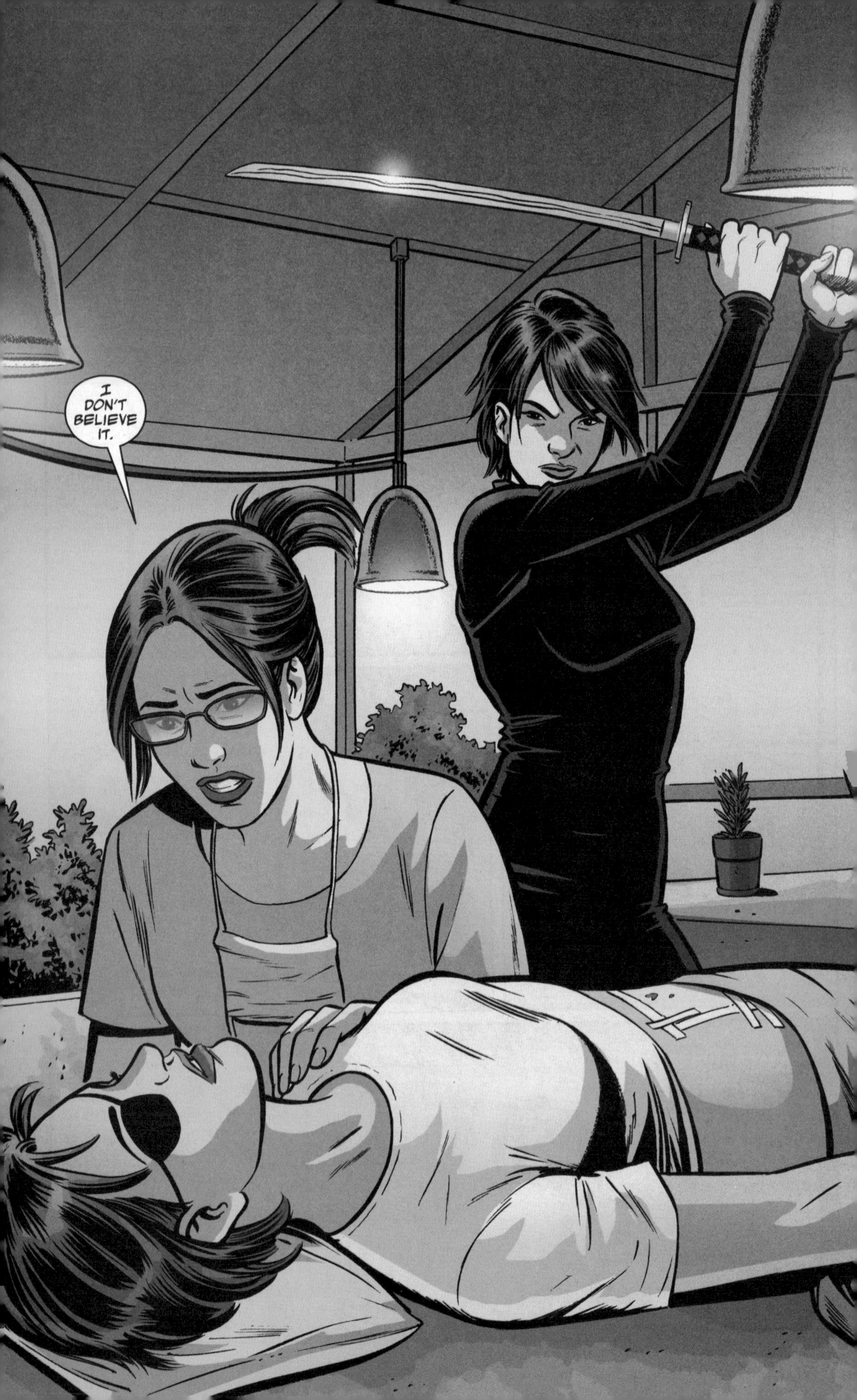
I DON'T BELIEVE IT.

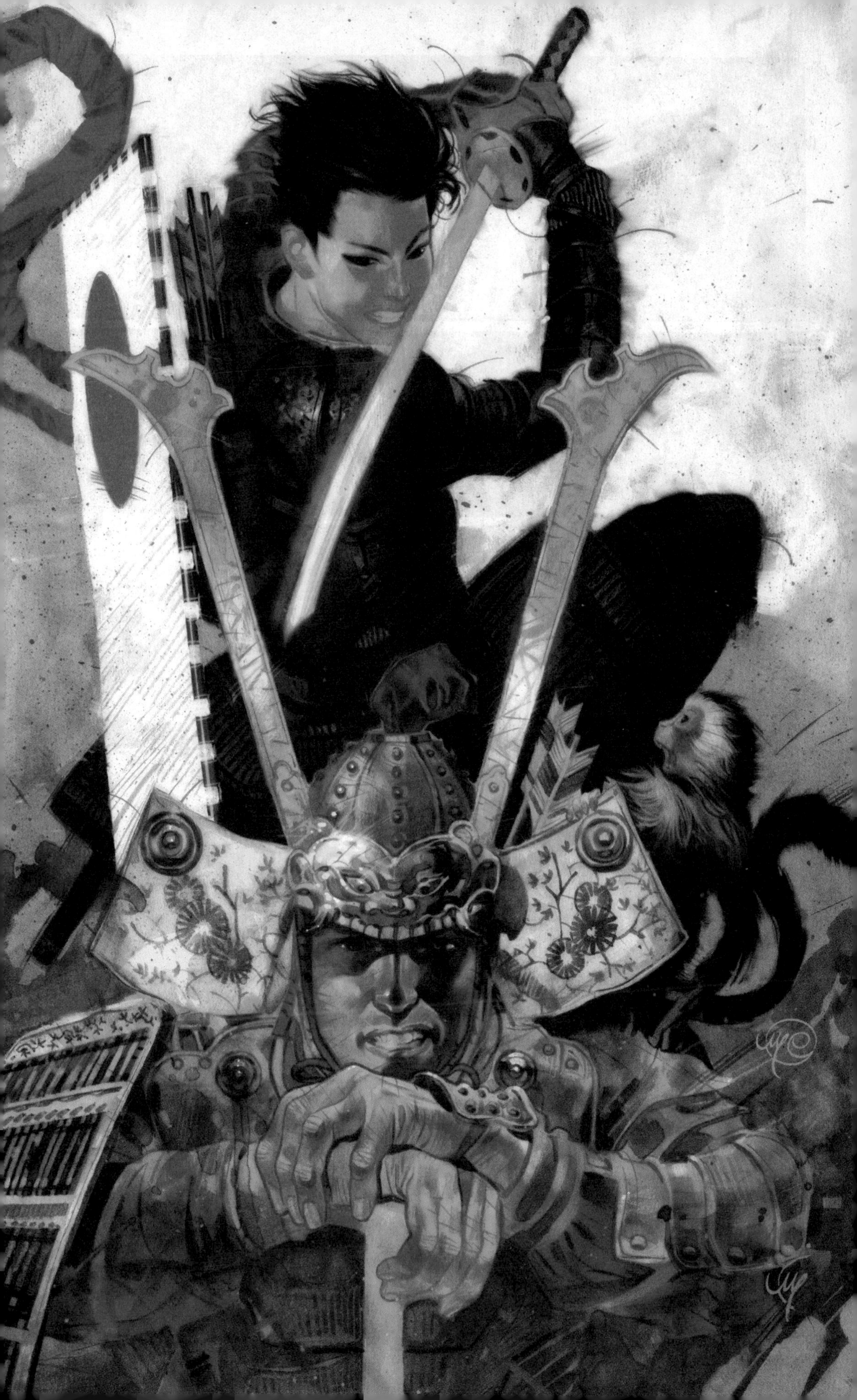

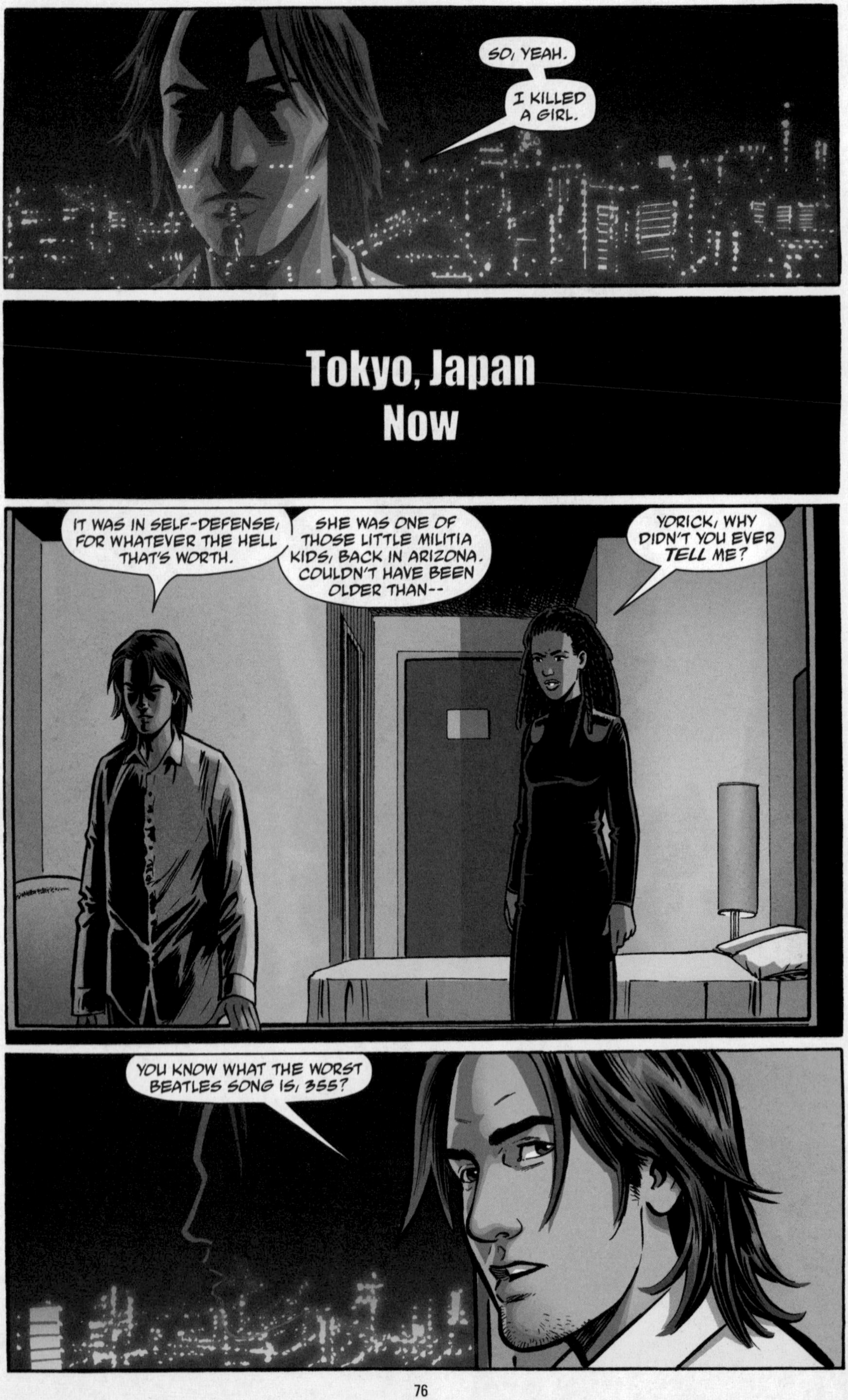
SO, YEAH.
I KILLED A GIRL.
Tokyo, Japan Now
IT WAS IN SELF-DEFENSE, FOR WHATEVER THE HELL THAT'S WORTH.
SHE WAS ONE OF THOSE LITTLE MILITIA KIDS, BACK IN ARIZONA. COULDN'T HAVE BEEN OLDER THAN--
YORICK, WHY DIDN'T YOU EVER TELL ME?
YOU KNOW WHAT THE WORST BEATLES SONG IS, 355?

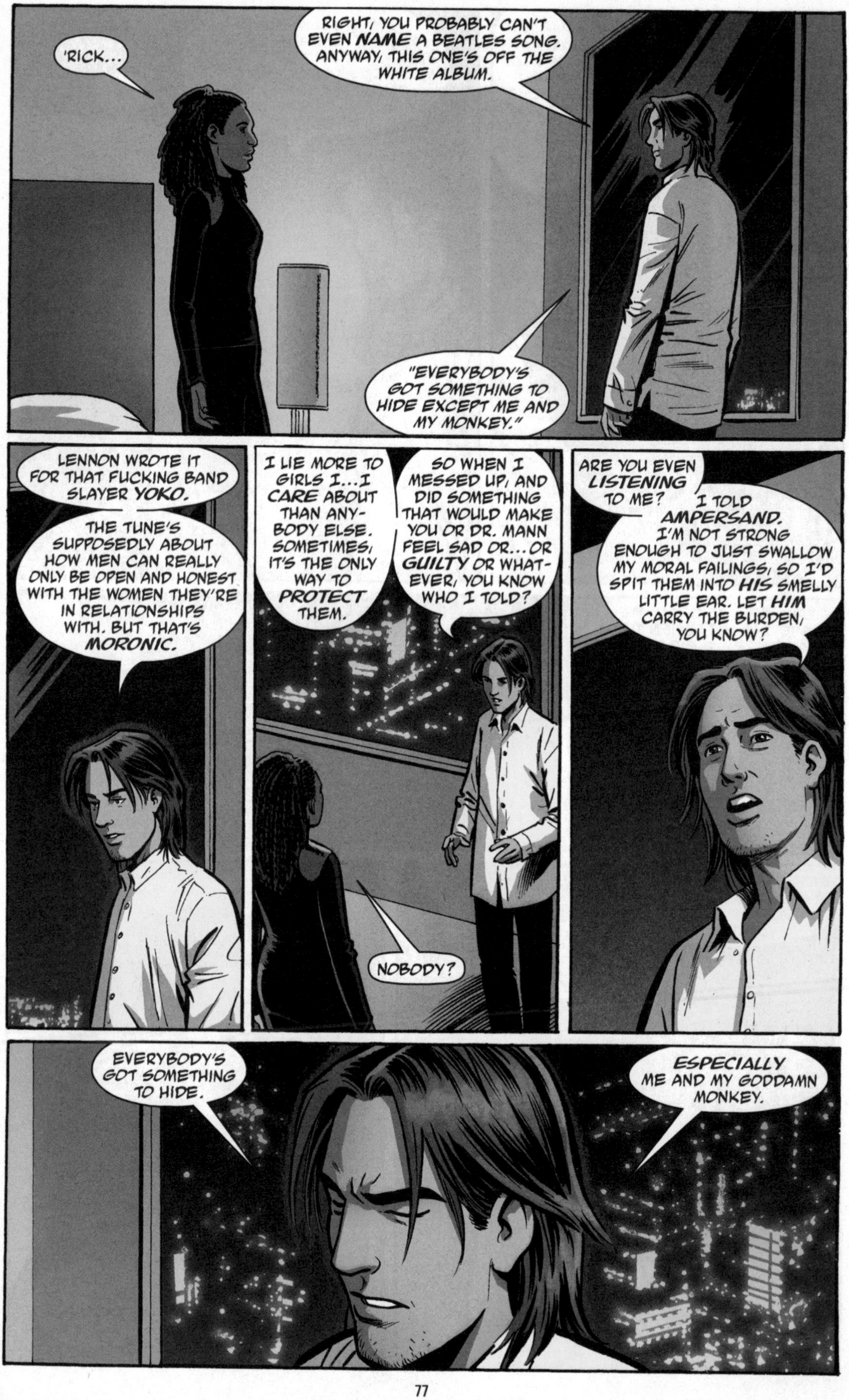
'RICK...
RIGHT, YOU PROBABLY CAN'T EVEN NAME A BEATLES SONG. ANYWAY, THIS ONE'S OFF THE WHITE ALBUM.
"EVERYBODY'S GOT SOMETHING TO HIDE EXCEPT ME AND MY MONKEY."
LENNON WROTE IT FOR THAT FUCKING BAND SLAYER YOKO.
THE TUNE'S SUPPOSEDLY ABOUT HOW MEN CAN REALLY ONLY BE OPEN AND HONEST WITH THE WOMEN THEY'RE IN RELATIONSHIPS WITH. BUT THAT'S MORONIC.
I LIE MORE TO GIRLS I...I CARE ABOUT THAN ANYBODY ELSE. SOMETIMES, IT'S THE ONLY WAY TO PROTECT THEM.
SO WHEN I MESSED UP, AND DID SOMETHING THAT WOULD MAKE YOU OR DR. MANN FEEL SAD OR...OR GUILTY OR WHATEVER, YOU KNOW WHO I TOLD?
NOBODY?
ARE YOU EVEN LISTENING TO ME?
I TOLD AMPERSAND. I'M NOT STRONG ENOUGH TO JUST SWALLOW MY MORAL FAILINGS, SO I'D SPIT THEM INTO HIS SMELLY LITTLE EAR. LET HIM CARRY THE BURDEN, YOU KNOW?
EVERYBODY'S GOT SOMETHING TO HIDE.
ESPECIALLY ME AND MY GODDAMN MONKEY.

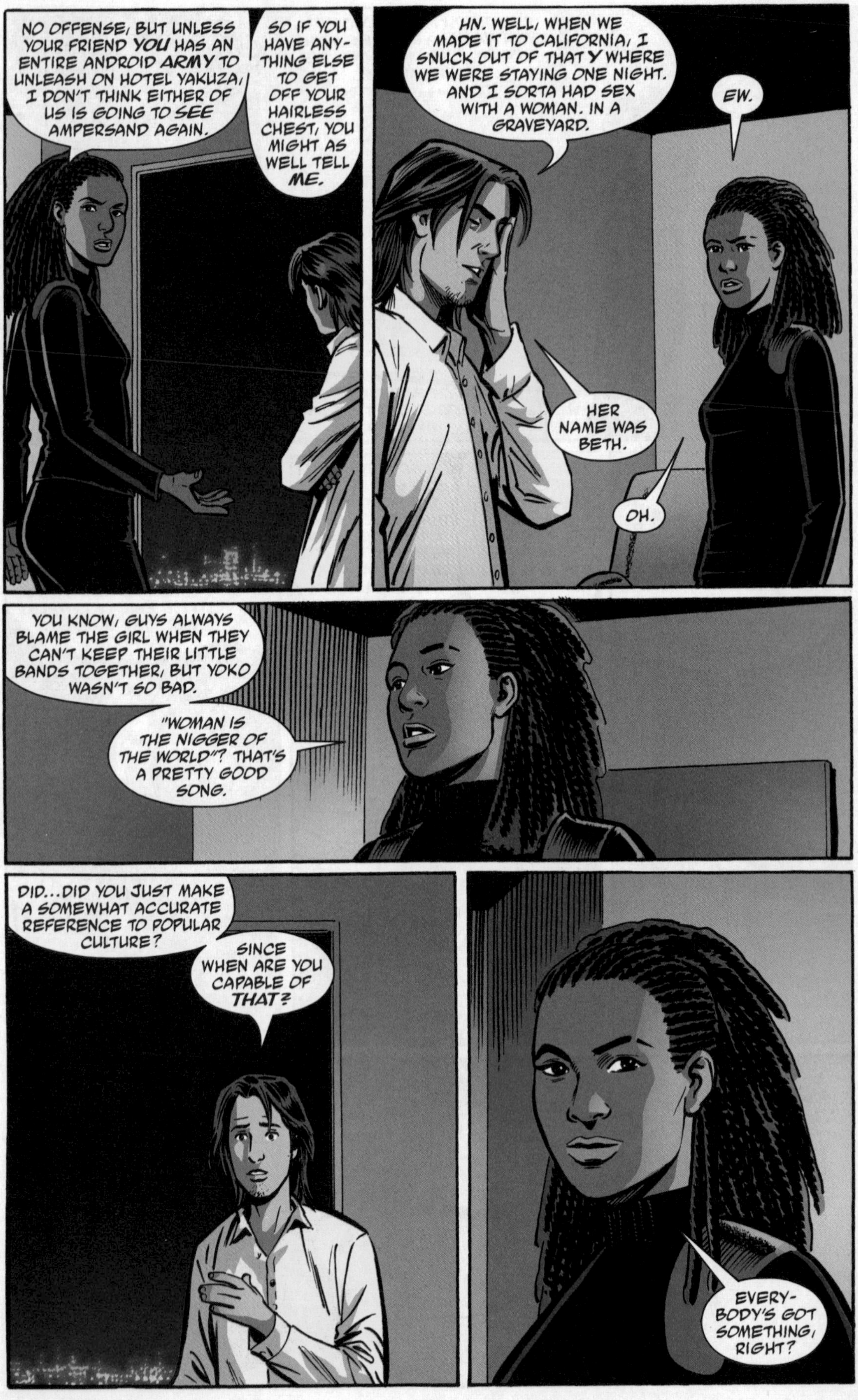
NO OFFENSE, BUT UNLESS YOUR FRIEND YOU HAS AN ENTIRE ANDROID ARMY TO UNLEASH ON HOTEL YAKUZA, I DON'T THINK EITHER OF US IS GOING TO SEE AMPERSAND AGAIN.
SO IF YOU HAVE ANYTHING ELSE TO GET OFF YOUR HAIRLESS CHEST, YOU MIGHT AS WELL TELL ME.
HN. WELL, WHEN WE MADE IT TO CALIFORNIA, I SNUCK OUT OF THAT Y WHERE WE WERE STAYING ONE NIGHT. AND I SORTA HAD SEX WITH A WOMAN. IN A GRAVEYARD.
EW.
HER NAME WAS BETH.
OH.
YOU KNOW, GUYS ALWAYS BLAME THE GIRL WHEN THEY CAN'T KEEP THEIR LITTLE BANDS TOGETHER, BUT YOKO WASN'T SO BAD.
"WOMAN IS THE NIGGER OF THE WORLD"? THAT'S A PRETTY GOOD SONG.
DID...DID YOU JUST MAKE A SOMEWHAT ACCURATE REFERENCE TO POPULAR CULTURE?
SINCE WHEN ARE YOU CAPABLE OF THAT?
EVERY-BODY'S GOT SOMETHING, RIGHT?

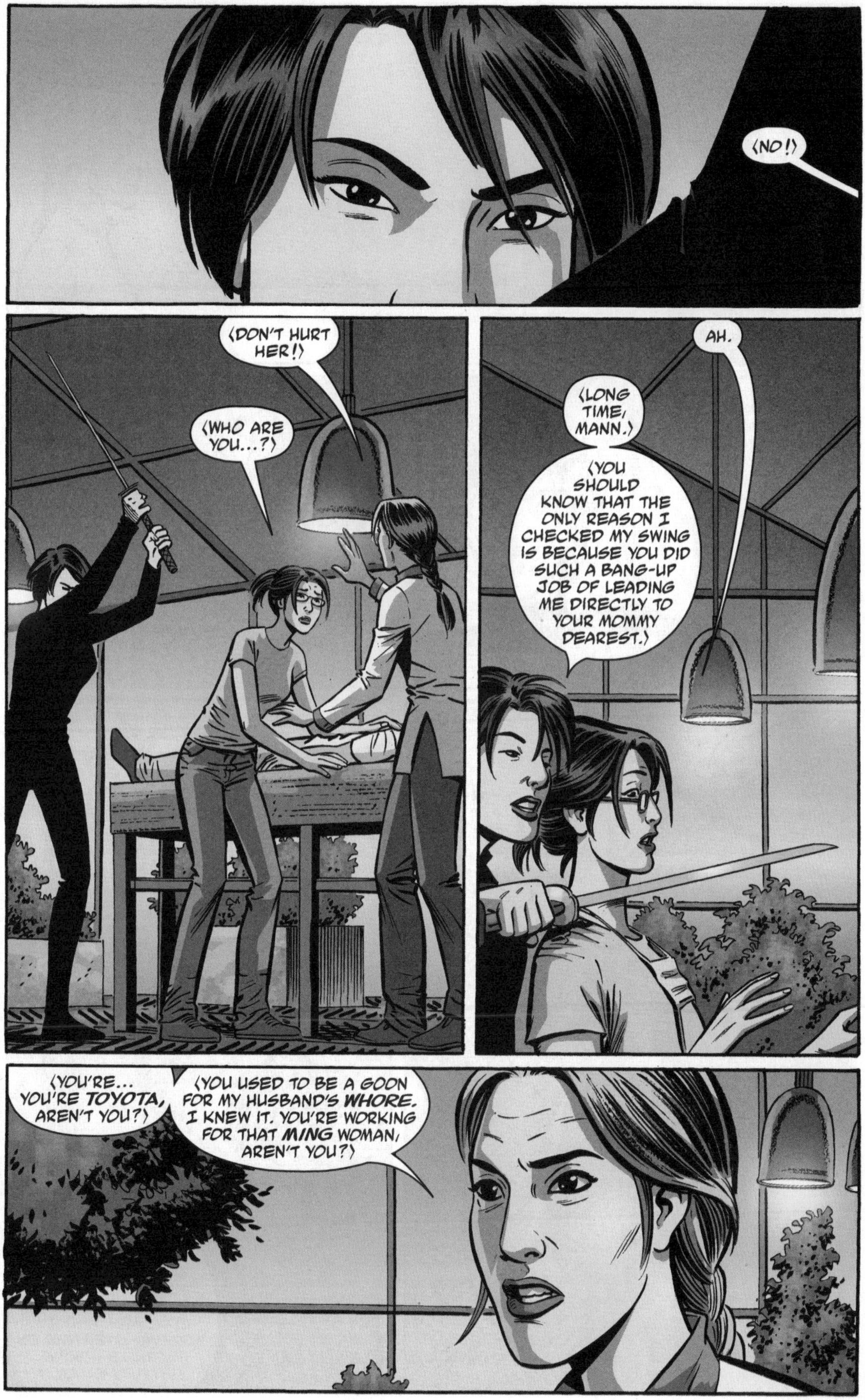

‹NO!›
‹DON'T HURT HER!›
‹WHO ARE YOU...?›
AH.
‹LONG TIME, MANN.›
‹YOU SHOULD KNOW THAT THE ONLY REASON I CHECKED MY SWING IS BECAUSE YOU DID SUCH A BANG-UP JOB OF LEADING ME DIRECTLY TO YOUR MOMMY DEAREST.›
‹YOU'RE... YOU'RE TOYOTA, AREN'T YOU?›
‹YOU USED TO BE A GOON FOR MY HUSBAND'S WHORE. I KNEW IT. YOU'RE WORKING FOR THAT MING WOMAN, AREN'T YOU?›

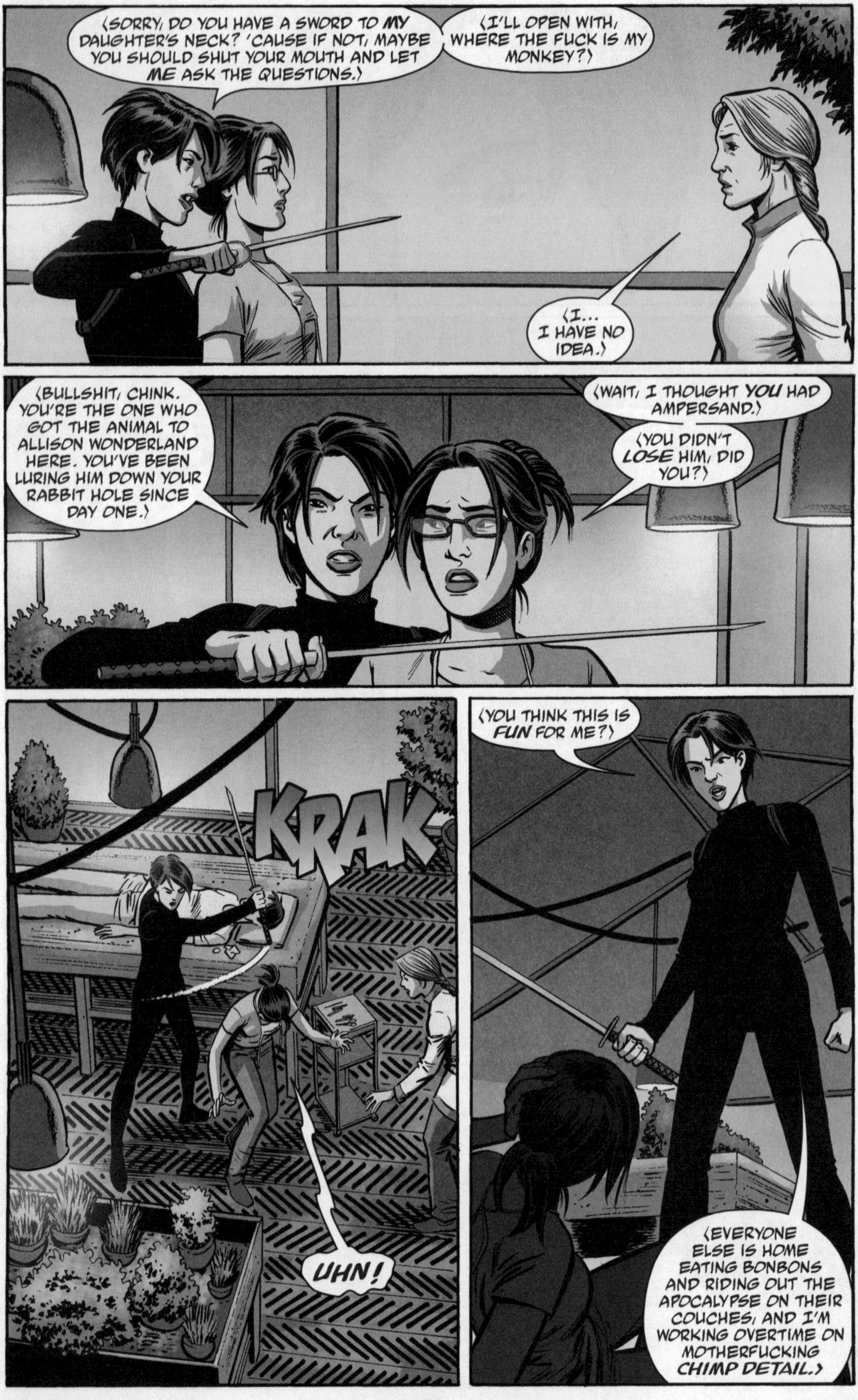

<SORRY, DO YOU HAVE A SWORD TO MY DAUGHTER'S NECK? 'CAUSE IF NOT, MAYBE YOU SHOULD SHUT YOUR MOUTH AND LET ME ASK THE QUESTIONS.>
<I'LL OPEN WITH, WHERE THE FUCK IS MY MONKEY?>
<I... I HAVE NO IDEA.>
<BULLSHIT, CHINK. YOU'RE THE ONE WHO GOT THE ANIMAL TO ALLISON WONDERLAND HERE. YOU'VE BEEN LURING HIM DOWN YOUR RABBIT HOLE SINCE DAY ONE.>
<WAIT, I THOUGHT YOU HAD AMPERSAND.>
<YOU DIDN'T LOSE HIM, DID YOU?>
KRAK
UHN!
<YOU THINK THIS IS FUN FOR ME?>
<EVERYONE ELSE IS HOME EATING BONBONS AND RIDING OUT THE APOCALYPSE ON THEIR COUCHES, AND I'M WORKING OVERTIME ON MOTHERFUCKING CHIMP DETAIL.>

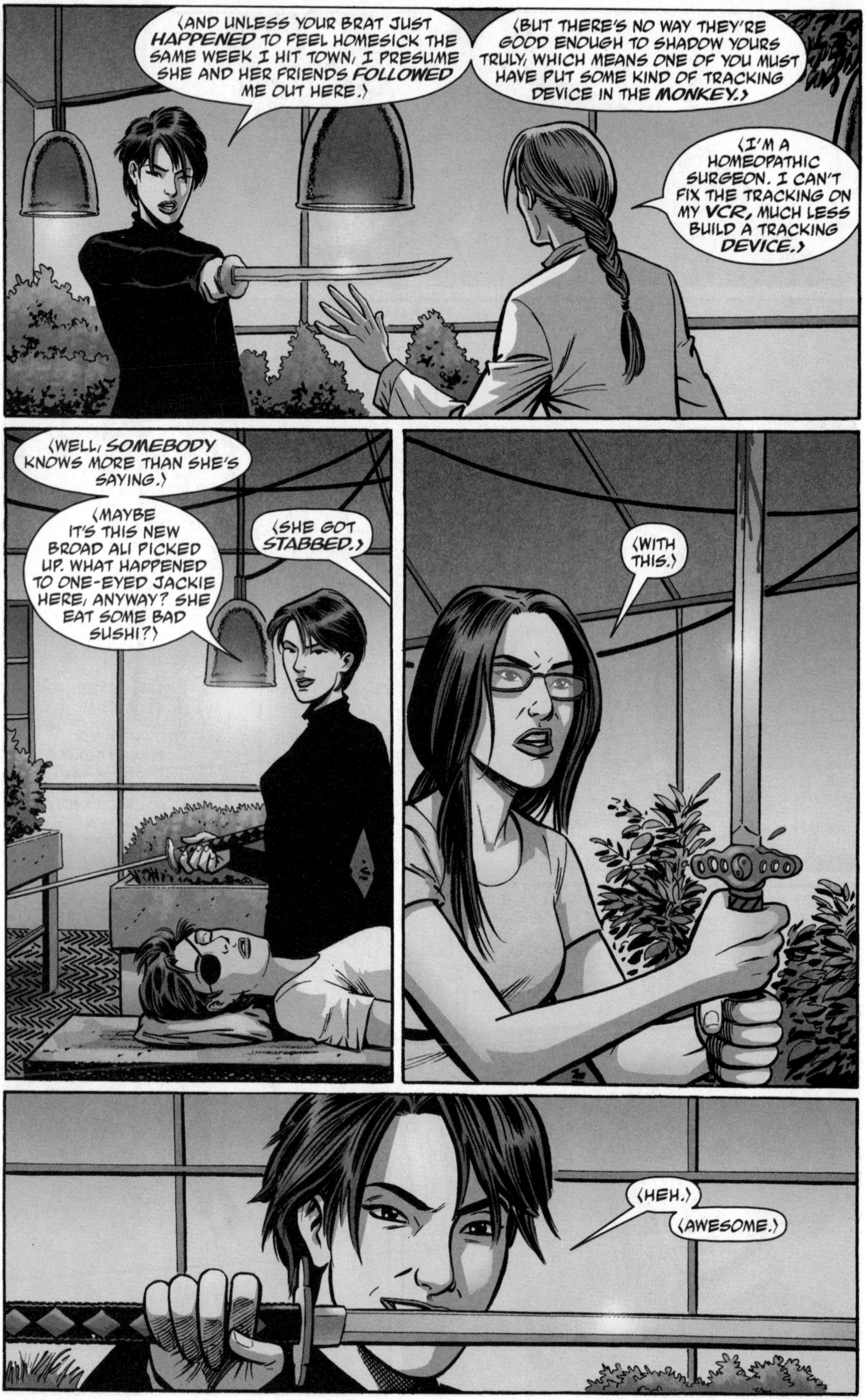
(AND UNLESS YOUR BRAT JUST HAPPENED TO FEEL HOMESICK THE SAME WEEK I HIT TOWN, I PRESUME SHE AND HER FRIENDS FOLLOWED ME OUT HERE.)
(BUT THERE'S NO WAY THEY'RE GOOD ENOUGH TO SHADOW YOURS TRULY, WHICH MEANS ONE OF YOU MUST HAVE PUT SOME KIND OF TRACKING DEVICE IN THE MONKEY.)
(I'M A HOMEOPATHIC SURGEON. I CAN'T FIX THE TRACKING ON MY VCR, MUCH LESS BUILD A TRACKING DEVICE.)
(WELL, SOMEBODY KNOWS MORE THAN SHE'S SAYING.)
(MAYBE IT'S THIS NEW BROAD ALI PICKED UP. WHAT HAPPENED TO ONE-EYED JACKIE HERE, ANYWAY? SHE EAT SOME BAD SUSHI?)
(SHE GOT STABBED.)
(WITH THIS.)
(HEH.)
(AWESOME.)

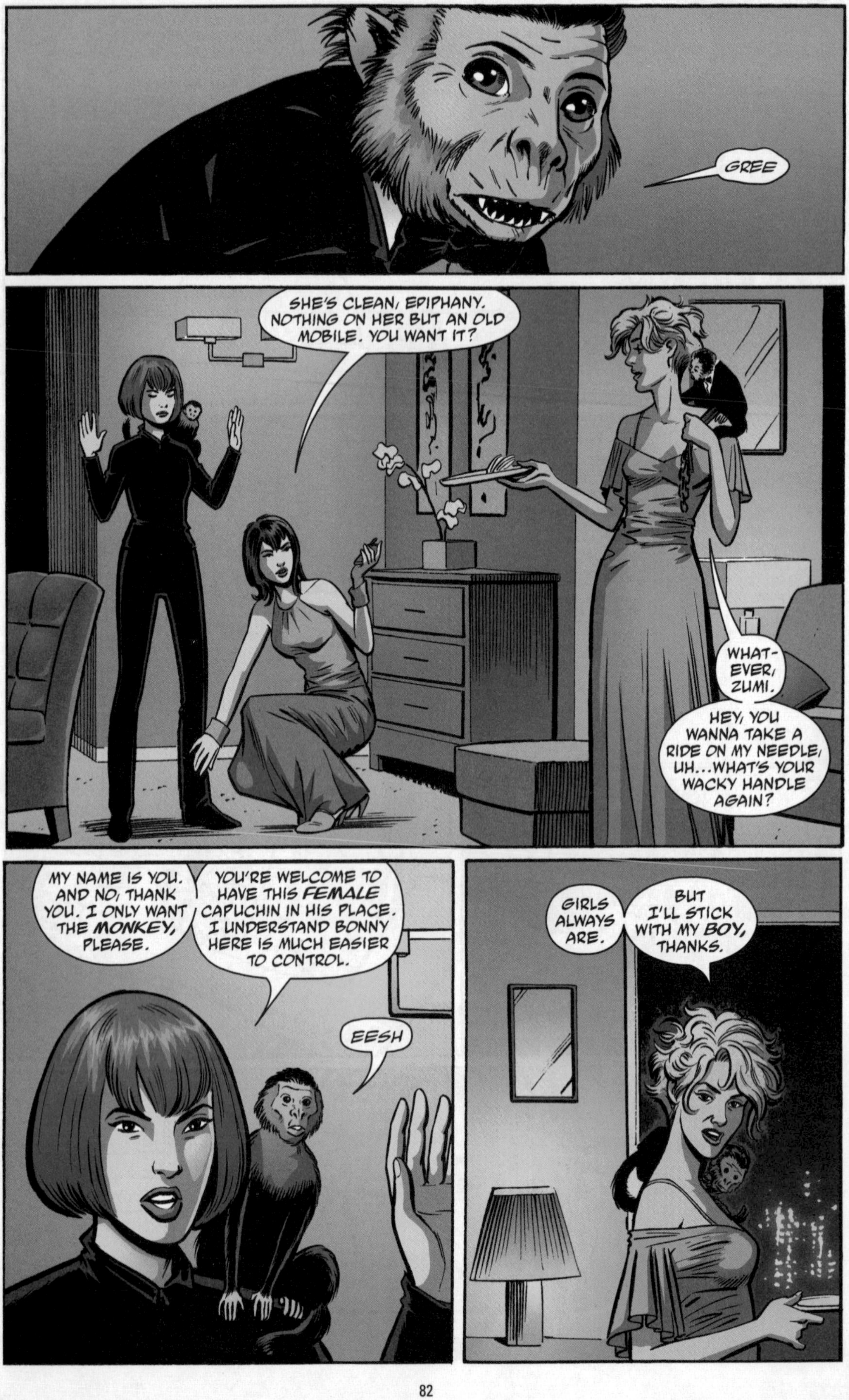
GREE
SHE'S CLEAN, EPIPHANY. NOTHING ON HER BUT AN OLD MOBILE. YOU WANT IT?
WHAT-EVER, ZUMI.
HEY, YOU WANNA TAKE A RIDE ON MY NEEDLE, UH...WHAT'S YOUR WACKY HANDLE AGAIN?
MY NAME IS YOU. AND NO, THANK YOU. I ONLY WANT THE MONKEY, PLEASE.
YOU'RE WELCOME TO HAVE THIS FEMALE CAPUCHIN IN HIS PLACE. I UNDERSTAND BONNY HERE IS MUCH EASIER TO CONTROL.
EESH
GIRLS ALWAYS ARE.
BUT I'LL STICK WITH MY BOY, THANKS.

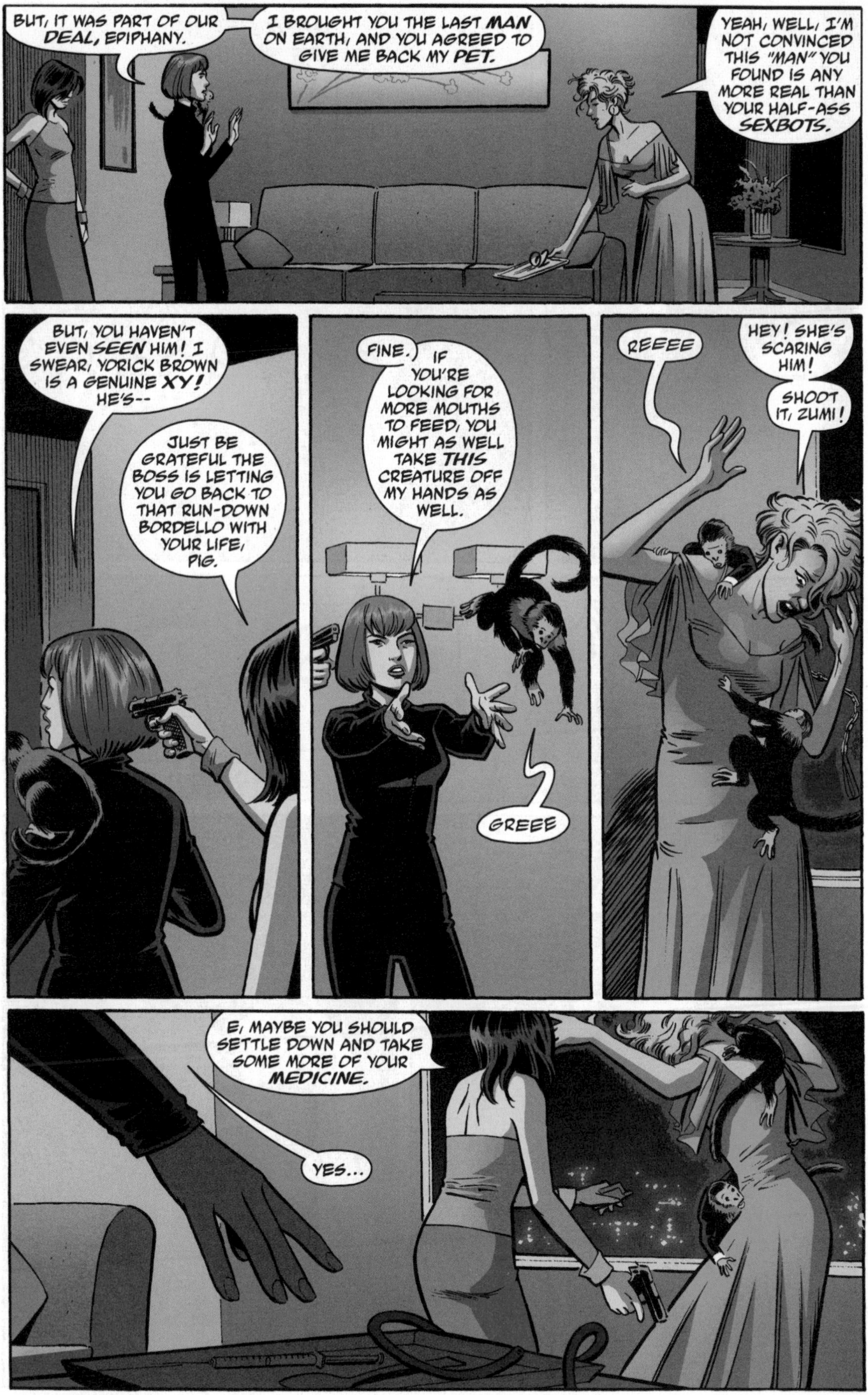
BUT, IT WAS PART OF OUR DEAL, EPIPHANY.
I BROUGHT YOU THE LAST MAN ON EARTH, AND YOU AGREED TO GIVE ME BACK MY PET.
YEAH, WELL, I'M NOT CONVINCED THIS "MAN" YOU FOUND IS ANY MORE REAL THAN YOUR HALF-ASS SEXBOTS.
BUT, YOU HAVEN'T EVEN SEEN HIM! I SWEAR, YORICK BROWN IS A GENUINE XY! HE'S--
JUST BE GRATEFUL THE BOSS IS LETTING YOU GO BACK TO THAT RUN-DOWN BORDELLO WITH YOUR LIFE, PIG.
FINE.
IF YOU'RE LOOKING FOR MORE MOUTHS TO FEED, YOU MIGHT AS WELL TAKE THIS CREATURE OFF MY HANDS AS WELL.
GREEE
REEEE
HEY! SHE'S SCARING HIM!
SHOOT IT, ZUMI!
E, MAYBE YOU SHOULD SETTLE DOWN AND TAKE SOME MORE OF YOUR MEDICINE.
YES...

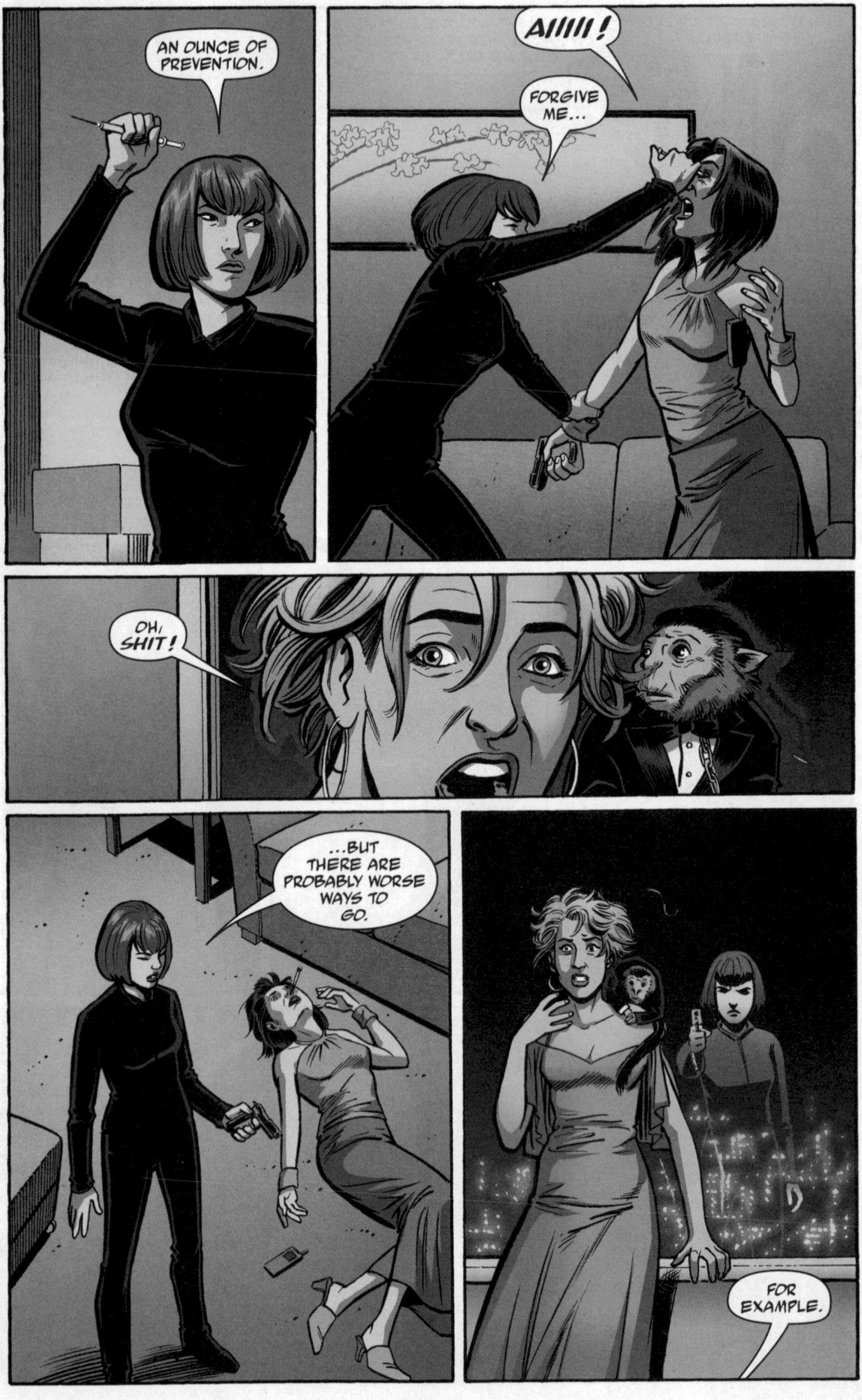
AN OUNCE OF PREVENTION.
AIIIII!
FORGIVE ME...
OH, SHIT!
...BUT THERE ARE PROBABLY WORSE WAYS TO GO.
FOR EXAMPLE.

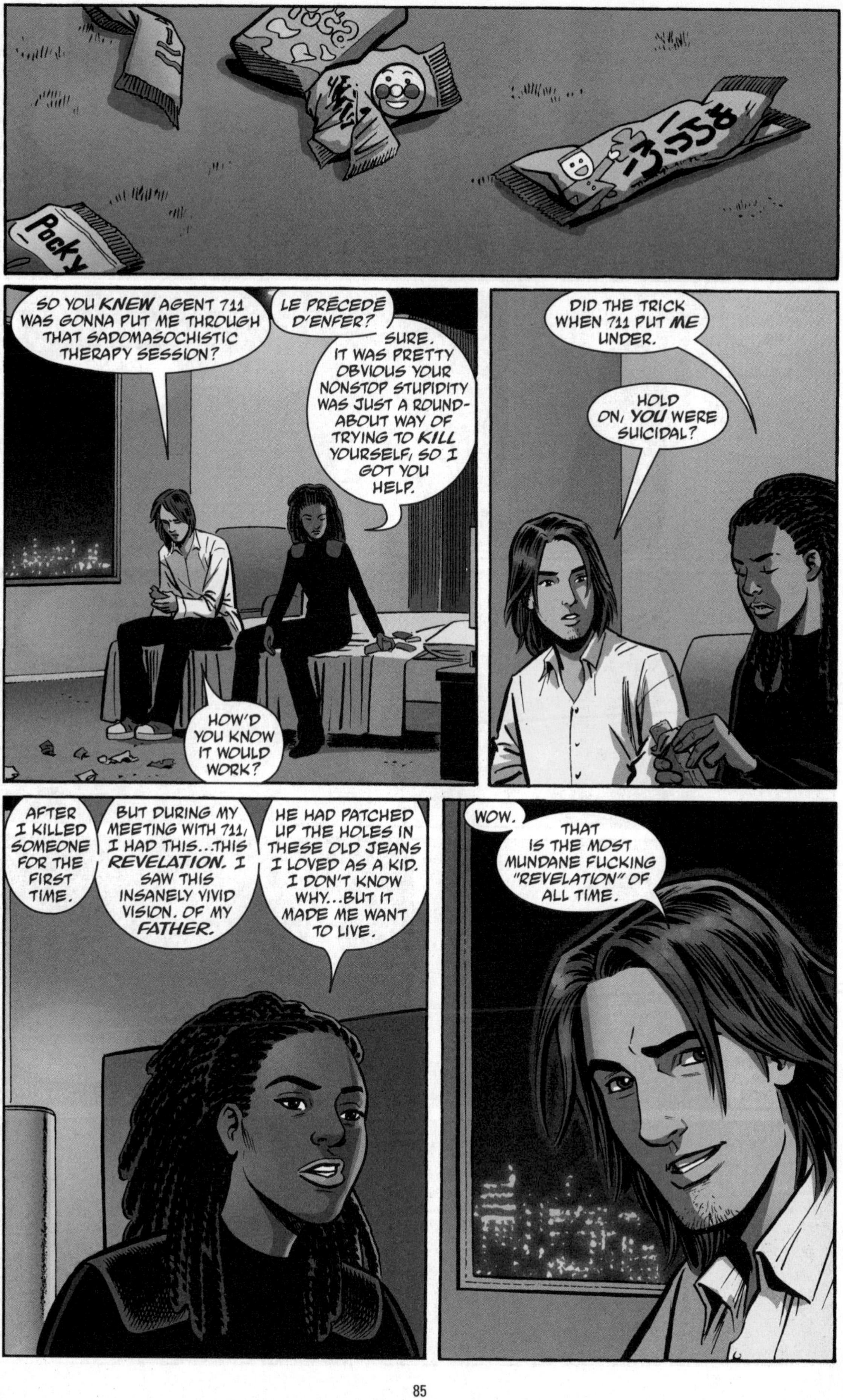
Pocky
SO YOU KNEW AGENT 711 WAS GONNA PUT ME THROUGH THAT SADOMASOCHISTIC THERAPY SESSION?
LE PRÉCEDÉ D'ENFER?
SURE. IT WAS PRETTY OBVIOUS YOUR NONSTOP STUPIDITY WAS JUST A ROUND-ABOUT WAY OF TRYING TO KILL YOURSELF, SO I GOT YOU HELP.
HOW'D YOU KNOW IT WOULD WORK?
DID THE TRICK WHEN 711 PUT ME UNDER.
HOLD ON, YOU WERE SUICIDAL?
AFTER I KILLED SOMEONE FOR THE FIRST TIME.
BUT DURING MY MEETING WITH 711, I HAD THIS...THIS REVELATION. I SAW THIS INSANELY VIVID VISION. OF MY FATHER.
HE HAD PATCHED UP THE HOLES IN THESE OLD JEANS I LOVED AS A KID. I DON'T KNOW WHY...BUT IT MADE ME WANT TO LIVE.
WOW.
THAT IS THE MOST MUNDANE FUCKING "REVELATION" OF ALL TIME.

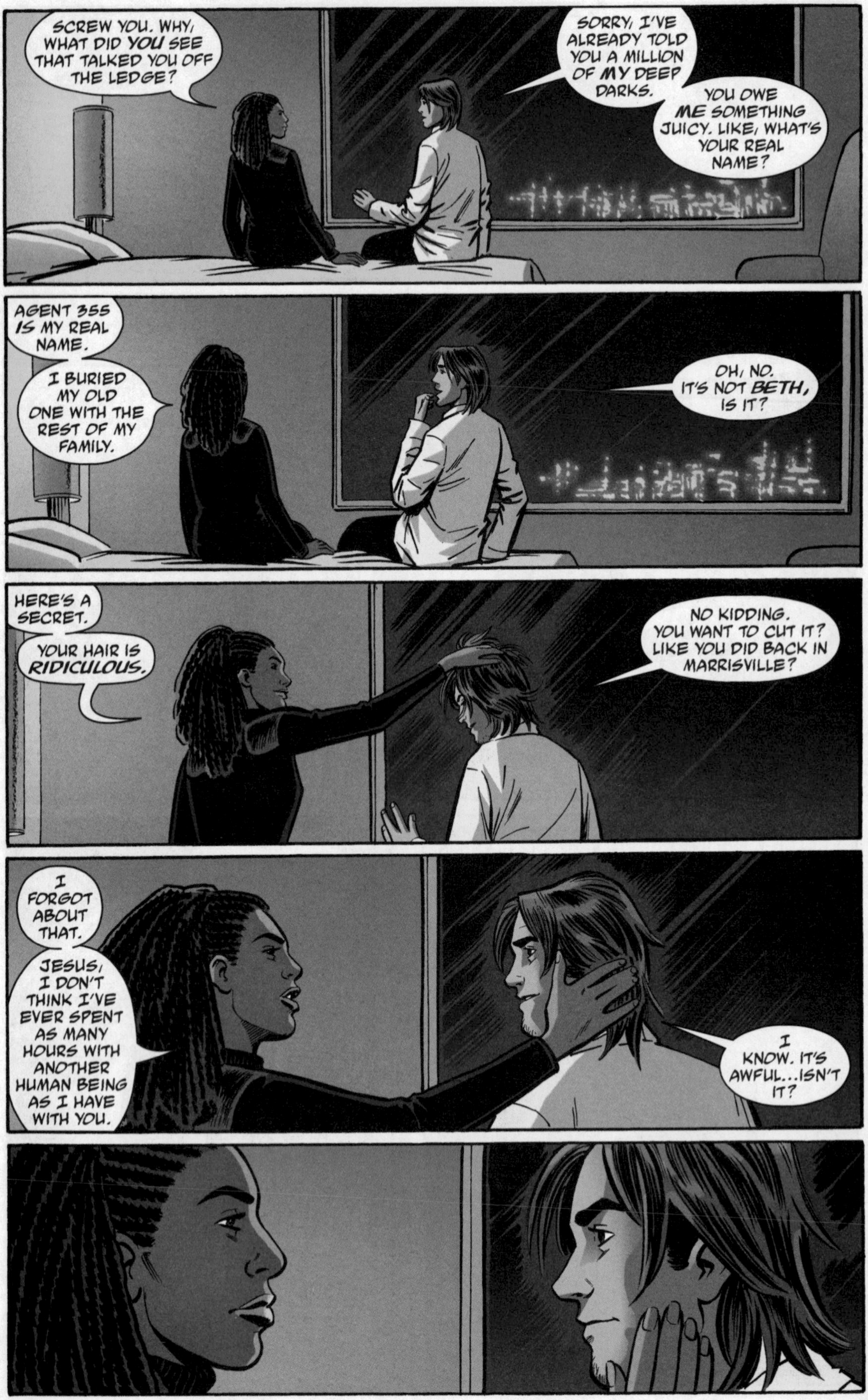
SCREW YOU. WHY, WHAT DID YOU SEE THAT TALKED YOU OFF THE LEDGE?
SORRY, I'VE ALREADY TOLD YOU A MILLION OF MY DEEP DARKS.
YOU OWE ME SOMETHING JUICY. LIKE, WHAT'S YOUR REAL NAME?
AGENT 355 IS MY REAL NAME.
I BURIED MY OLD ONE WITH THE REST OF MY FAMILY.
OH, NO. IT'S NOT BETH, IS IT?
HERE'S A SECRET.
YOUR HAIR IS RIDICULOUS.
NO KIDDING. YOU WANT TO CUT IT? LIKE YOU DID BACK IN MARRISVILLE?
I FORGOT ABOUT THAT.
JESUS, I DON'T THINK I'VE EVER SPENT AS MANY HOURS WITH ANOTHER HUMAN BEING AS I HAVE WITH YOU.
I KNOW. IT'S AWFUL...ISN'T IT?

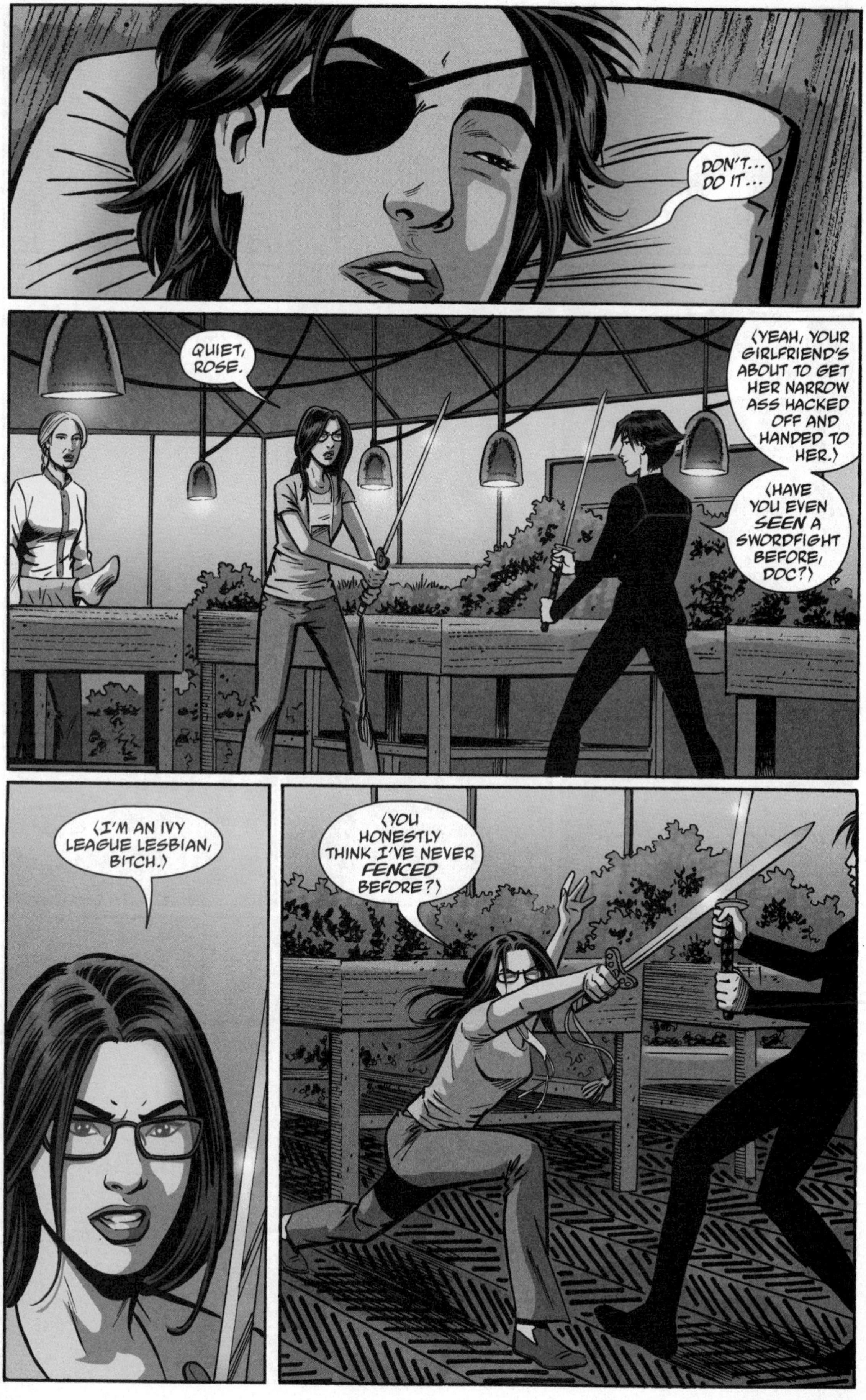
DON'T... DO IT...
QUIET, ROSE.
‹YEAH, YOUR GIRLFRIEND'S ABOUT TO GET HER NARROW ASS HACKED OFF AND HANDED TO HER.›
‹HAVE YOU EVEN SEEN A SWORDFIGHT BEFORE, DOC?›
‹I'M AN IVY LEAGUE LESBIAN, BITCH.›
‹YOU HONESTLY THINK I'VE NEVER FENCED BEFORE?›

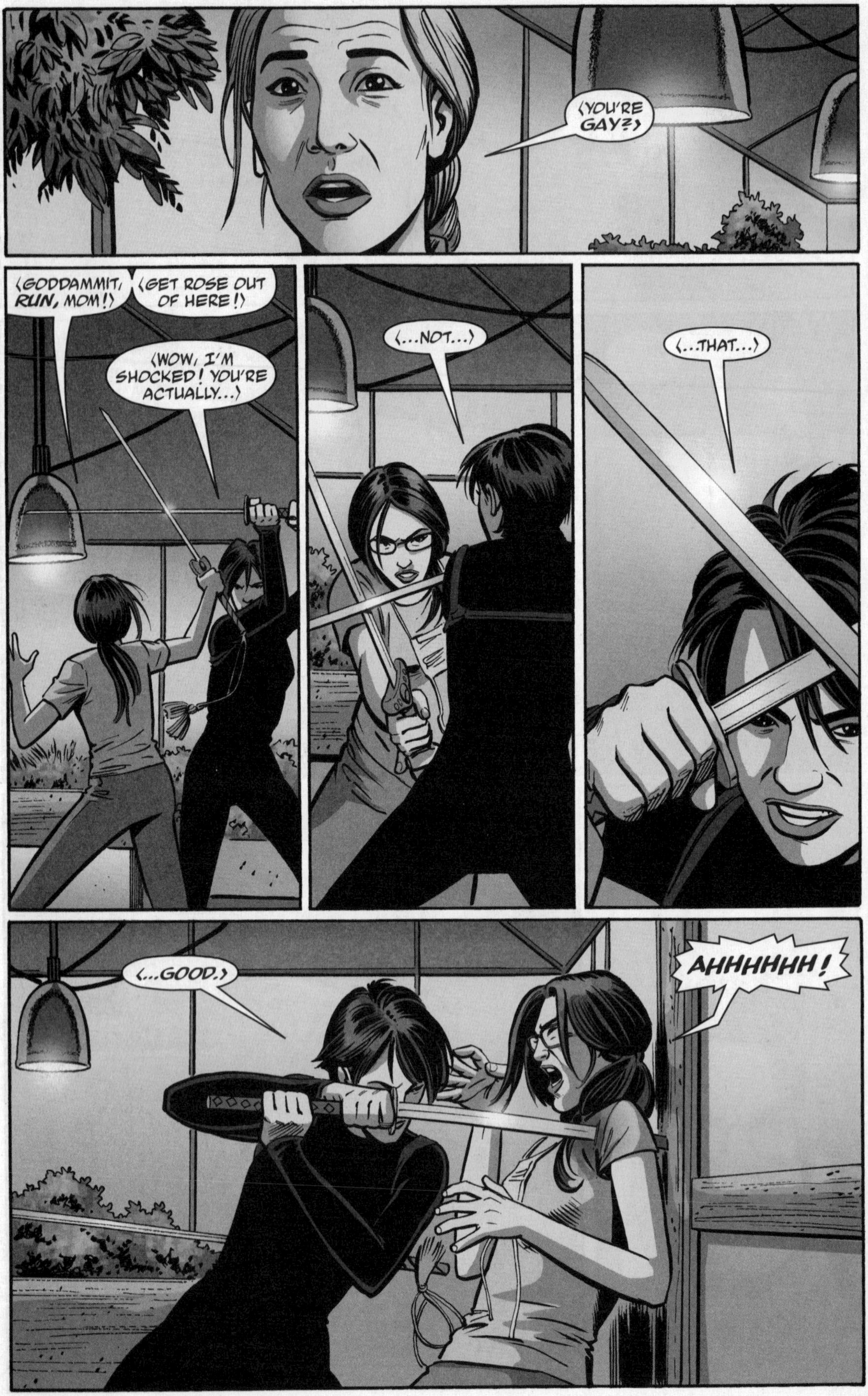
(YOU'RE GAY?)
(GODDAMMIT, RUN, MOM!)
(GET ROSE OUT OF HERE!)
(WOW, I'M SHOCKED! YOU'RE ACTUALLY...)
(...NOT...)
(...THAT...)
(...GOOD.)
AHHHHHH!

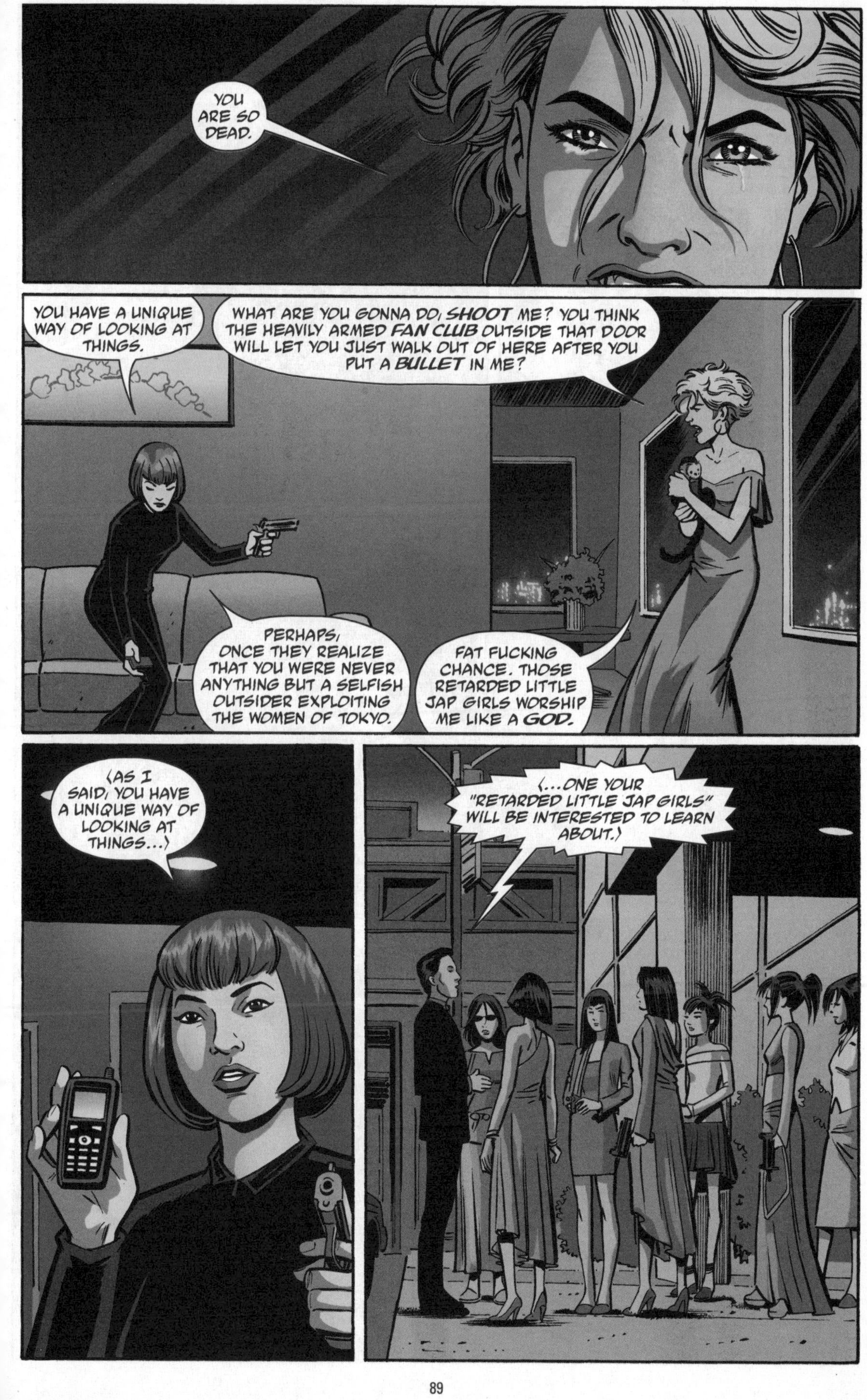
YOU ARE SO DEAD.
YOU HAVE A UNIQUE WAY OF LOOKING AT THINGS.
WHAT ARE YOU GONNA DO, SHOOT ME? YOU THINK THE HEAVILY ARMED FAN CLUB OUTSIDE THAT DOOR WILL LET YOU JUST WALK OUT OF HERE AFTER YOU PUT A BULLET IN ME?
PERHAPS, ONCE THEY REALIZE THAT YOU WERE NEVER ANYTHING BUT A SELFISH OUTSIDER EXPLOITING THE WOMEN OF TOKYO.
FAT FUCKING CHANCE. THOSE RETARDED LITTLE JAP GIRLS WORSHIP ME LIKE A GOD.
(AS I SAID, YOU HAVE A UNIQUE WAY OF LOOKING AT THINGS...)
(...ONE YOUR "RETARDED LITTLE JAP GIRLS" WILL BE INTERESTED TO LEARN ABOUT.)

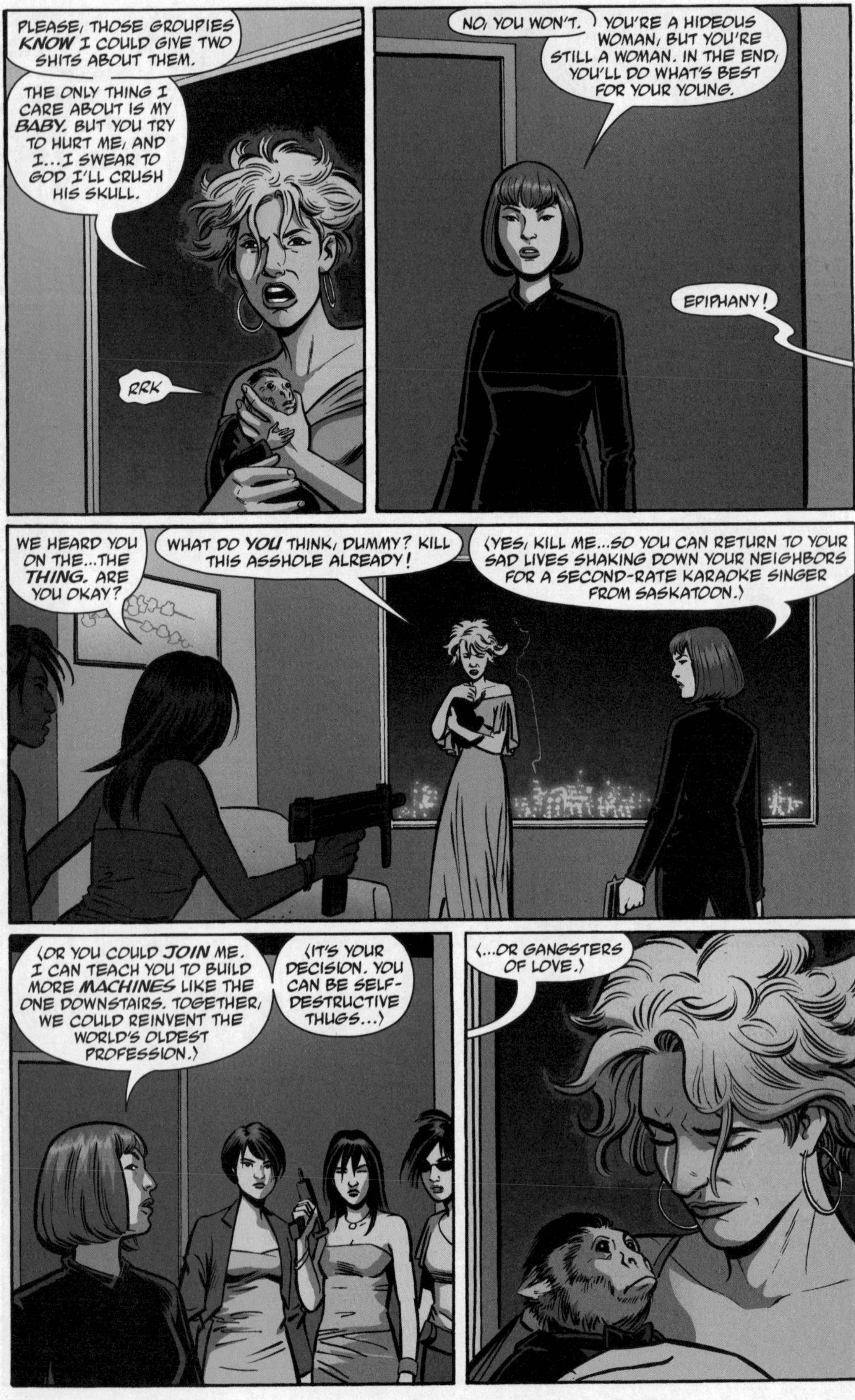
PLEASE, THOSE GROUPIES KNOW I COULD GIVE TWO SHITS ABOUT THEM.
THE ONLY THING I CARE ABOUT IS MY BABY. BUT YOU TRY TO HURT ME, AND I...I SWEAR TO GOD I'LL CRUSH HIS SKULL.
RRK
NO, YOU WON'T.
YOU'RE A HIDEOUS WOMAN, BUT YOU'RE STILL A WOMAN. IN THE END, YOU'LL DO WHAT'S BEST FOR YOUR YOUNG.
EPIPHANY!
WE HEARD YOU ON THE...THE THING. ARE YOU OKAY?
WHAT DO YOU THINK, DUMMY? KILL THIS ASSHOLE ALREADY!
⟨YES, KILL ME...SO YOU CAN RETURN TO YOUR SAD LIVES SHAKING DOWN YOUR NEIGHBORS FOR A SECOND-RATE KARAOKE SINGER FROM SASKATOON.⟩
⟨OR YOU COULD JOIN ME. I CAN TEACH YOU TO BUILD MORE MACHINES LIKE THE ONE DOWNSTAIRS. TOGETHER, WE COULD REINVENT THE WORLD'S OLDEST PROFESSION.⟩
⟨IT'S YOUR DECISION. YOU CAN BE SELF-DESTRUCTIVE THUGS...⟩
⟨...OR GANGSTERS OF LOVE.⟩

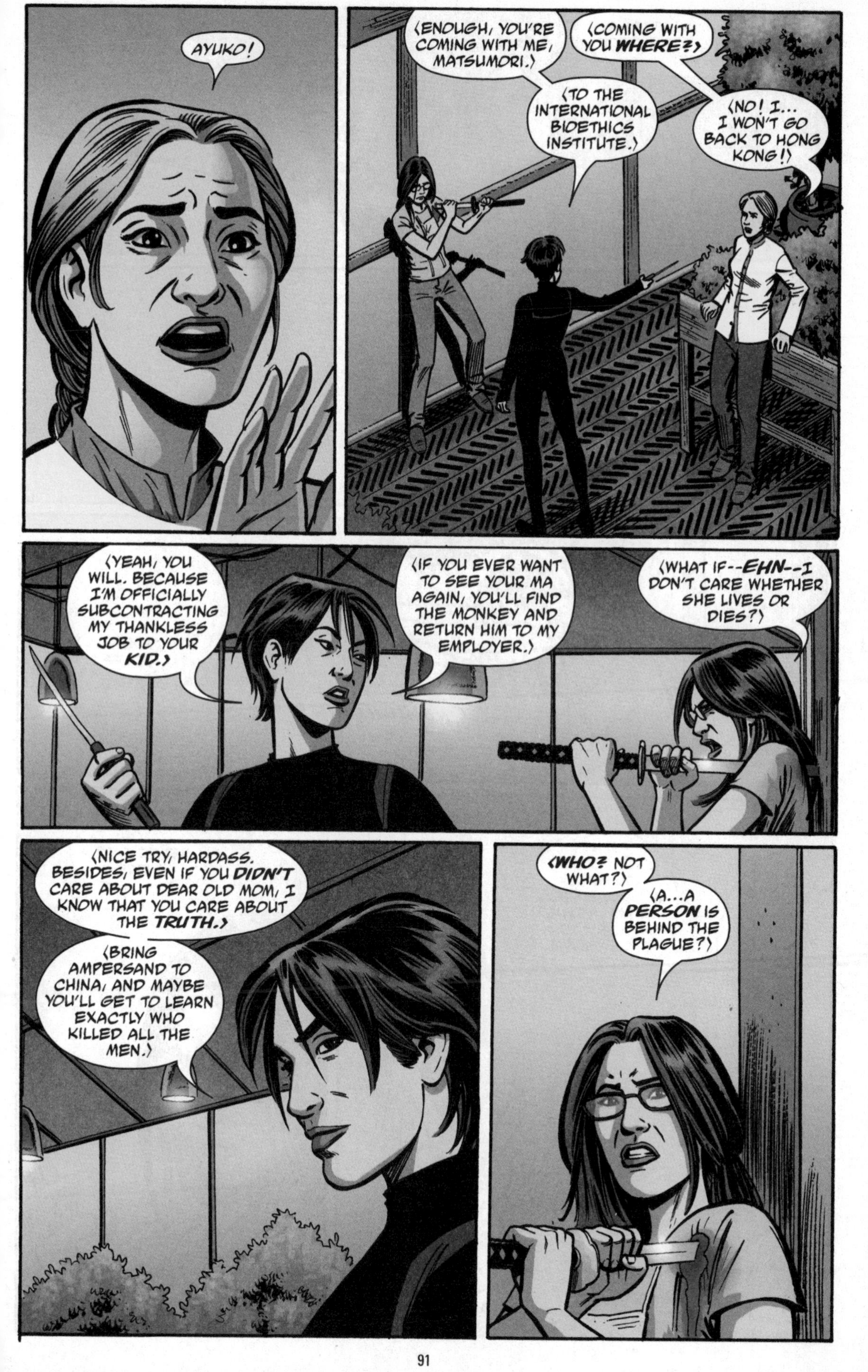
AYUKO!
⟨ENOUGH, YOU'RE COMING WITH ME, MATSUMORI.⟩
⟨COMING WITH YOU **WHERE?**⟩
⟨TO THE INTERNATIONAL BIOETHICS INSTITUTE.⟩
⟨NO! I... I WON'T GO BACK TO HONG KONG!⟩
⟨YEAH, YOU WILL. BECAUSE I'M OFFICIALLY SUBCONTRACTING MY THANKLESS JOB TO YOUR **KID.**⟩
⟨IF YOU EVER WANT TO SEE YOUR MA AGAIN, YOU'LL FIND THE MONKEY AND RETURN HIM TO MY EMPLOYER.⟩
⟨WHAT IF--**EHN**--I DON'T CARE WHETHER SHE LIVES OR DIES?⟩
⟨NICE TRY, HARDASS. BESIDES, EVEN IF YOU **DIDN'T** CARE ABOUT DEAR OLD MOM, I KNOW THAT YOU CARE ABOUT THE **TRUTH.**⟩
⟨BRING AMPERSAND TO CHINA, AND MAYBE YOU'LL GET TO LEARN EXACTLY WHO KILLED ALL THE MEN.⟩
⟨**WHO?** NOT WHAT?⟩
⟨A...A **PERSON** IS BEHIND THE PLAGUE?⟩

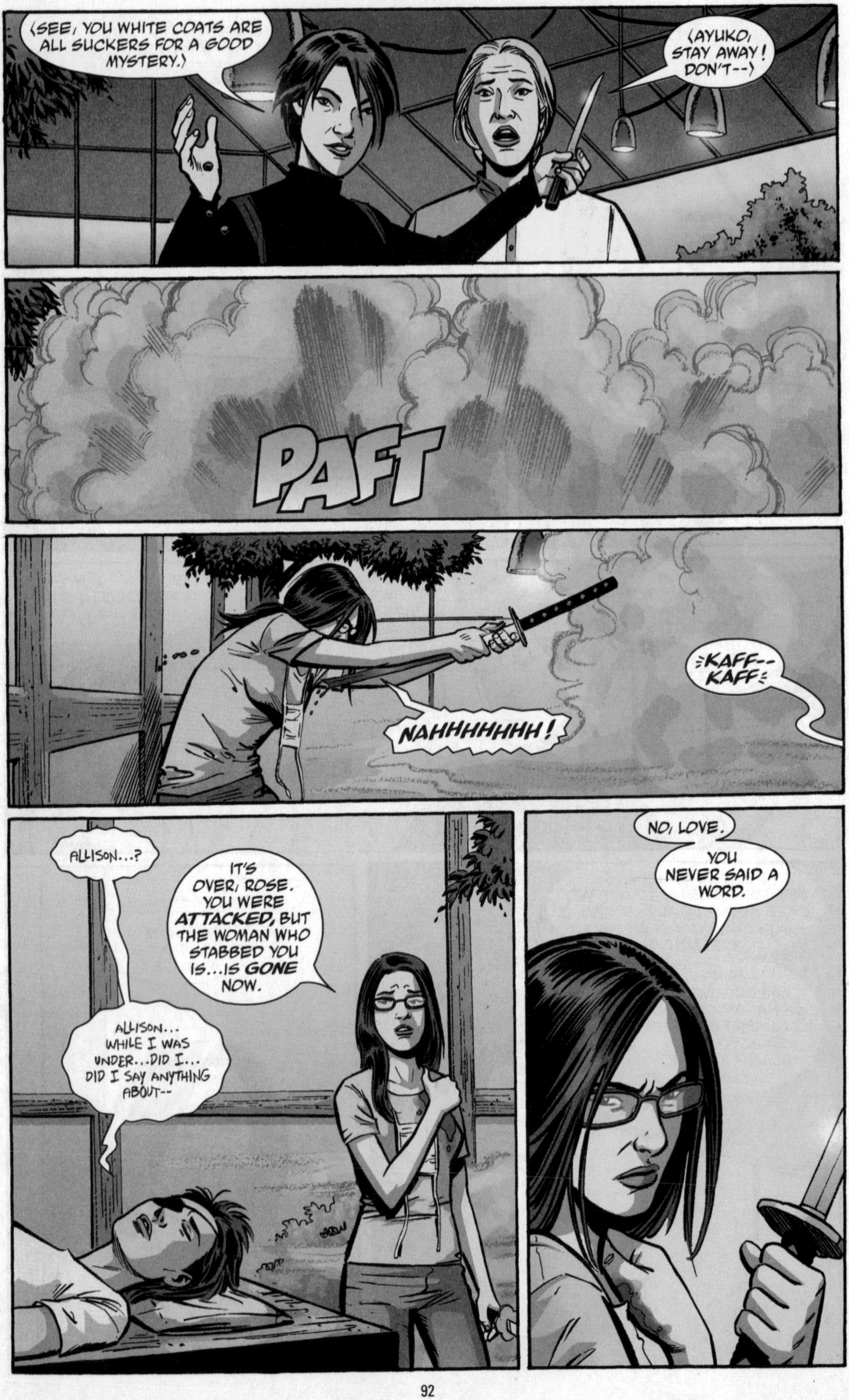

⟨SEE, YOU WHITE COATS ARE ALL SUCKERS FOR A GOOD MYSTERY.⟩
⟨AYUKO, STAY AWAY! DON'T--⟩
PAFT
KAFF--KAFF
NAHHHHHHH!
ALLISON...?
IT'S OVER, ROSE. YOU WERE ATTACKED, BUT THE WOMAN WHO STABBED YOU IS...IS GONE NOW.
ALLISON... WHILE I WAS UNDER...DID I... DID I SAY ANYTHING ABOUT--
NO, LOVE.
YOU NEVER SAID A WORD.

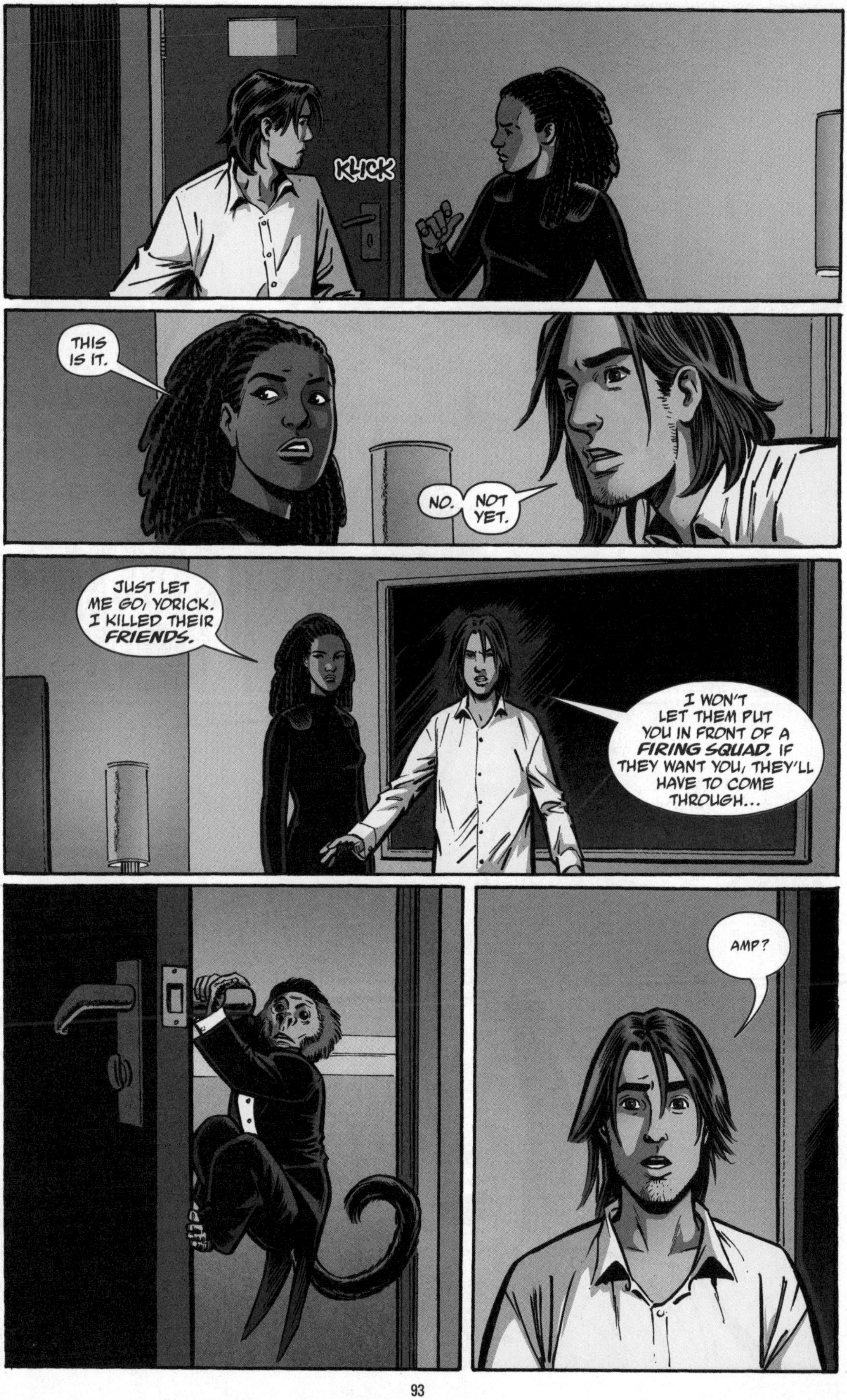
KLICK
THIS IS IT.
NO.
NOT YET.
JUST LET ME GO, YORICK. I KILLED THEIR FRIENDS.
I WON'T LET THEM PUT YOU IN FRONT OF A FIRING SQUAD. IF THEY WANT YOU, THEY'LL HAVE TO COME THROUGH...
AMP?

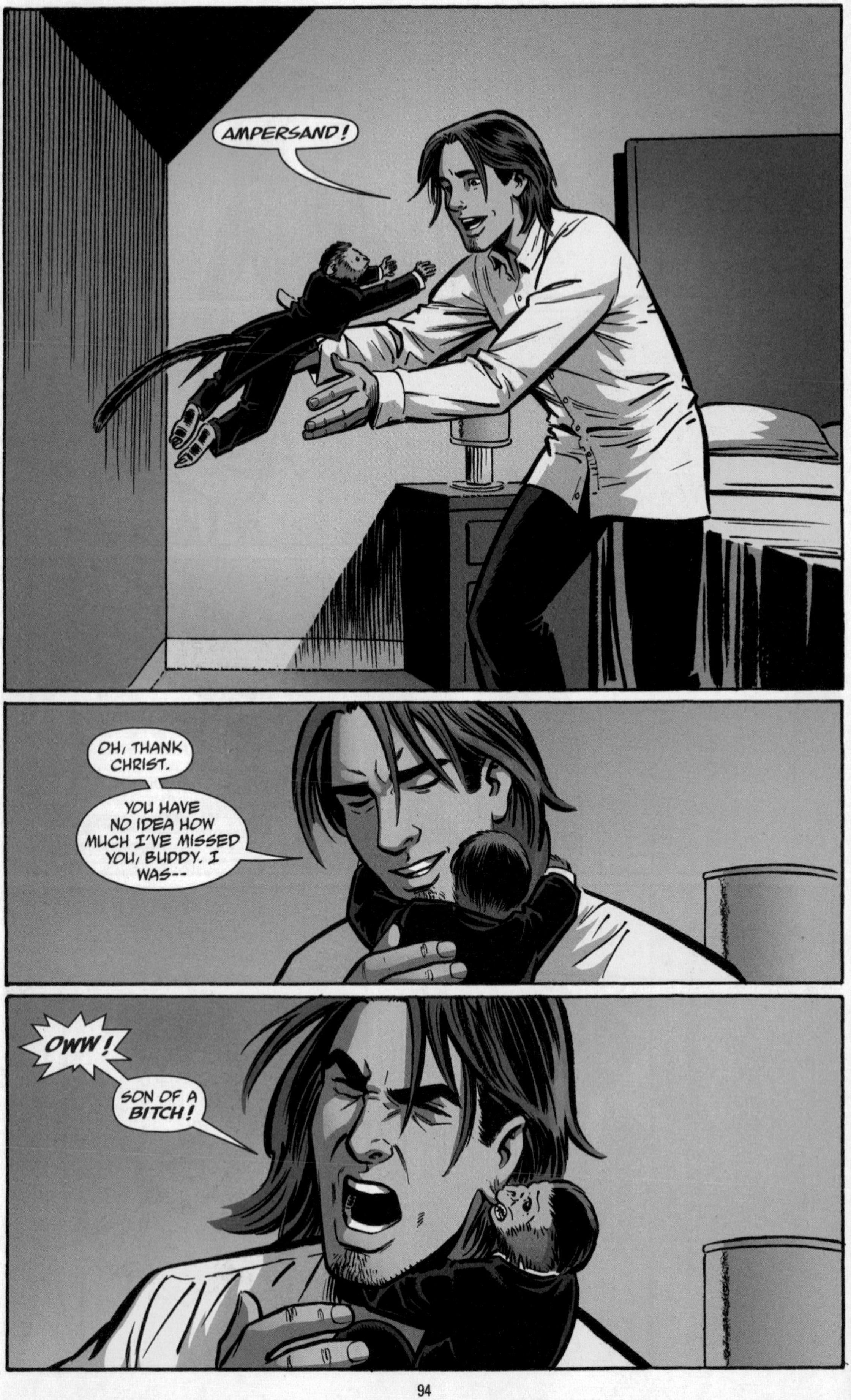
AMPERSAND!
OH, THANK CHRIST.
YOU HAVE NO IDEA HOW MUCH I'VE MISSED YOU, BUDDY. I WAS--
OWW!
SON OF A BITCH!

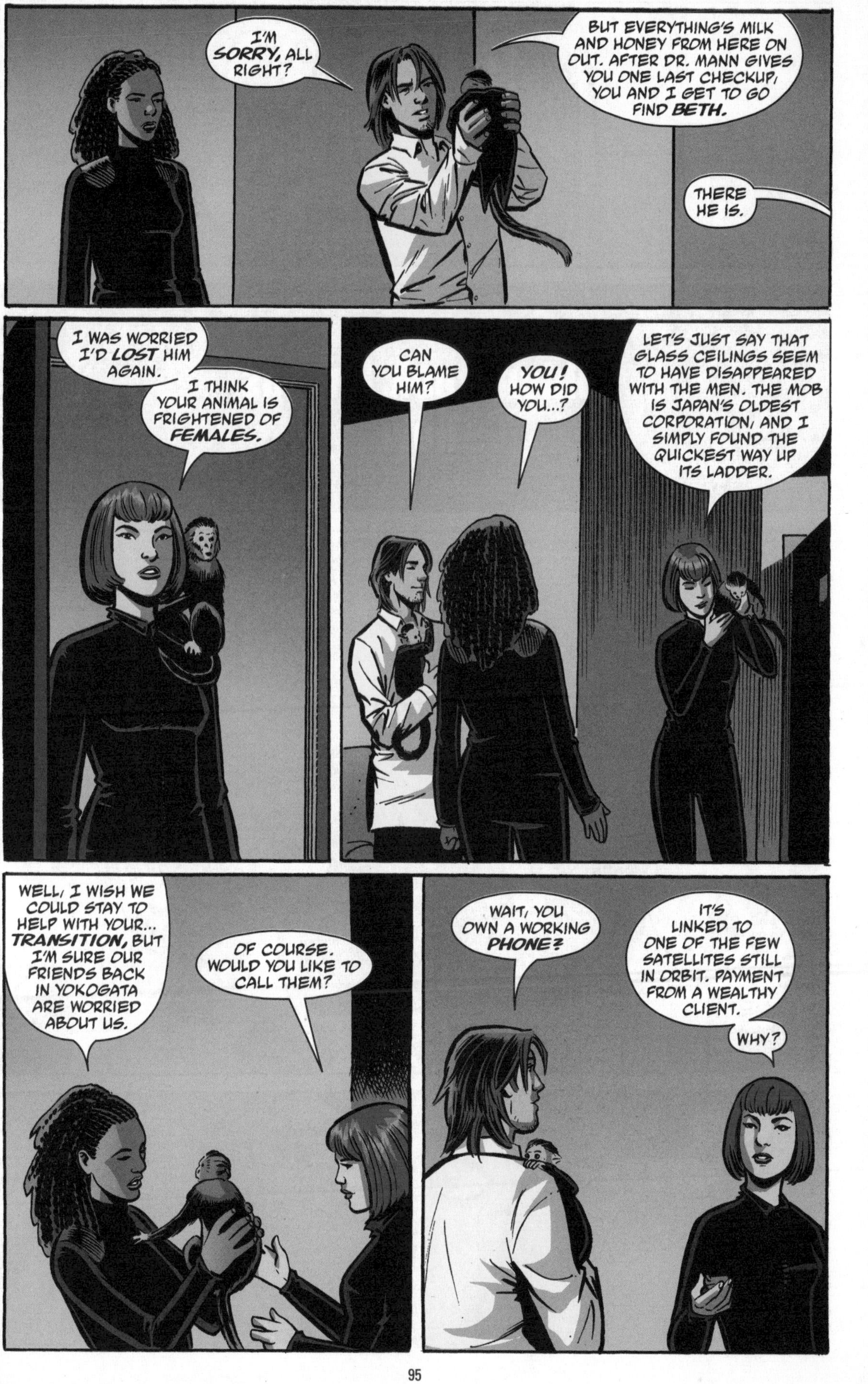
I'M SORRY, ALL RIGHT?
BUT EVERYTHING'S MILK AND HONEY FROM HERE ON OUT. AFTER DR. MANN GIVES YOU ONE LAST CHECKUP, YOU AND I GET TO GO FIND BETH.
THERE HE IS.
I WAS WORRIED I'D LOST HIM AGAIN.
I THINK YOUR ANIMAL IS FRIGHTENED OF FEMALES.
CAN YOU BLAME HIM?
YOU! HOW DID YOU...?
LET'S JUST SAY THAT GLASS CEILINGS SEEM TO HAVE DISAPPEARED WITH THE MEN. THE MOB IS JAPAN'S OLDEST CORPORATION, AND I SIMPLY FOUND THE QUICKEST WAY UP ITS LADDER.
WELL, I WISH WE COULD STAY TO HELP WITH YOUR... TRANSITION, BUT I'M SURE OUR FRIENDS BACK IN YOKOGATA ARE WORRIED ABOUT US.
OF COURSE. WOULD YOU LIKE TO CALL THEM?
WAIT, YOU OWN A WORKING PHONE?
IT'S LINKED TO ONE OF THE FEW SATELLITES STILL IN ORBIT. PAYMENT FROM A WEALTHY CLIENT.
WHY?

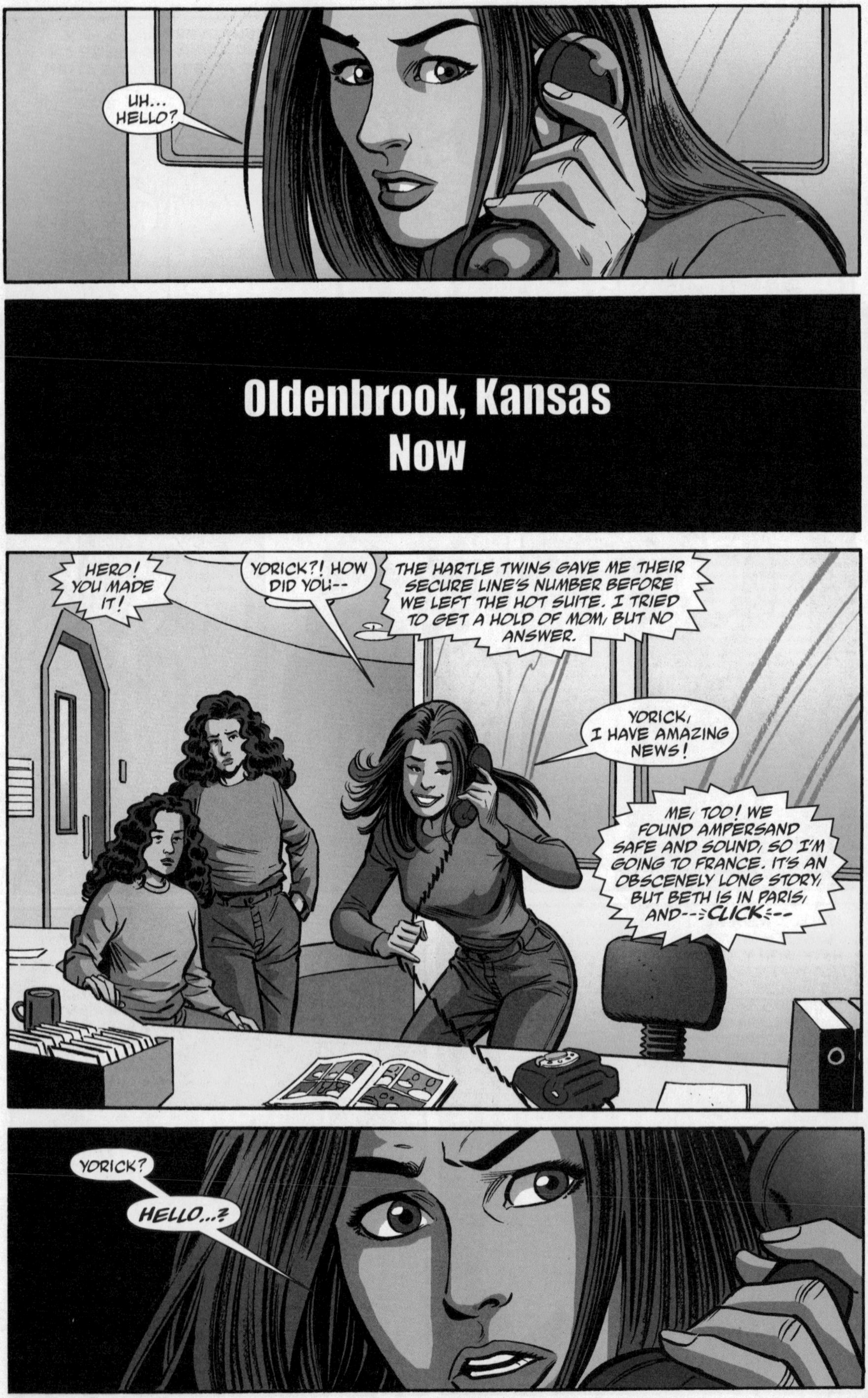
UH... HELLO?
Oldenbrook, Kansas
Now
HERO! YOU MADE IT!
YORICK?! HOW DID YOU--
THE HARTLE TWINS GAVE ME THEIR SECURE LINE'S NUMBER BEFORE WE LEFT THE HOT SUITE. I TRIED TO GET A HOLD OF MOM, BUT NO ANSWER.
YORICK, I HAVE AMAZING NEWS!
ME, TOO! WE FOUND AMPERSAND SAFE AND SOUND, SO I'M GOING TO FRANCE. IT'S AN OBSCENELY LONG STORY, BUT BETH IS IN PARIS, AND--CLICK--
YORICK?
HELLO...?

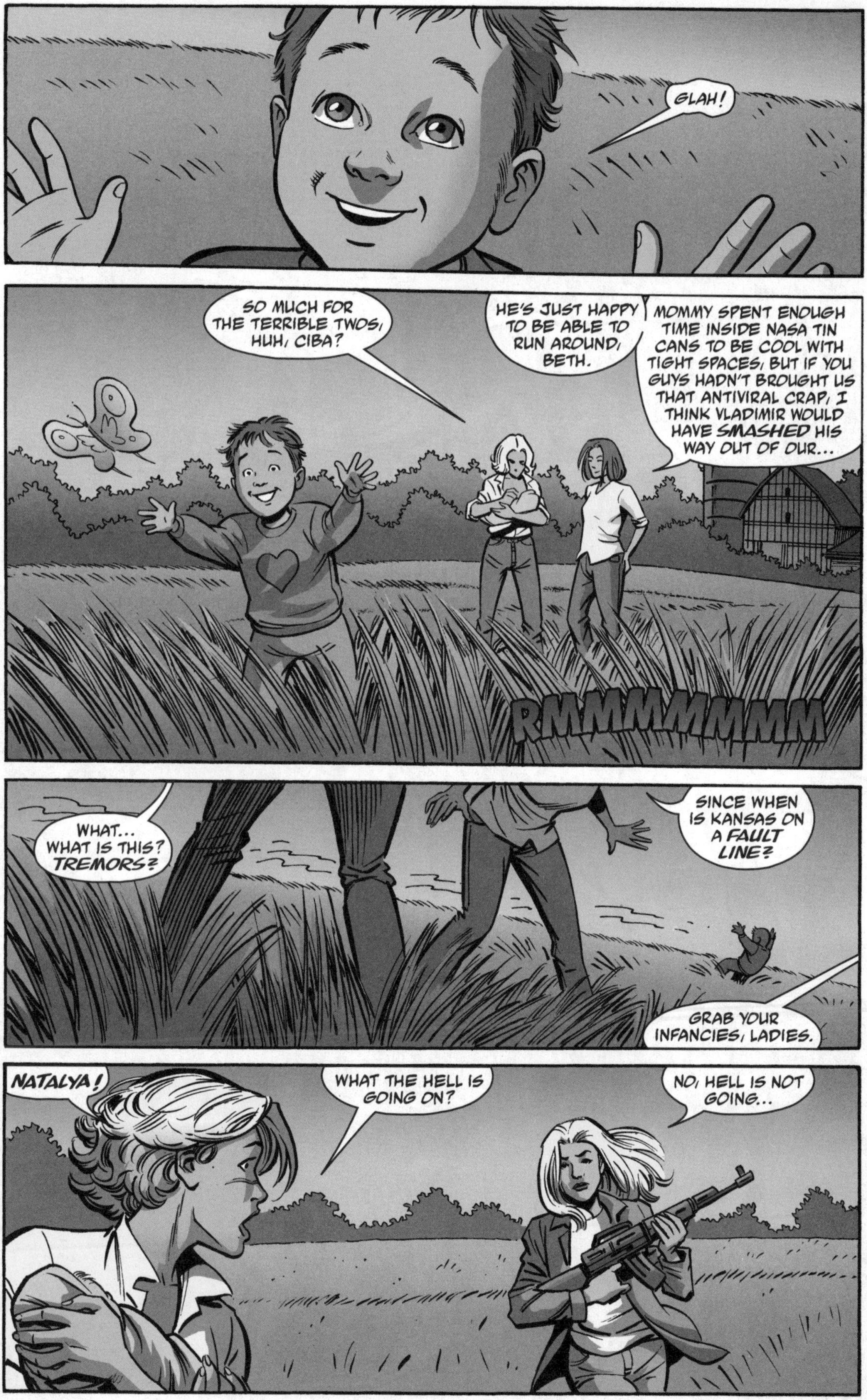
GLAH!
SO MUCH FOR THE TERRIBLE TWOS, HUH, CIBA?
HE'S JUST HAPPY TO BE ABLE TO RUN AROUND, BETH.
MOMMY SPENT ENOUGH TIME INSIDE NASA TIN CANS TO BE COOL WITH TIGHT SPACES, BUT IF YOU GUYS HADN'T BROUGHT US THAT ANTIVIRAL CRAP, I THINK VLADIMIR WOULD HAVE SMASHED HIS WAY OUT OF OUR...
RMMMMMMMM
WHAT... WHAT IS THIS? TREMORS?
SINCE WHEN IS KANSAS ON A FAULT LINE?
GRAB YOUR INFANCIES, LADIES.
NATALYA!
WHAT THE HELL IS GOING ON?
NO, HELL IS NOT GOING...

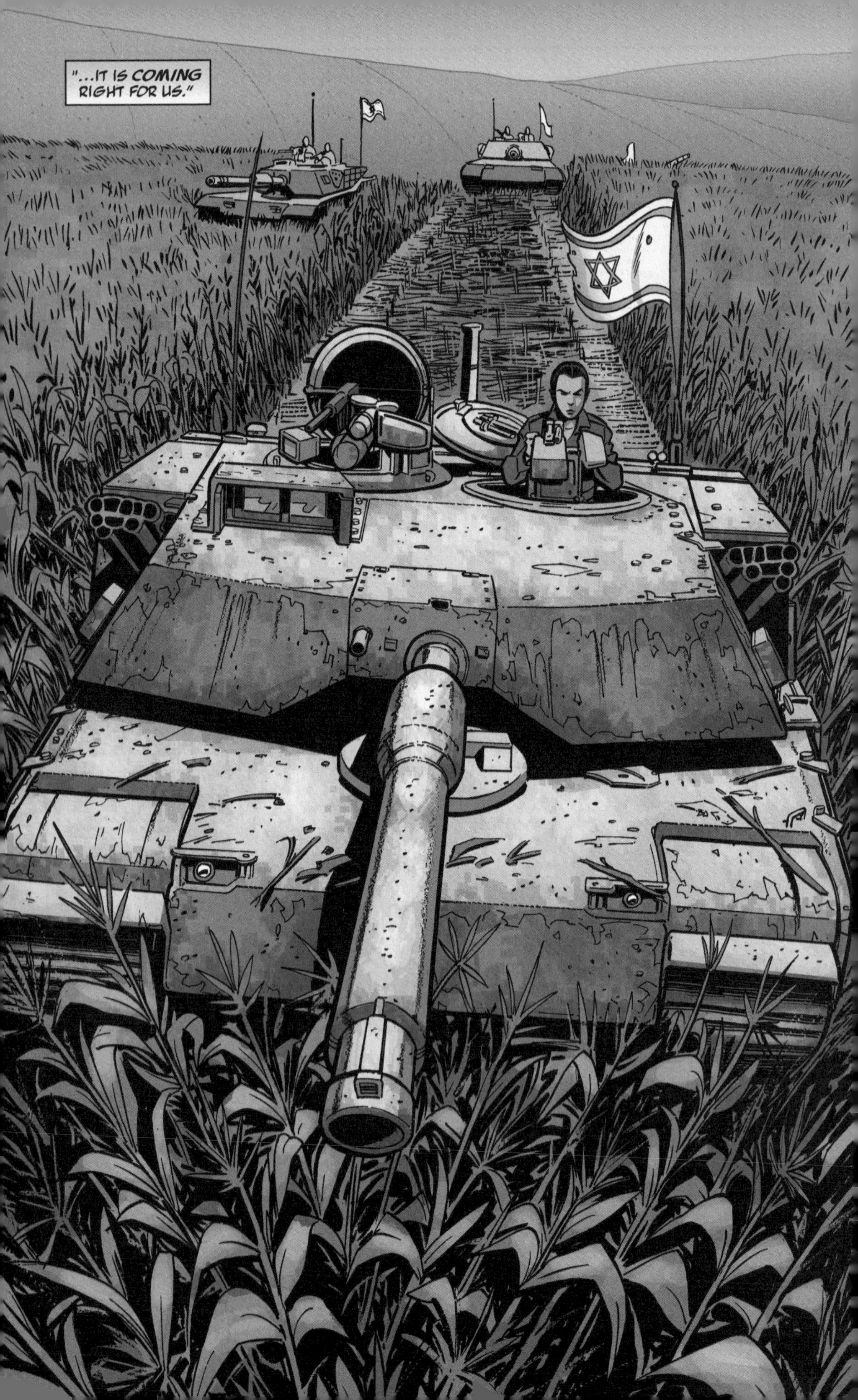
"...IT IS COMING RIGHT FOR US."

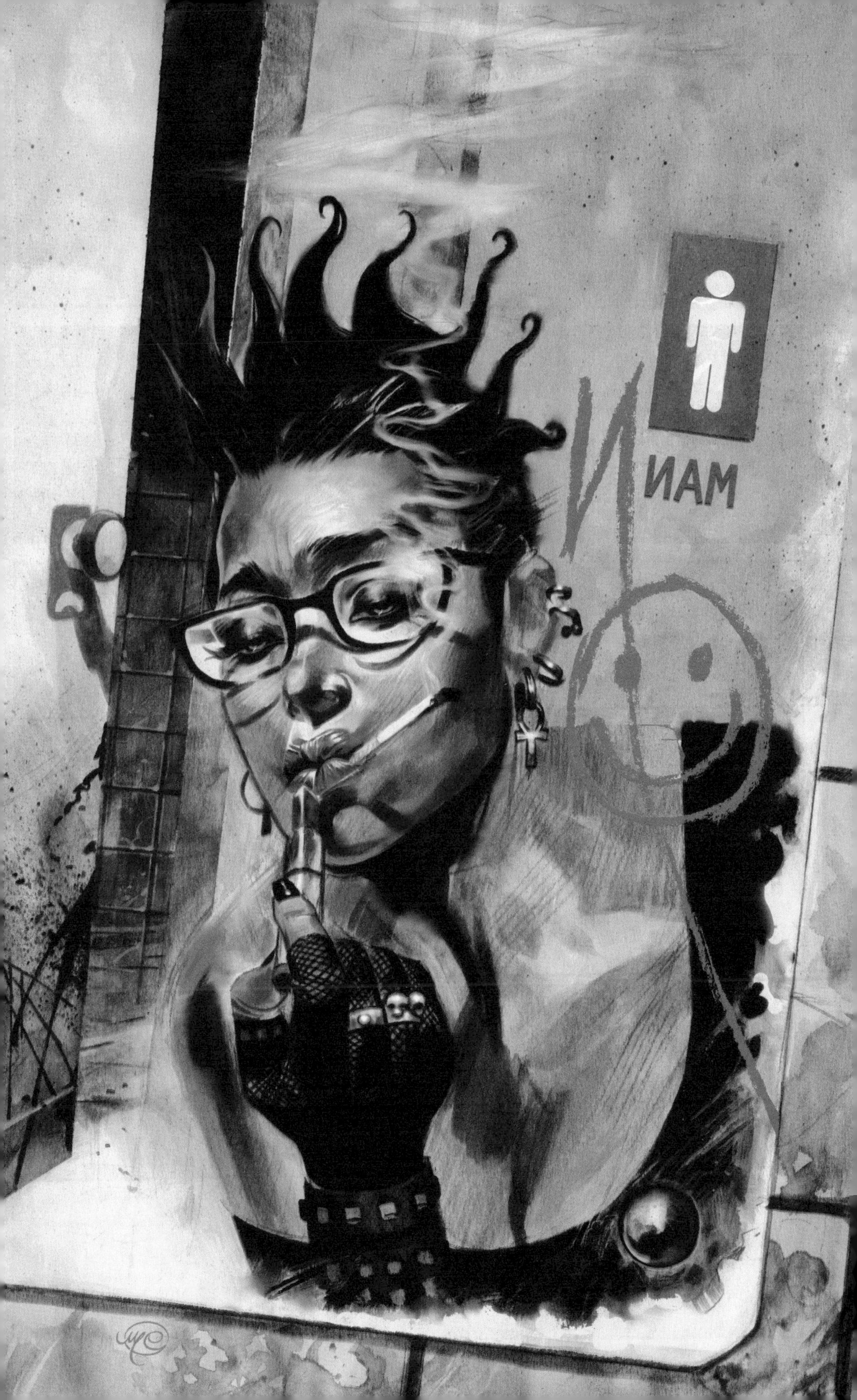

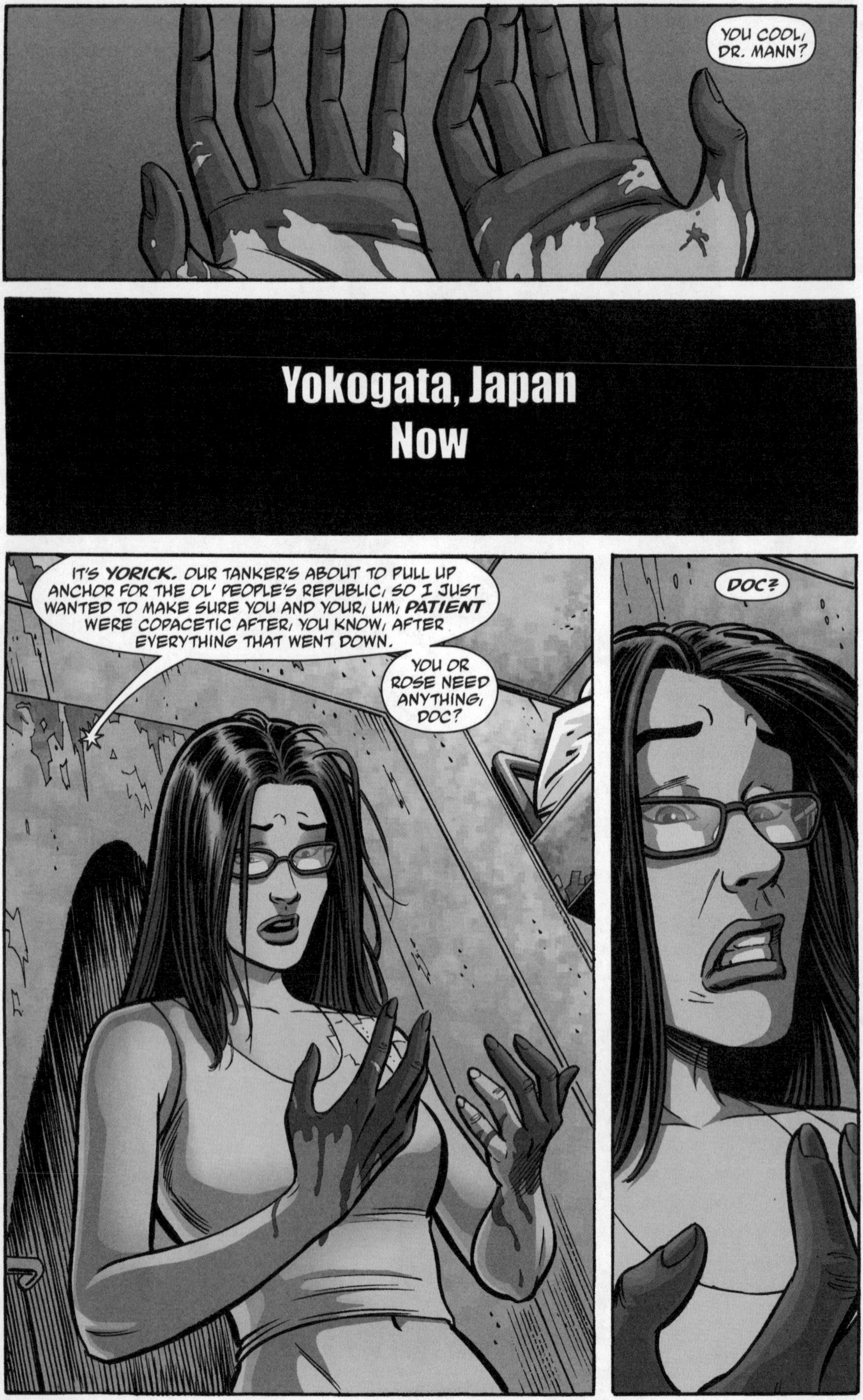
YOU COOL, DR. MANN?
Yokogata, Japan
Now
IT'S YORICK. OUR TANKER'S ABOUT TO PULL UP ANCHOR FOR THE OL' PEOPLE'S REPUBLIC, SO I JUST WANTED TO MAKE SURE YOU AND YOUR, UM, PATIENT WERE COPACETIC AFTER, YOU KNOW, AFTER EVERYTHING THAT WENT DOWN.
YOU OR ROSE NEED ANYTHING, DOC?
DOC?

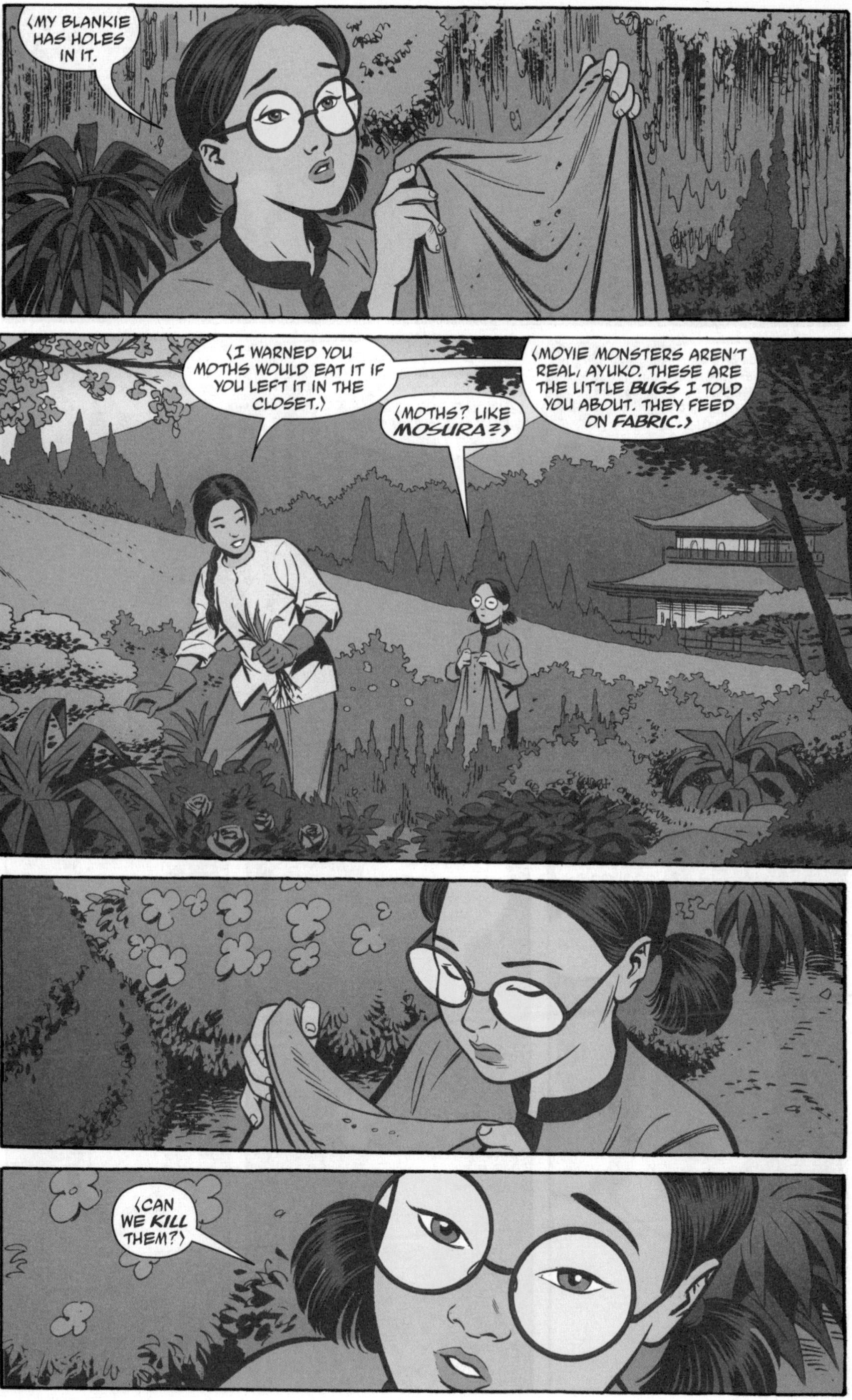
⟨MY BLANKIE HAS HOLES IN IT.
⟨I WARNED YOU MOTHS WOULD EAT IT IF YOU LEFT IT IN THE CLOSET.⟩
⟨MOTHS? LIKE MOSURA?⟩
⟨MOVIE MONSTERS AREN'T REAL, AYUKO. THESE ARE THE LITTLE BUGS I TOLD YOU ABOUT. THEY FEED ON FABRIC.⟩
⟨CAN WE KILL THEM?⟩

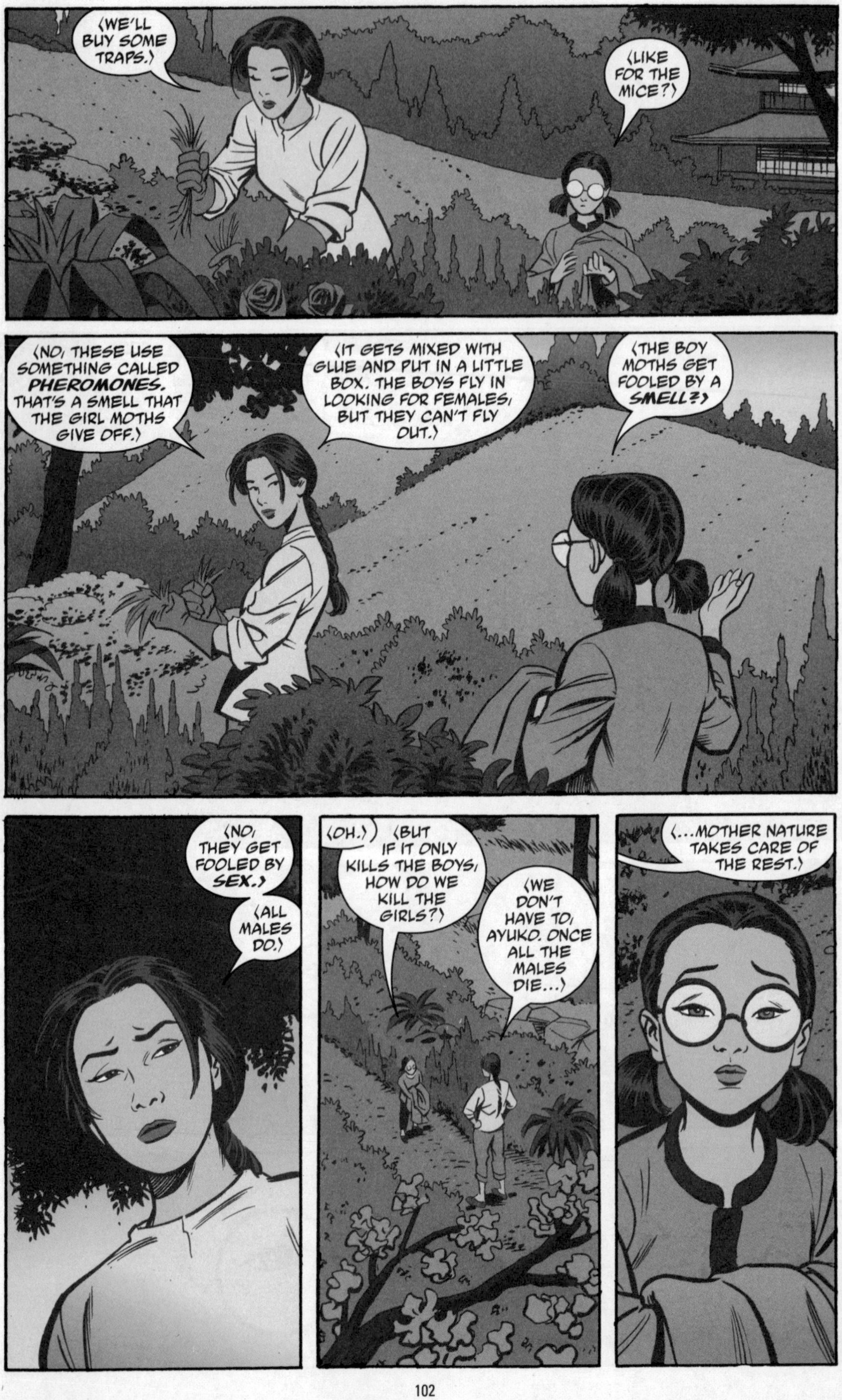
⟨WE'LL BUY SOME TRAPS.⟩
⟨LIKE FOR THE MICE?⟩
⟨NO, THESE USE SOMETHING CALLED PHEROMONES. THAT'S A SMELL THAT THE GIRL MOTHS GIVE OFF.⟩
⟨IT GETS MIXED WITH GLUE AND PUT IN A LITTLE BOX. THE BOYS FLY IN LOOKING FOR FEMALES, BUT THEY CAN'T FLY OUT.⟩
⟨THE BOY MOTHS GET FOOLED BY A SMELL?⟩
⟨NO, THEY GET FOOLED BY SEX.⟩
⟨ALL MALES DO.⟩
⟨OH.⟩
⟨BUT IF IT ONLY KILLS THE BOYS, HOW DO WE KILL THE GIRLS?⟩
⟨WE DON'T HAVE TO, AYUKO. ONCE ALL THE MALES DIE...⟩
⟨...MOTHER NATURE TAKES CARE OF THE REST.⟩

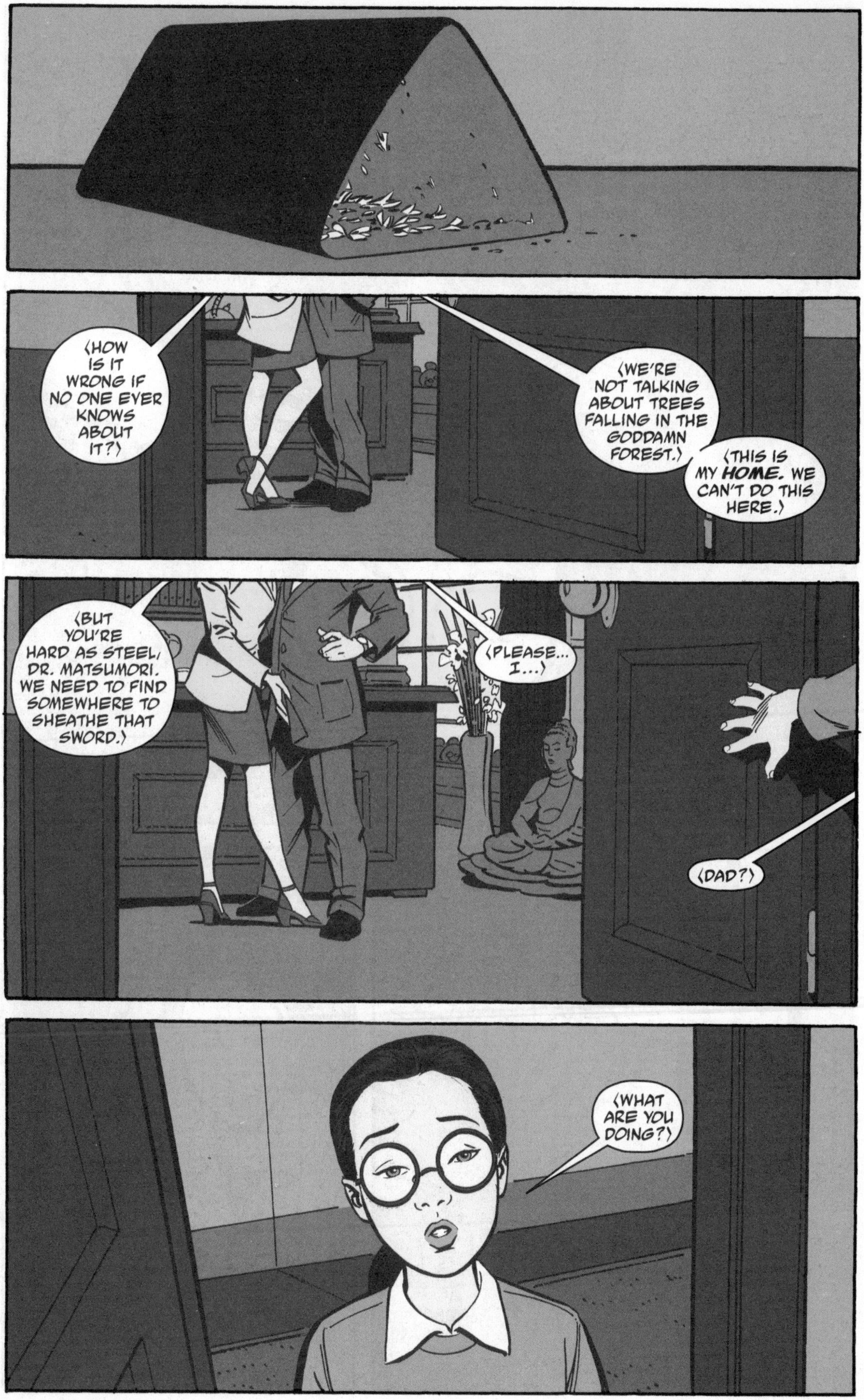
‹HOW IS IT WRONG IF NO ONE EVER KNOWS ABOUT IT?›
‹WE'RE NOT TALKING ABOUT TREES FALLING IN THE GODDAMN FOREST.›
‹THIS IS MY **HOME.** WE CAN'T DO THIS HERE.›
‹BUT YOU'RE HARD AS STEEL, DR. MATSUMORI. WE NEED TO FIND SOMEWHERE TO SHEATHE THAT SWORD.›
‹PLEASE... I...›
‹DAD?›
‹WHAT ARE YOU DOING?›

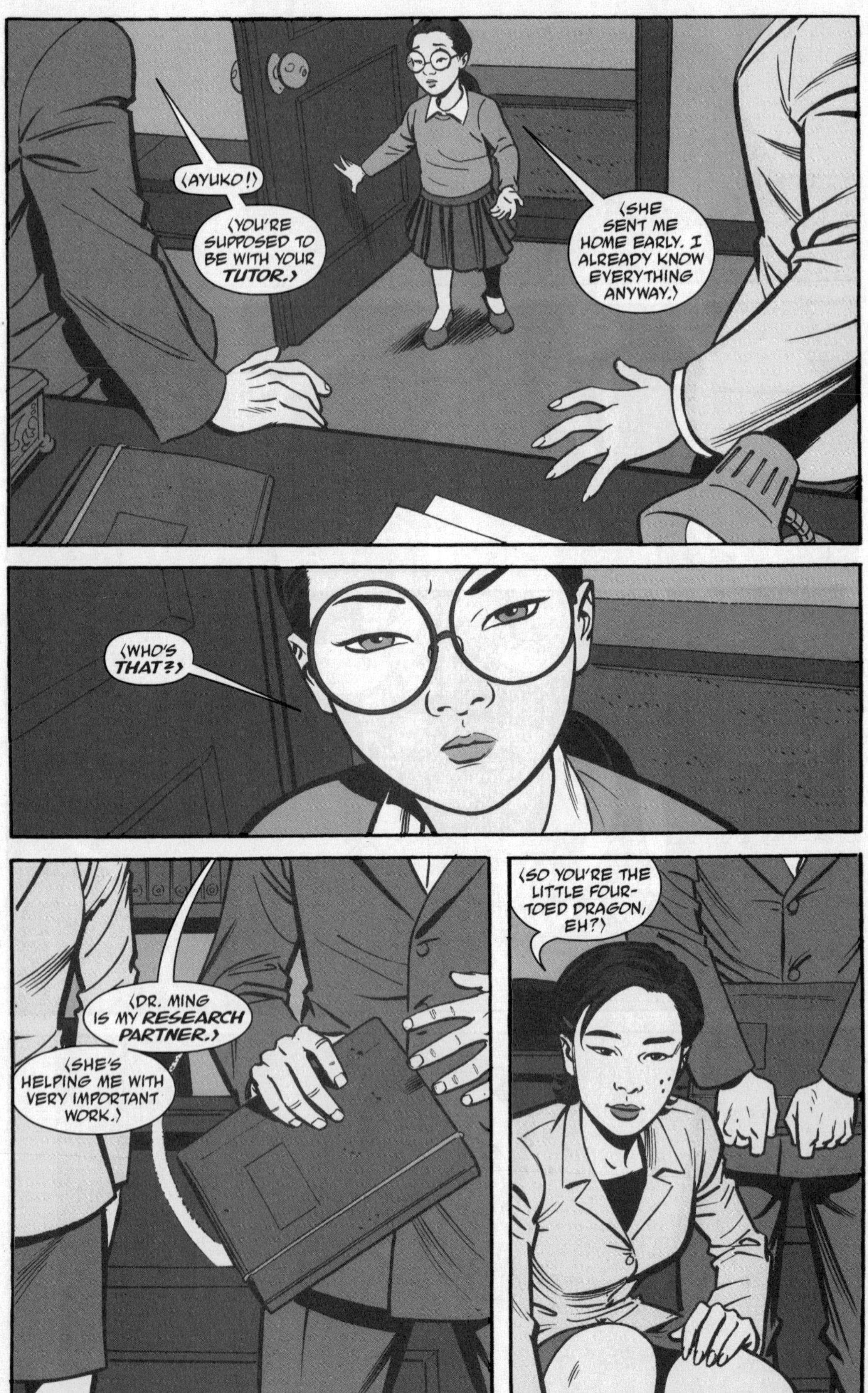
‹AYUKO!›
‹YOU'RE SUPPOSED TO BE WITH YOUR TUTOR.›
‹SHE SENT ME HOME EARLY. I ALREADY KNOW EVERYTHING ANYWAY.›
‹WHO'S THAT?›
‹DR. MING IS MY RESEARCH PARTNER.›
‹SHE'S HELPING ME WITH VERY IMPORTANT WORK.›
‹SO YOU'RE THE LITTLE FOUR-TOED DRAGON, EH?›

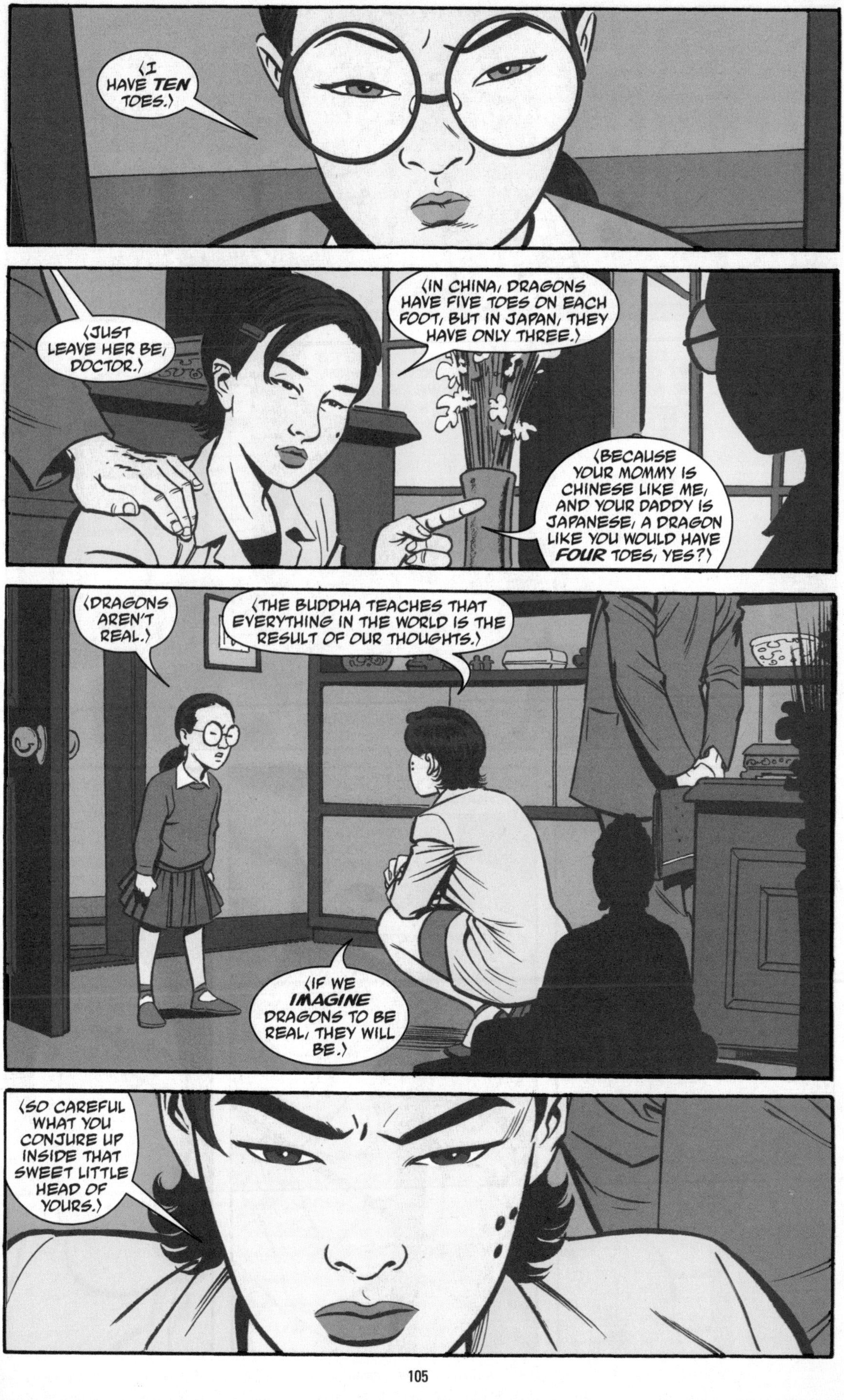
⟨I HAVE TEN TOES.⟩
⟨JUST LEAVE HER BE, DOCTOR.⟩
⟨IN CHINA, DRAGONS HAVE FIVE TOES ON EACH FOOT, BUT IN JAPAN, THEY HAVE ONLY THREE.⟩
⟨BECAUSE YOUR MOMMY IS CHINESE LIKE ME, AND YOUR DADDY IS JAPANESE, A DRAGON LIKE YOU WOULD HAVE FOUR TOES, YES?⟩
⟨DRAGONS AREN'T REAL.⟩
⟨THE BUDDHA TEACHES THAT EVERYTHING IN THE WORLD IS THE RESULT OF OUR THOUGHTS.⟩
⟨IF WE IMAGINE DRAGONS TO BE REAL, THEY WILL BE.⟩
⟨SO CAREFUL WHAT YOU CONJURE UP INSIDE THAT SWEET LITTLE HEAD OF YOURS.⟩

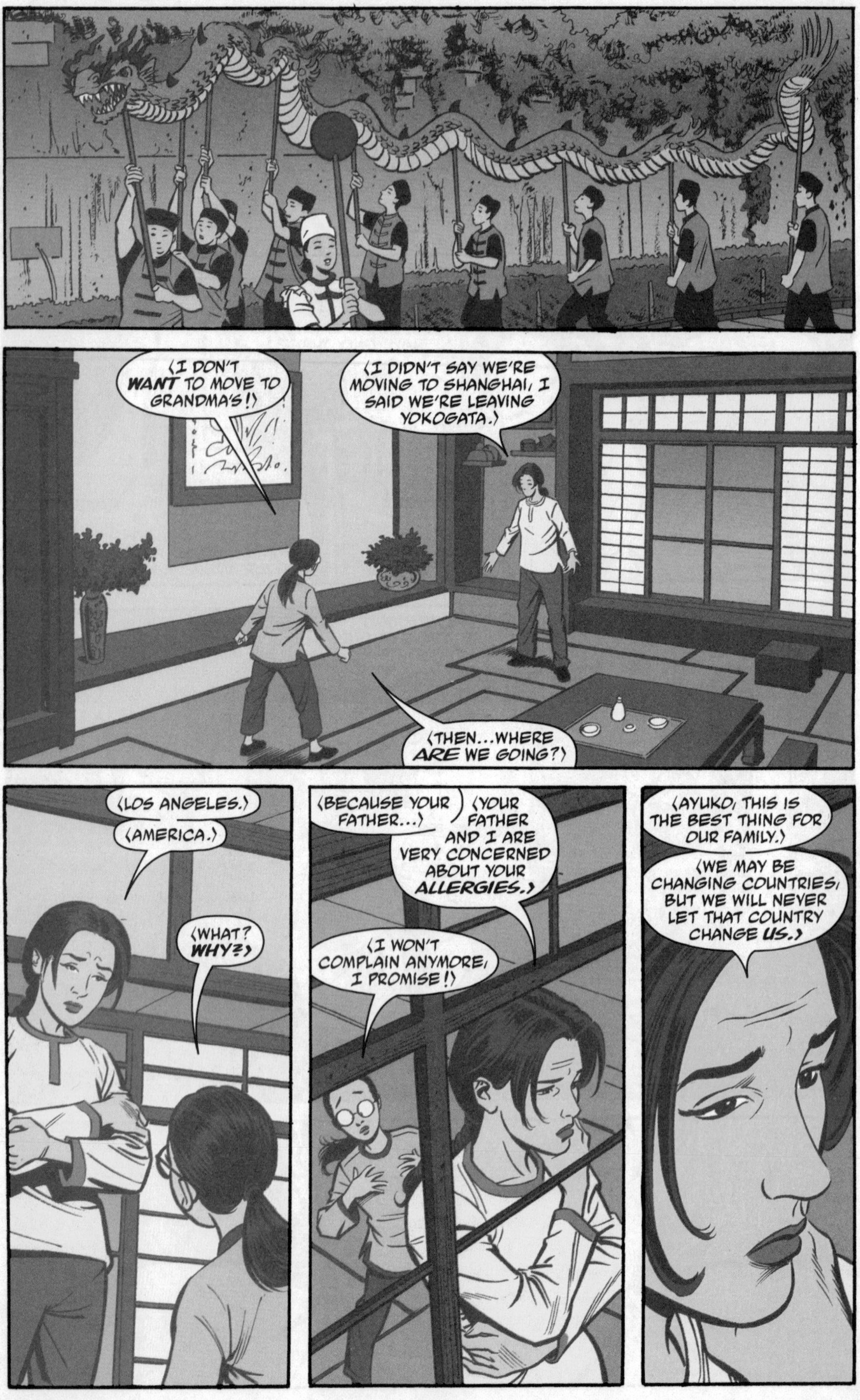
⟨I DON'T WANT TO MOVE TO GRANDMA'S!⟩
⟨I DIDN'T SAY WE'RE MOVING TO SHANGHAI, I SAID WE'RE LEAVING YOKOGATA.⟩
⟨THEN...WHERE ARE WE GOING?⟩
⟨LOS ANGELES.⟩
⟨AMERICA.⟩
⟨WHAT? WHY?⟩
⟨BECAUSE YOUR FATHER...⟩
⟨YOUR FATHER AND I ARE VERY CONCERNED ABOUT YOUR ALLERGIES.⟩
⟨I WON'T COMPLAIN ANYMORE, I PROMISE!⟩
⟨AYUKO, THIS IS THE BEST THING FOR OUR FAMILY.⟩
⟨WE MAY BE CHANGING COUNTRIES, BUT WE WILL NEVER LET THAT COUNTRY CHANGE US.⟩

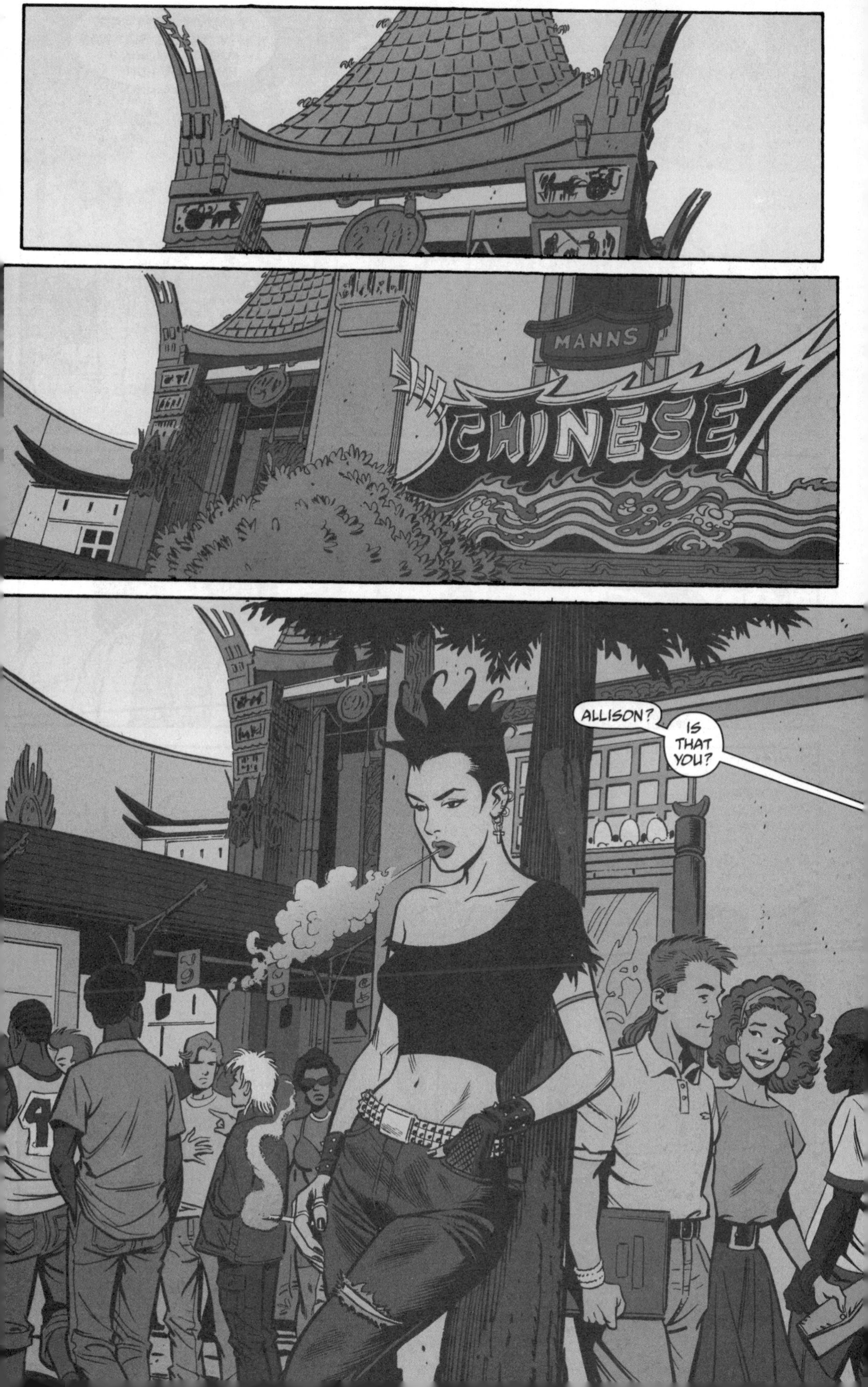

MANNS
CHINESE
ALLISON?
IS THAT YOU?

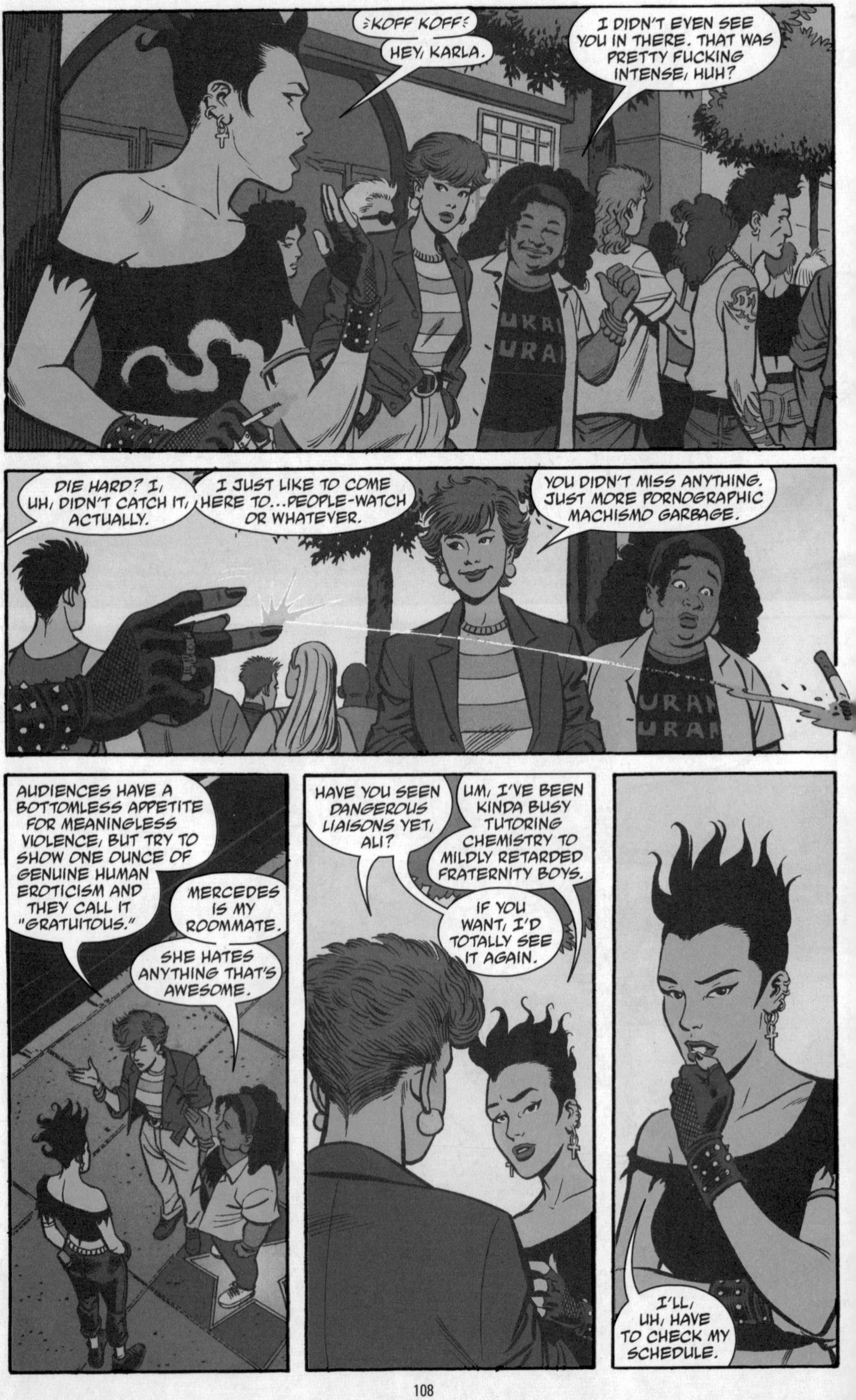

KOFF KOFF
HEY, KARLA.
I DIDN'T EVEN SEE YOU IN THERE. THAT WAS PRETTY FUCKING INTENSE, HUH?
DIE HARD? I, UH, DIDN'T CATCH IT, ACTUALLY.
I JUST LIKE TO COME HERE TO...PEOPLE-WATCH OR WHATEVER.
YOU DIDN'T MISS ANYTHING. JUST MORE PORNOGRAPHIC MACHISMO GARBAGE.
AUDIENCES HAVE A BOTTOMLESS APPETITE FOR MEANINGLESS VIOLENCE, BUT TRY TO SHOW ONE OUNCE OF GENUINE HUMAN EROTICISM AND THEY CALL IT "GRATUITOUS."
MERCEDES IS MY ROOMMATE.
SHE HATES ANYTHING THAT'S AWESOME.
HAVE YOU SEEN DANGEROUS LIAISONS YET, ALI?
UM, I'VE BEEN KINDA BUSY TUTORING CHEMISTRY TO MILDLY RETARDED FRATERNITY BOYS.
IF YOU WANT, I'D TOTALLY SEE IT AGAIN.
I'LL, UH, HAVE TO CHECK MY SCHEDULE.

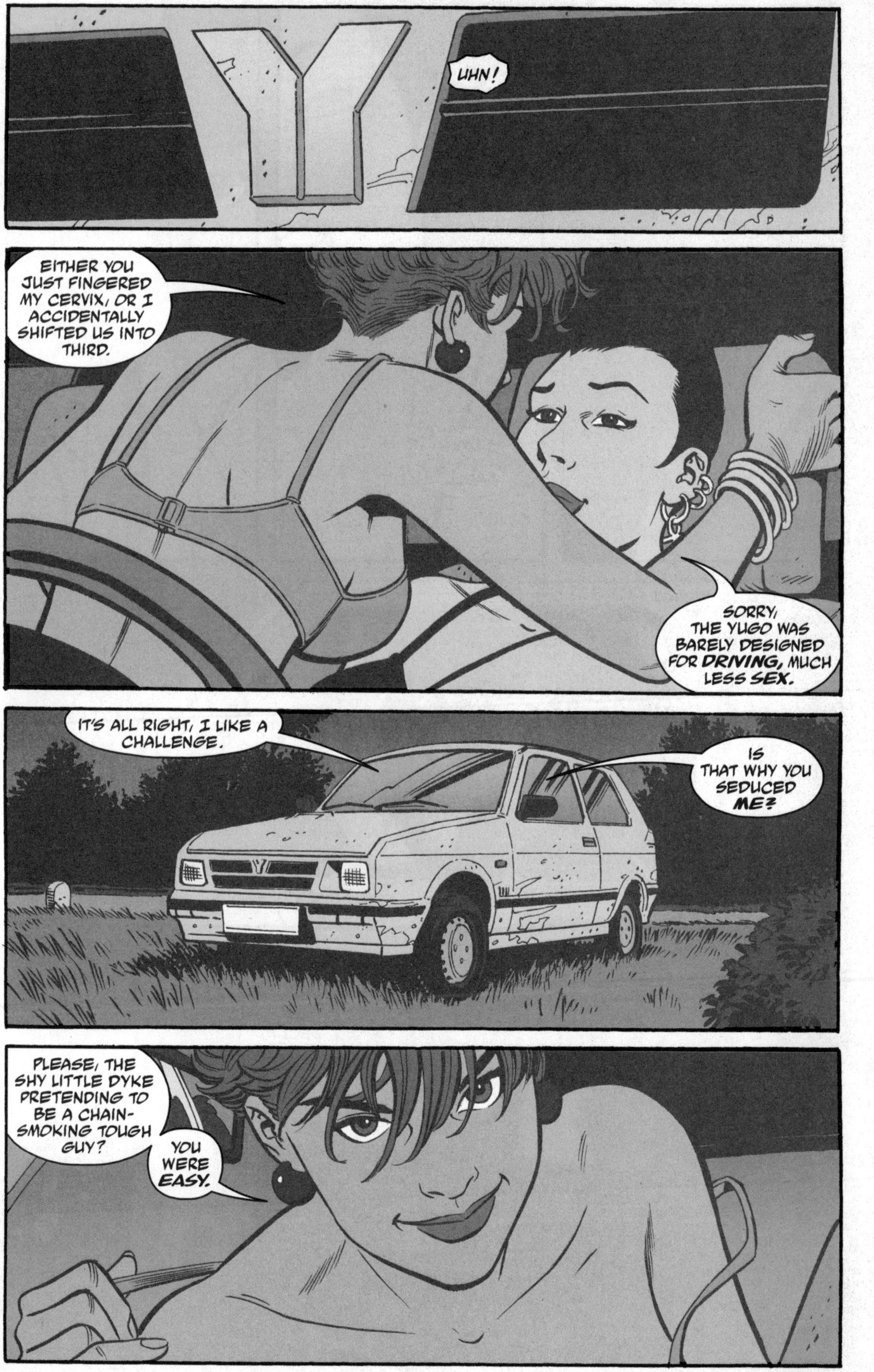
UHN!
EITHER YOU JUST FINGERED MY CERVIX, OR I ACCIDENTALLY SHIFTED US INTO THIRD.
SORRY, THE YUGO WAS BARELY DESIGNED FOR DRIVING, MUCH LESS SEX.
IT'S ALL RIGHT, I LIKE A CHALLENGE.
IS THAT WHY YOU SEDUCED ME?
PLEASE, THE SHY LITTLE DYKE PRETENDING TO BE A CHAIN-SMOKING TOUGH GUY?
YOU WERE EASY.

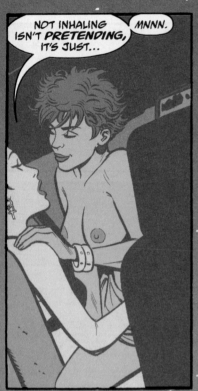

NOT INHALING ISN'T *PRETENDING,* IT'S JUST... MNNN.

I LOVE THE WAY YOU SMELL.

HHN.

I LOVE THE WAY YOU *TASTE.*

ALI, I... I THINK I LOVE *YOU.*

YOU *THINK?*

ABOUT YOU?

EVERY SECOND OF EVERY DAY.

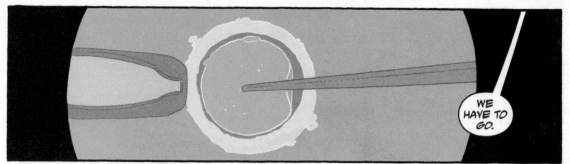

WE HAVE TO GO.

WHAT ARE YOU TALKING ABOUT?

THE U.S. IS MADE UP OF MORALIZING COWARDS.

I'LL HAVE TO CONTINUE MY WORK ELSE-WHERE.

I'M NOT COMING WITH YOU.

OH, REALLY? SO YOU PLAN TO PAY FOR UNIVERSITY ON YOUR OWN?

HOW HARD DO YOU THINK IT WILL BE FOR ME TO GET A SCHOLARSHIP, DAD?

YOU NEVER EVEN OPEN A BOOK.

I DON'T NEED TO. SHIT YOU STRUGGLE TO COMPREHEND IS EASY FOR ME. I CAN SPEND TIME LIVING LIFE INSTEAD OF JUST OBSERVING IT.

IF THIS IS ABOUT BOYS, YOU'LL HAVE MILLIONS TO CHOOSE FROM WHERE WE'RE GOING.

I FUCK GIRLS, DAD.

JUST LIKE YOU.

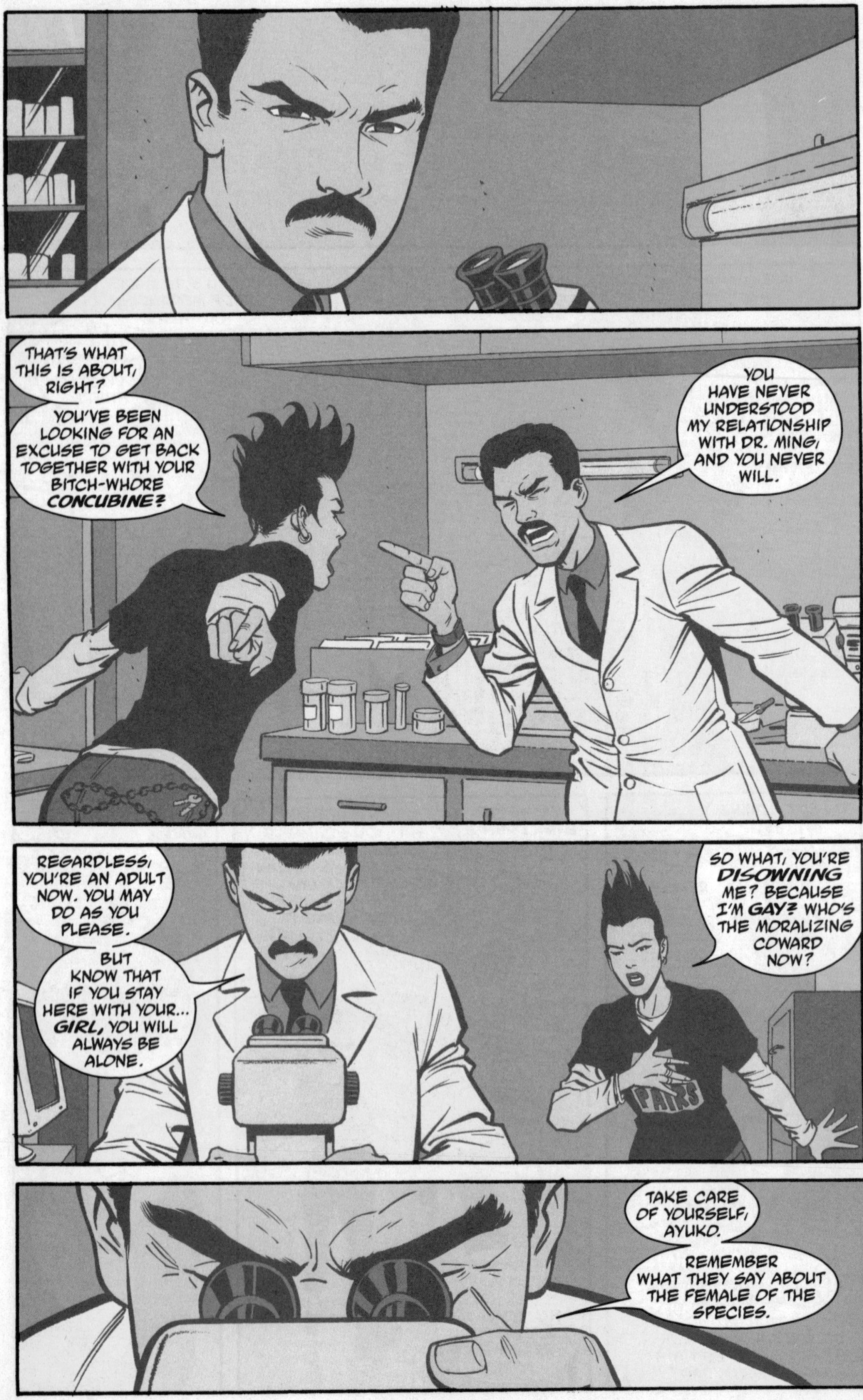
THAT'S WHAT THIS IS ABOUT, RIGHT?
YOU'VE BEEN LOOKING FOR AN EXCUSE TO GET BACK TOGETHER WITH YOUR BITCH-WHORE CONCUBINE?
YOU HAVE NEVER UNDERSTOOD MY RELATIONSHIP WITH DR. MING, AND YOU NEVER WILL.
REGARDLESS, YOU'RE AN ADULT NOW. YOU MAY DO AS YOU PLEASE.
BUT KNOW THAT IF YOU STAY HERE WITH YOUR... GIRL, YOU WILL ALWAYS BE ALONE.
SO WHAT, YOU'RE DISOWNING ME? BECAUSE I'M GAY? WHO'S THE MORALIZING COWARD NOW?
PAIRS
TAKE CARE OF YOURSELF, AYUKO.
REMEMBER WHAT THEY SAY ABOUT THE FEMALE OF THE SPECIES.

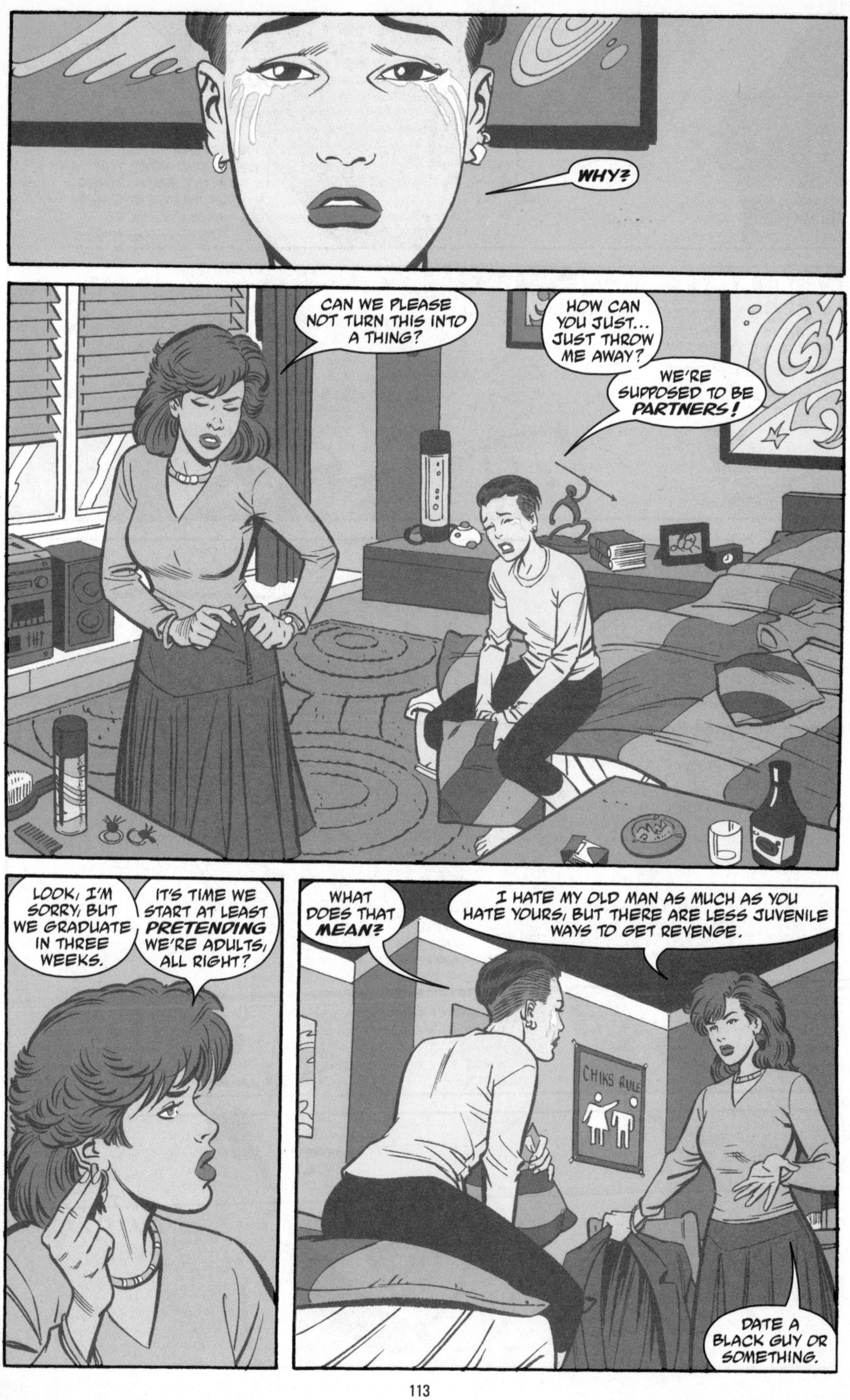
WHY?
CAN WE PLEASE NOT TURN THIS INTO A THING?
HOW CAN YOU JUST... JUST THROW ME AWAY?
WE'RE SUPPOSED TO BE PARTNERS!
LOOK, I'M SORRY, BUT WE GRADUATE IN THREE WEEKS.
IT'S TIME WE START AT LEAST PRETENDING WE'RE ADULTS, ALL RIGHT?
WHAT DOES THAT MEAN?
I HATE MY OLD MAN AS MUCH AS YOU HATE YOURS, BUT THERE ARE LESS JUVENILE WAYS TO GET REVENGE.
CHIKS RULE
DATE A BLACK GUY OR SOMETHING.

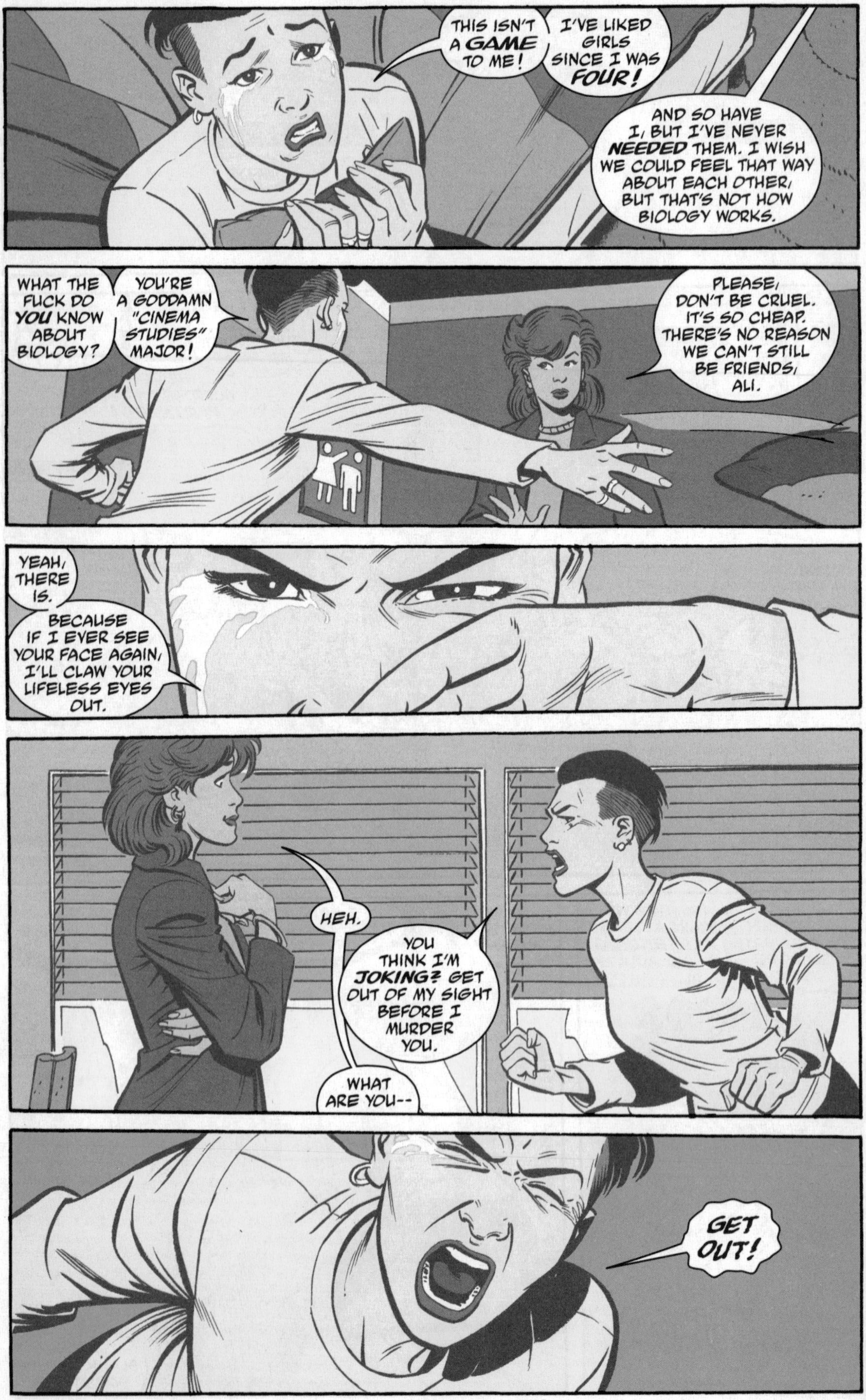
THIS ISN'T A GAME TO ME!
I'VE LIKED GIRLS SINCE I WAS FOUR!
AND SO HAVE I, BUT I'VE NEVER NEEDED THEM. I WISH WE COULD FEEL THAT WAY ABOUT EACH OTHER, BUT THAT'S NOT HOW BIOLOGY WORKS.
WHAT THE FUCK DO YOU KNOW ABOUT BIOLOGY?
YOU'RE A GODDAMN "CINEMA STUDIES" MAJOR!
PLEASE, DON'T BE CRUEL. IT'S SO CHEAP. THERE'S NO REASON WE CAN'T STILL BE FRIENDS, ALI.
YEAH, THERE IS.
BECAUSE IF I EVER SEE YOUR FACE AGAIN, I'LL CLAW YOUR LIFELESS EYES OUT.
HEH.
YOU THINK I'M JOKING? GET OUT OF MY SIGHT BEFORE I MURDER YOU.
WHAT ARE YOU--
GET OUT!

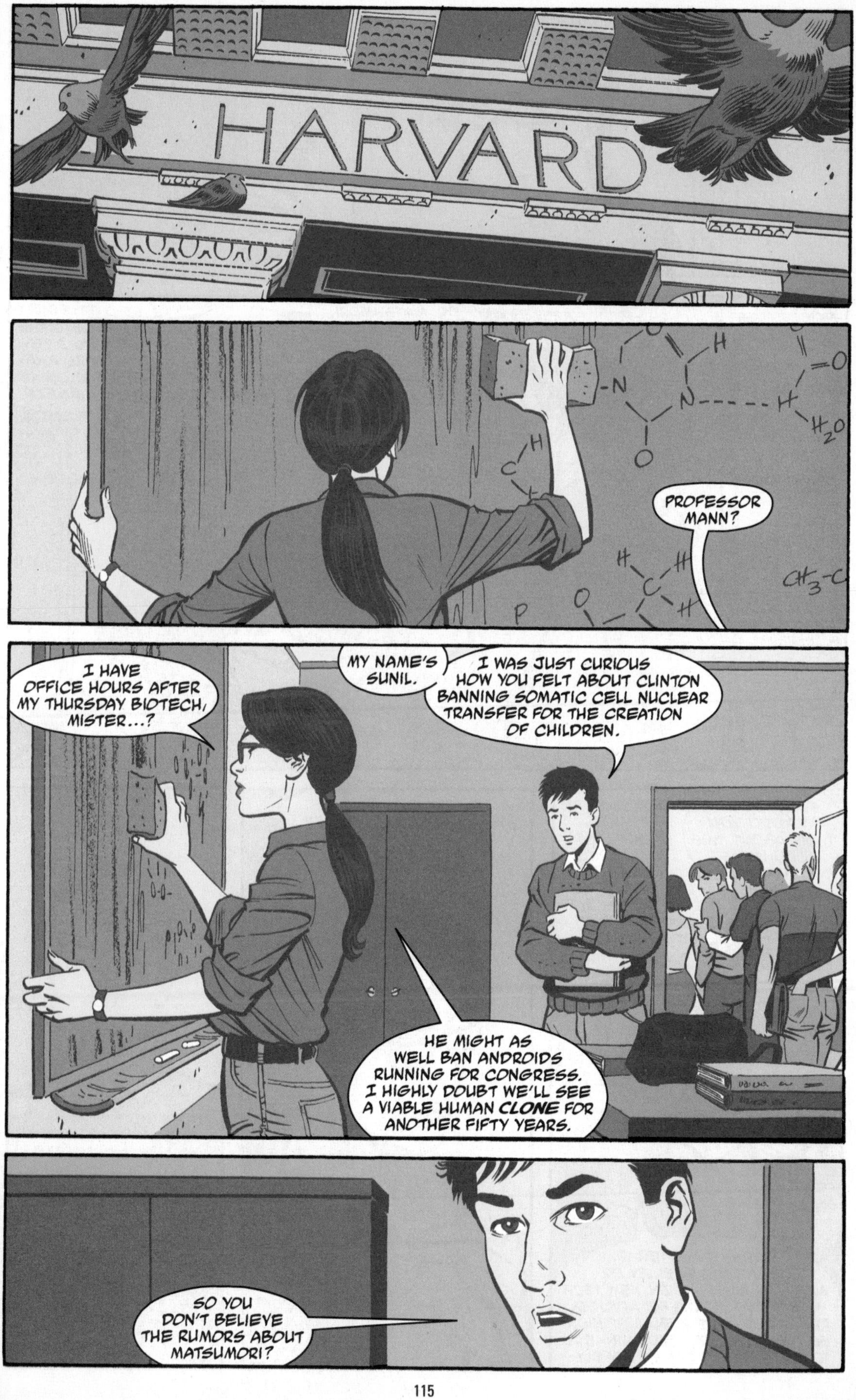
HARVARD
PROFESSOR MANN?
I HAVE OFFICE HOURS AFTER MY THURSDAY BIOTECH, MISTER...?
MY NAME'S SUNIL.
I WAS JUST CURIOUS HOW YOU FELT ABOUT CLINTON BANNING SOMATIC CELL NUCLEAR TRANSFER FOR THE CREATION OF CHILDREN.
HE MIGHT AS WELL BAN ANDROIDS RUNNING FOR CONGRESS. I HIGHLY DOUBT WE'LL SEE A VIABLE HUMAN CLONE FOR ANOTHER FIFTY YEARS.
SO YOU DON'T BELIEVE THE RUMORS ABOUT MATSUMORI?

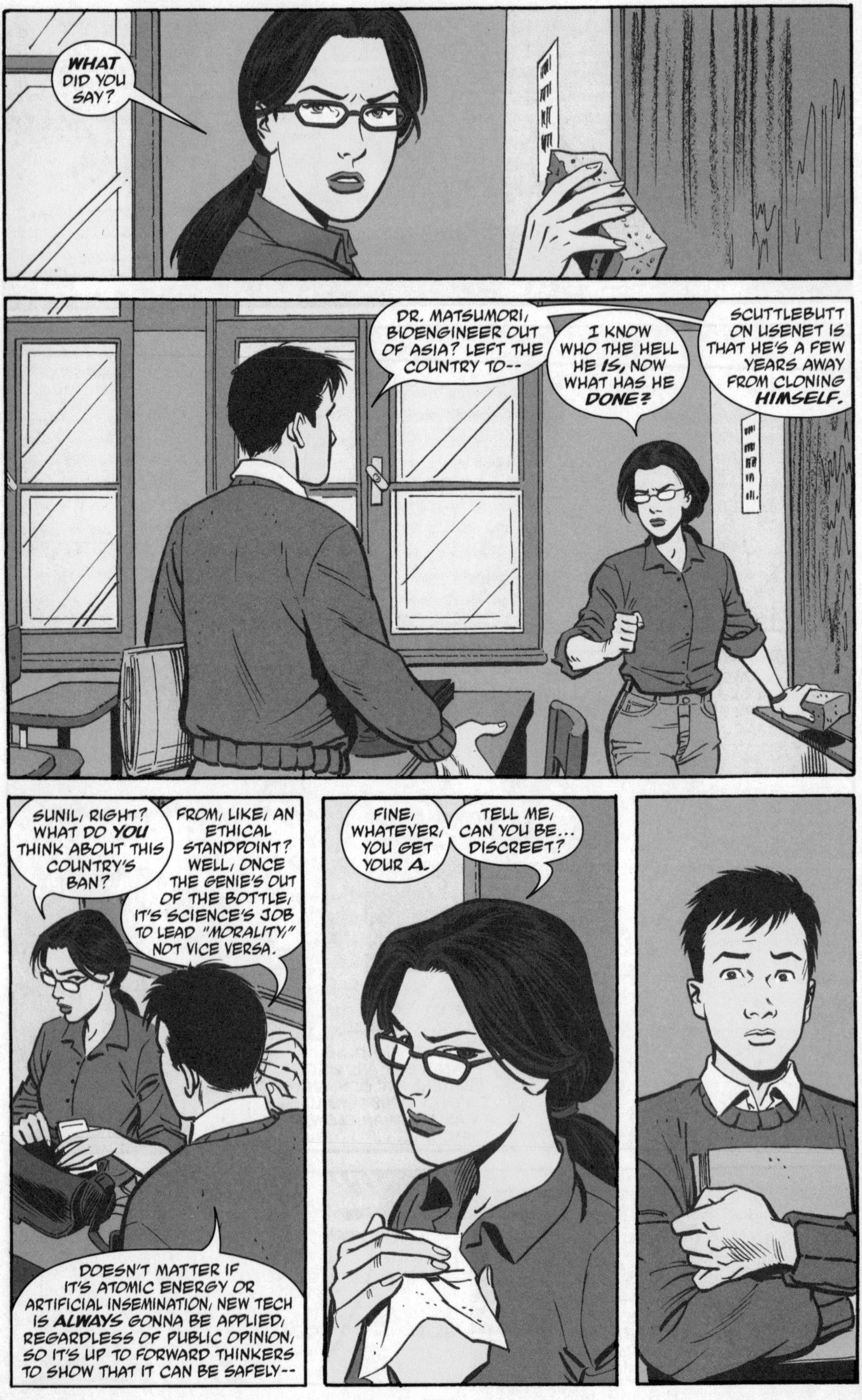

WHAT DID YOU SAY?
DR. MATSUMORI, BIOENGINEER OUT OF ASIA? LEFT THE COUNTRY TO--
I KNOW WHO THE HELL HE IS, NOW WHAT HAS HE DONE?
SCUTTLEBUTT ON USENET IS THAT HE'S A FEW YEARS AWAY FROM CLONING HIMSELF.
SUNIL, RIGHT? WHAT DO YOU THINK ABOUT THIS COUNTRY'S BAN?
FROM, LIKE, AN ETHICAL STANDPOINT? WELL, ONCE THE GENIE'S OUT OF THE BOTTLE, IT'S SCIENCE'S JOB TO LEAD "MORALITY," NOT VICE VERSA.
DOESN'T MATTER IF IT'S ATOMIC ENERGY OR ARTIFICIAL INSEMINATION, NEW TECH IS ALWAYS GONNA BE APPLIED, REGARDLESS OF PUBLIC OPINION, SO IT'S UP TO FORWARD THINKERS TO SHOW THAT IT CAN BE SAFELY--
FINE, WHATEVER, YOU GET YOUR A.
TELL ME, CAN YOU BE... DISCREET?

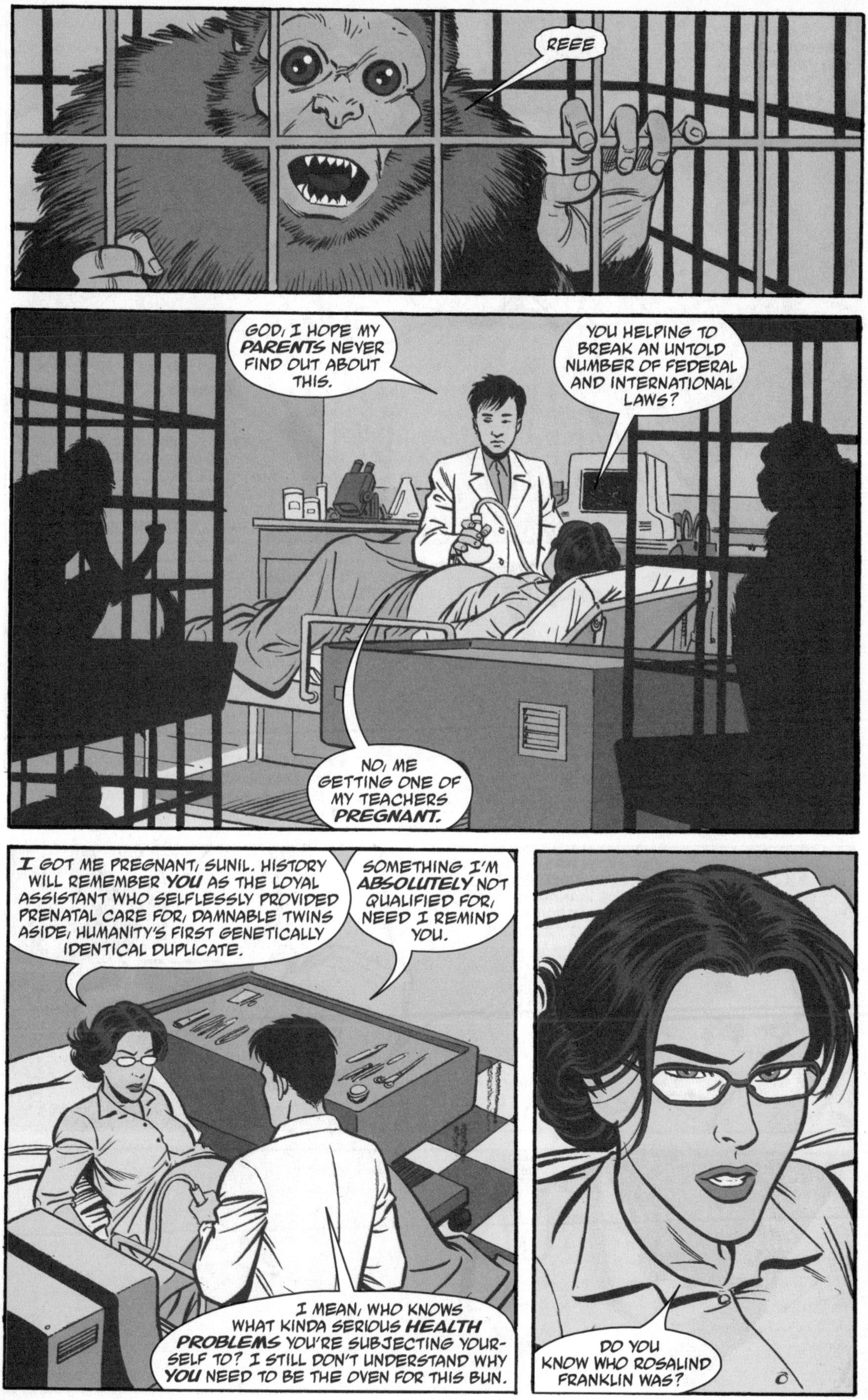
REEE
GOD, I HOPE MY PARENTS NEVER FIND OUT ABOUT THIS.
YOU HELPING TO BREAK AN UNTOLD NUMBER OF FEDERAL AND INTERNATIONAL LAWS?
NO, ME GETTING ONE OF MY TEACHERS PREGNANT.
I GOT ME PREGNANT, SUNIL. HISTORY WILL REMEMBER YOU AS THE LOYAL ASSISTANT WHO SELFLESSLY PROVIDED PRENATAL CARE FOR, DAMNABLE TWINS ASIDE, HUMANITY'S FIRST GENETICALLY IDENTICAL DUPLICATE.
SOMETHING I'M ABSOLUTELY NOT QUALIFIED FOR, NEED I REMIND YOU.
I MEAN, WHO KNOWS WHAT KINDA SERIOUS HEALTH PROBLEMS YOU'RE SUBJECTING YOURSELF TO? I STILL DON'T UNDERSTAND WHY YOU NEED TO BE THE OVEN FOR THIS BUN.
DO YOU KNOW WHO ROSALIND FRANKLIN WAS?

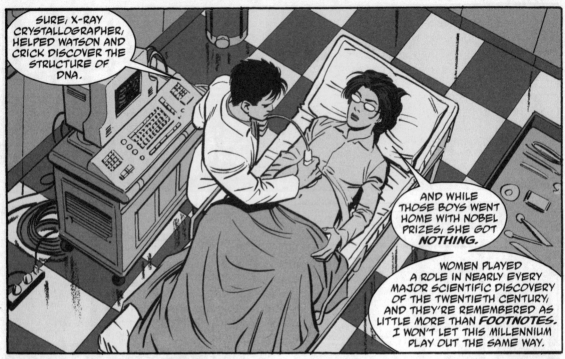

SURE, X-RAY CRYSTALLOGRAPHER, HELPED WATSON AND CRICK DISCOVER THE STRUCTURE OF DNA.

AND WHILE THOSE BOYS WENT HOME WITH NOBEL PRIZES, SHE GOT *NOTHING.*

WOMEN PLAYED A ROLE IN NEARLY EVERY MAJOR SCIENTIFIC DISCOVERY OF THE TWENTIETH CENTURY, AND THEY'RE REMEMBERED AS LITTLE MORE THAN *FOOTNOTES.* I WON'T LET THIS MILLENNIUM PLAY OUT THE SAME WAY.

DOCTOR, ROSALIND FRANKLIN WASN'T PASSED OVER FOR THE NOBEL BECAUSE SHE WAS A WOMAN, SHE WAS PASSED OVER BECAUSE THEY DON'T GIVE THE PRIZE *POSTHUMOUSLY.*

SHE DIED OF *CANCER,* PROBABLY BECAUSE OF ALL THE *RADIATION* FROM HER RESEARCH. I KNOW YOU'RE NOT A FAN OF ANECDOTAL EVIDENCE, BUT YOU KNOW A CAUTIONARY TALE WHEN YOU HEAR ONE, RIGHT?

CHILDBIRTH HAS ALWAYS BEEN A DANGEROUS UNDERTAKING, BUT AT LEAST I'VE MANAGED TO ELIMINATE THE MOST PAINFUL PART OF THE PROCESS.

WHAT'S THAT?

SEX?

LOVE.

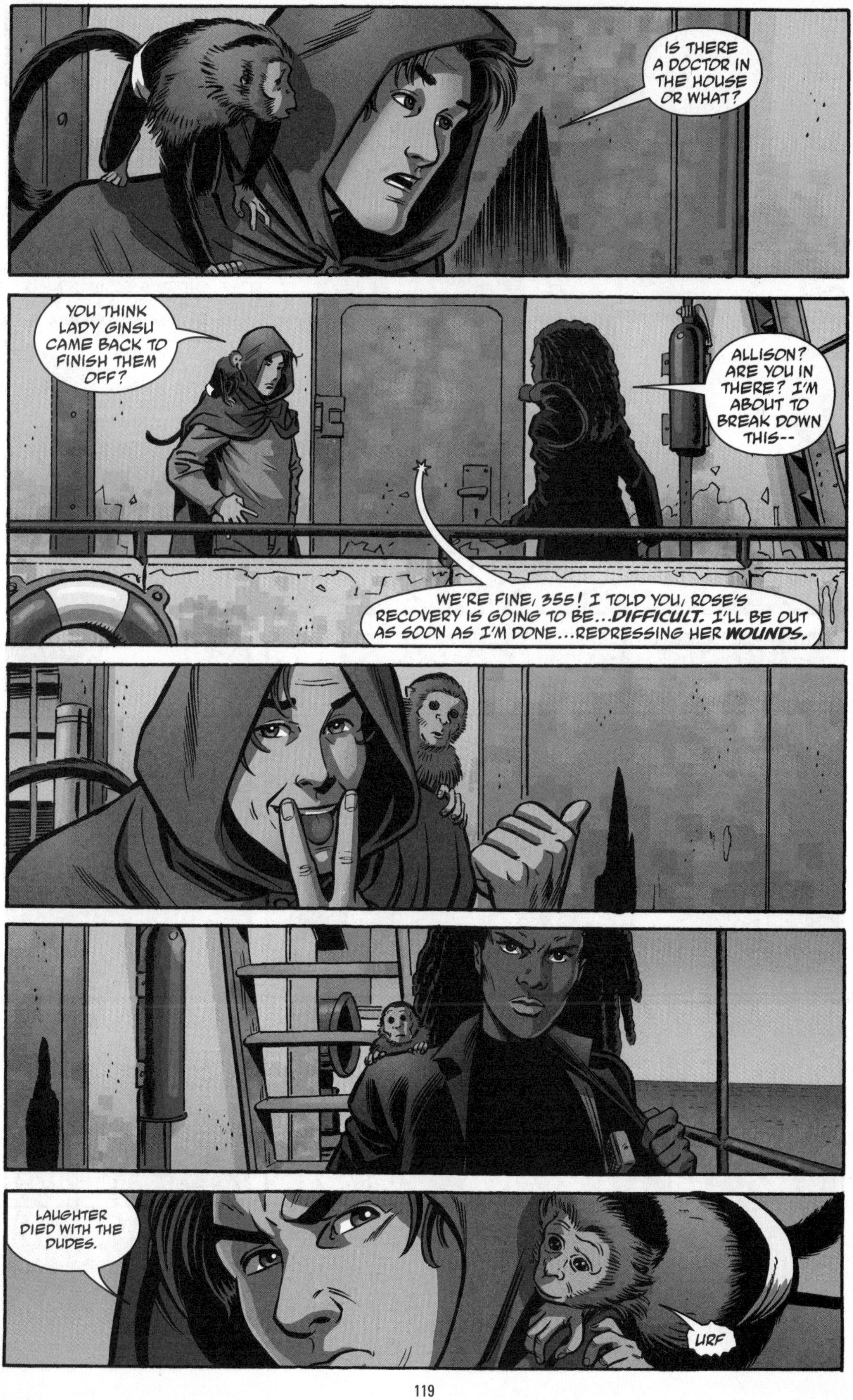
IS THERE A DOCTOR IN THE HOUSE OR WHAT?
YOU THINK LADY GINSU CAME BACK TO FINISH THEM OFF?
ALLISON? ARE YOU IN THERE? I'M ABOUT TO BREAK DOWN THIS--
WE'RE FINE, 355! I TOLD YOU, ROSE'S RECOVERY IS GOING TO BE...**DIFFICULT.** I'LL BE OUT AS SOON AS I'M DONE...REDRESSING HER **WOUNDS.**
LAUGHTER DIED WITH THE DUDES.
URF

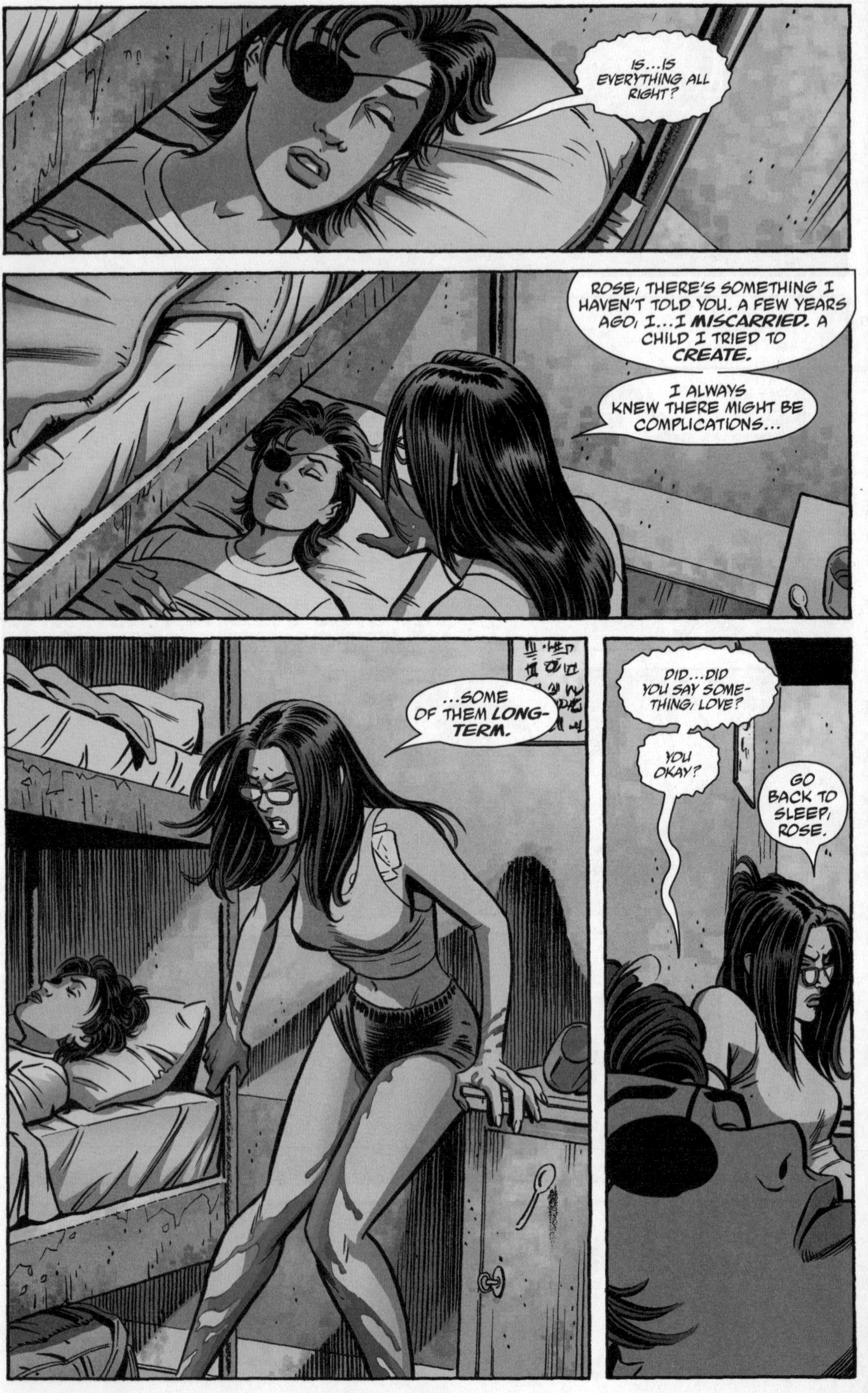
IS...IS EVERYTHING ALL RIGHT?
ROSE, THERE'S SOMETHING I HAVEN'T TOLD YOU. A FEW YEARS AGO, I...I **MISCARRIED.** A CHILD I TRIED TO **CREATE.**
I ALWAYS KNEW THERE MIGHT BE COMPLICATIONS...
...SOME OF THEM **LONG-TERM.**
DID...DID YOU SAY SOME-THING, LOVE?
YOU OKAY?
GO BACK TO SLEEP, ROSE.

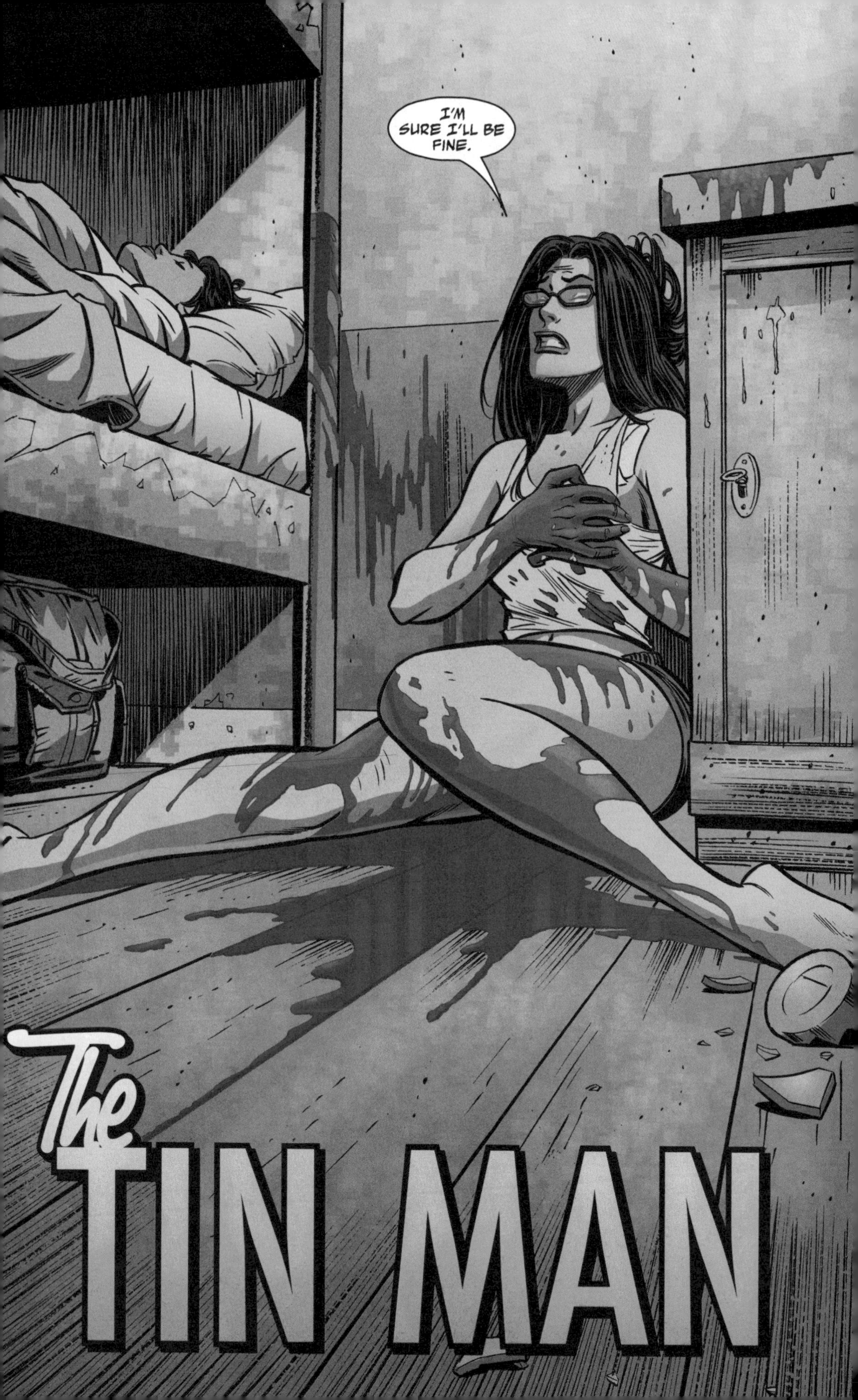
I'M SURE I'LL BE FINE.
The TIN MAN

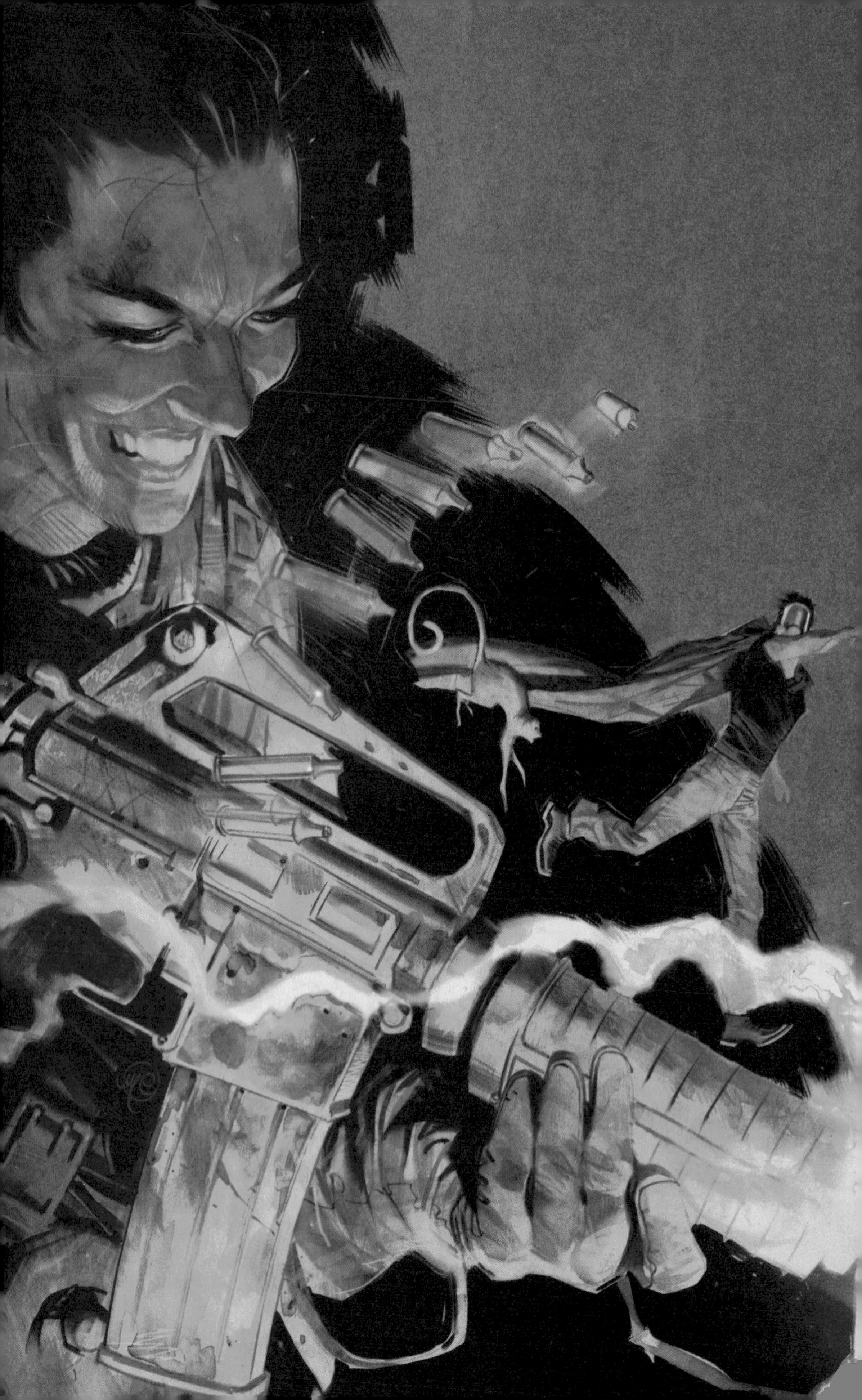

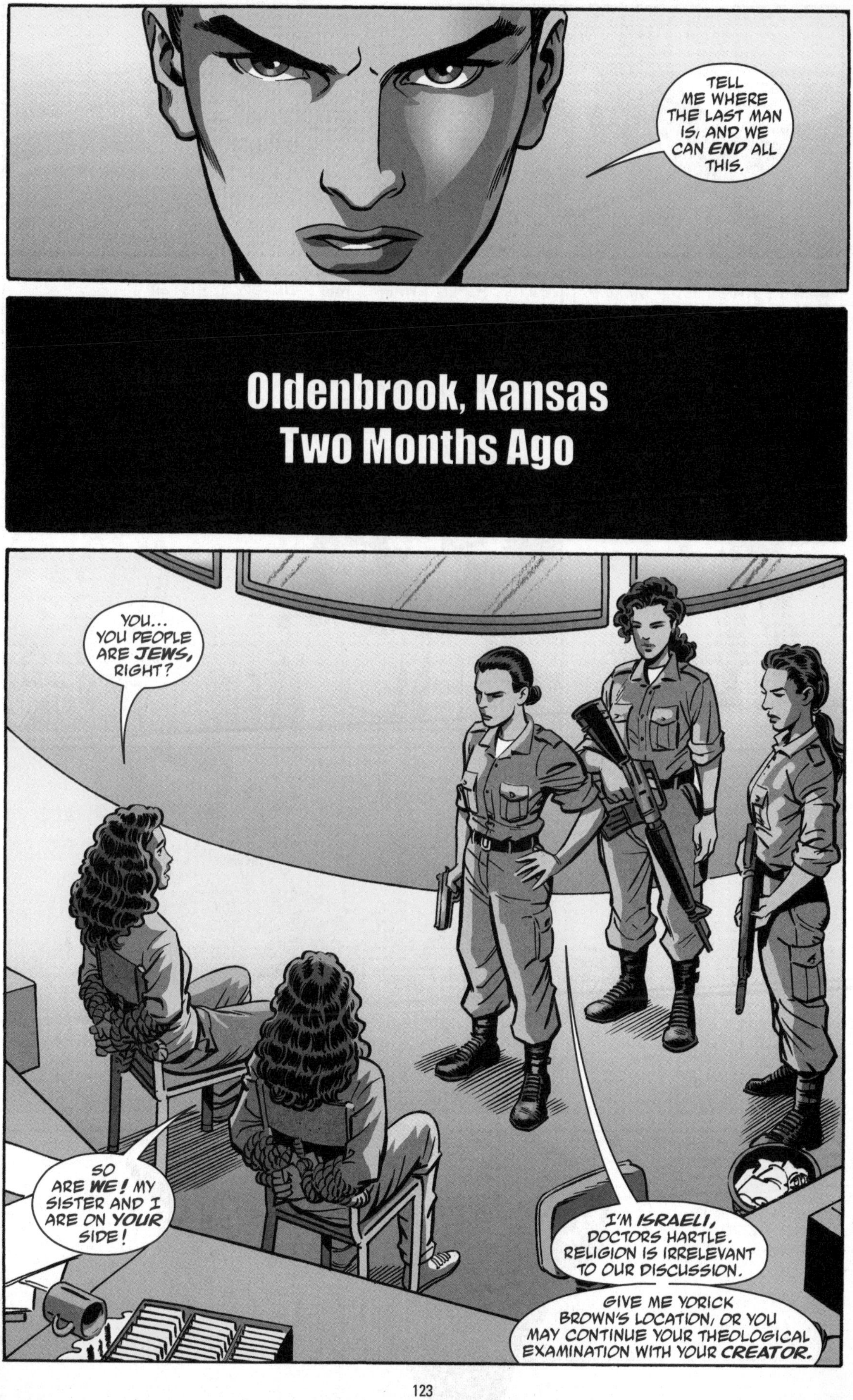
TELL ME WHERE THE LAST MAN IS, AND WE CAN END ALL THIS.
Oldenbrook, Kansas
Two Months Ago
YOU... YOU PEOPLE ARE JEWS, RIGHT?
SO ARE WE! MY SISTER AND I ARE ON YOUR SIDE!
I'M ISRAELI, DOCTORS HARTLE. RELIGION IS IRRELEVANT TO OUR DISCUSSION.
GIVE ME YORICK BROWN'S LOCATION, OR YOU MAY CONTINUE YOUR THEOLOGICAL EXAMINATION WITH YOUR CREATOR.

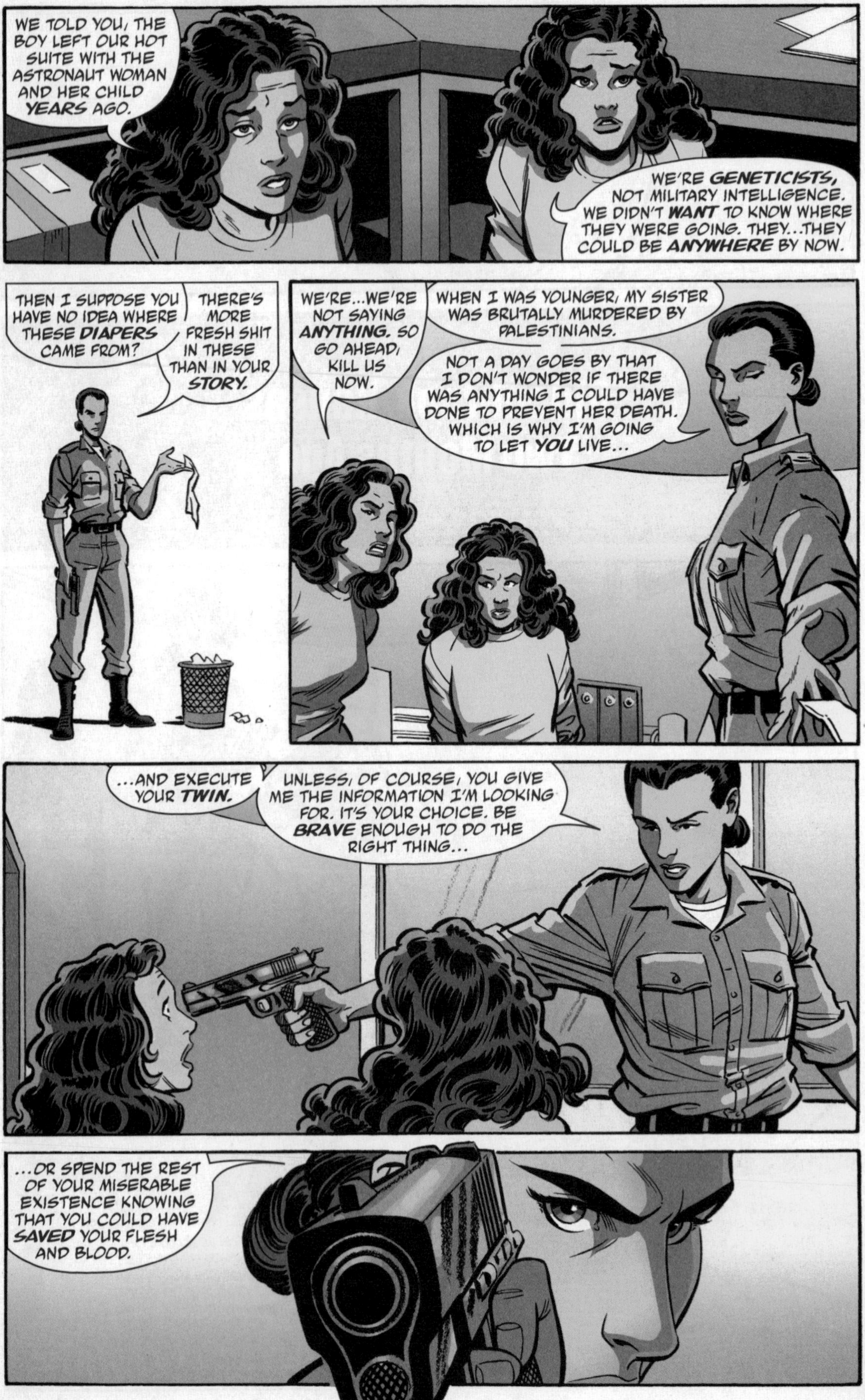
WE TOLD YOU, THE BOY LEFT OUR HOT SUITE WITH THE ASTRONAUT WOMAN AND HER CHILD YEARS AGO.
WE'RE GENETICISTS, NOT MILITARY INTELLIGENCE. WE DIDN'T WANT TO KNOW WHERE THEY WERE GOING. THEY...THEY COULD BE ANYWHERE BY NOW.
THEN I SUPPOSE YOU HAVE NO IDEA WHERE THESE DIAPERS CAME FROM?
THERE'S MORE FRESH SHIT IN THESE THAN IN YOUR STORY.
WE'RE...WE'RE NOT SAYING ANYTHING. SO GO AHEAD, KILL US NOW.
WHEN I WAS YOUNGER, MY SISTER WAS BRUTALLY MURDERED BY PALESTINIANS.
NOT A DAY GOES BY THAT I DON'T WONDER IF THERE WAS ANYTHING I COULD HAVE DONE TO PREVENT HER DEATH. WHICH IS WHY I'M GOING TO LET YOU LIVE...
...AND EXECUTE YOUR TWIN.
UNLESS, OF COURSE, YOU GIVE ME THE INFORMATION I'M LOOKING FOR. IT'S YOUR CHOICE. BE BRAVE ENOUGH TO DO THE RIGHT THING...
...OR SPEND THE REST OF YOUR MISERABLE EXISTENCE KNOWING THAT YOU COULD HAVE SAVED YOUR FLESH AND BLOOD.

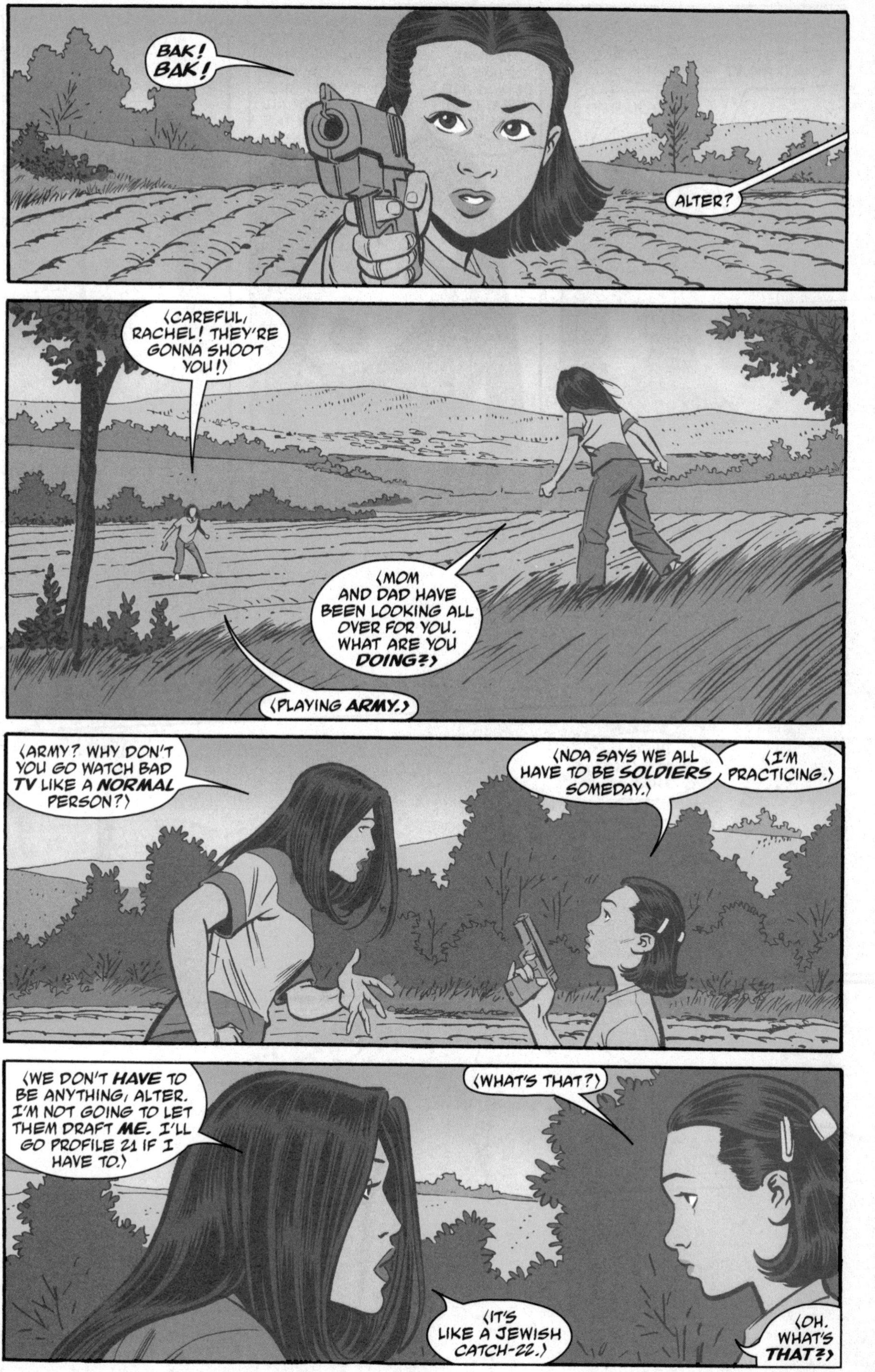
BAK! BAK!
ALTER?
(CAREFUL, RACHEL! THEY'RE GONNA SHOOT YOU!)
(MOM AND DAD HAVE BEEN LOOKING ALL OVER FOR YOU. WHAT ARE YOU DOING?)
(PLAYING ARMY.)
(ARMY? WHY DON'T YOU GO WATCH BAD TV LIKE A NORMAL PERSON?)
(NOA SAYS WE ALL HAVE TO BE SOLDIERS SOMEDAY.)
(I'M PRACTICING.)
(WE DON'T HAVE TO BE ANYTHING, ALTER. I'M NOT GOING TO LET THEM DRAFT ME. I'LL GO PROFILE 21 IF I HAVE TO.)
(WHAT'S THAT?)
(IT'S LIKE A JEWISH CATCH-22.)
(OH. WHAT'S THAT?)

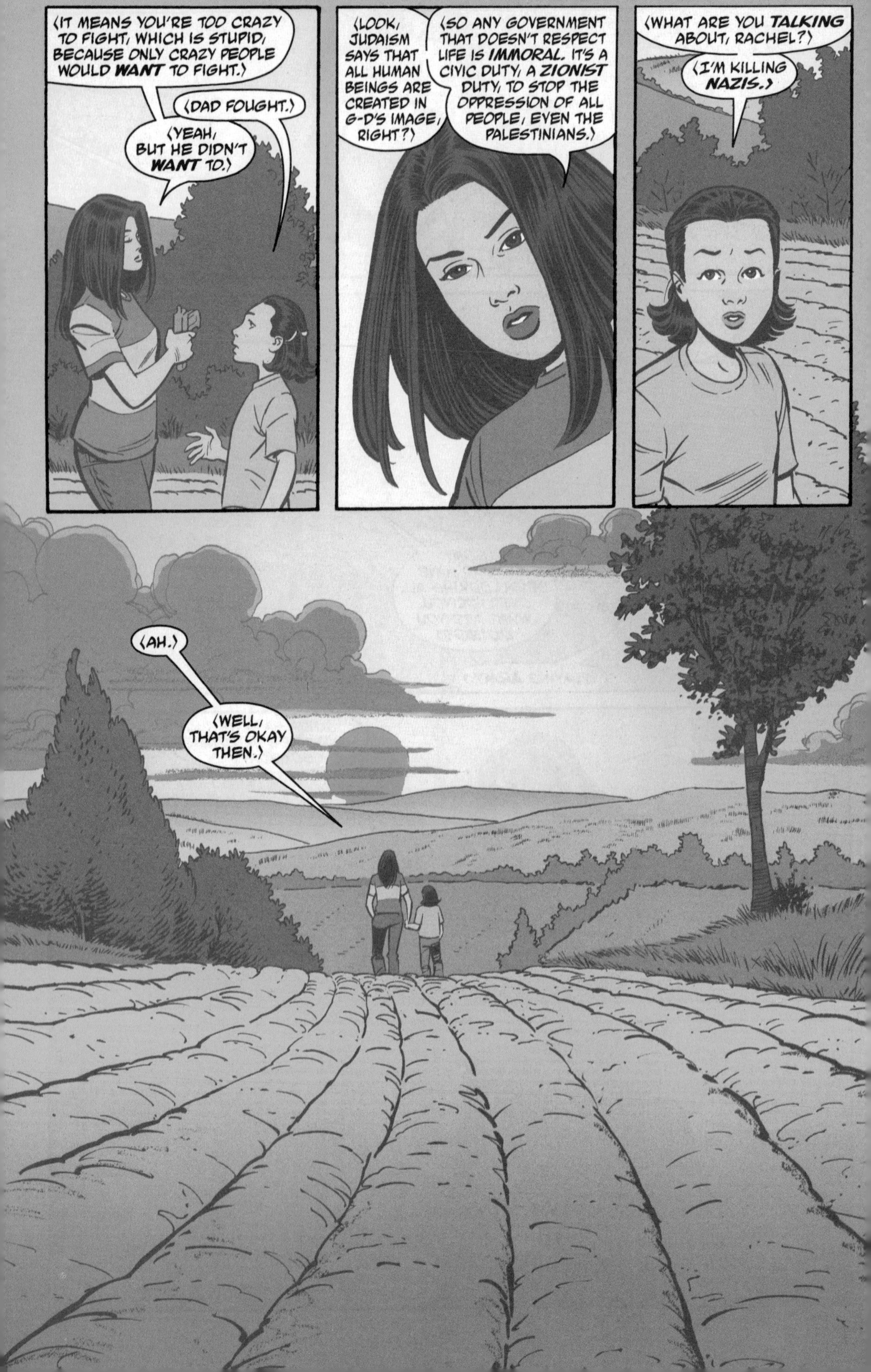
⟨IT MEANS YOU'RE TOO CRAZY TO FIGHT, WHICH IS STUPID, BECAUSE ONLY CRAZY PEOPLE WOULD **WANT** TO FIGHT.⟩
⟨DAD FOUGHT.⟩
⟨YEAH, BUT HE DIDN'T **WANT** TO.⟩
⟨LOOK, JUDAISM SAYS THAT ALL HUMAN BEINGS ARE CREATED IN G-D'S IMAGE, RIGHT?⟩
⟨SO ANY GOVERNMENT THAT DOESN'T RESPECT LIFE IS **IMMORAL**. IT'S A CIVIC DUTY, A **ZIONIST** DUTY, TO STOP THE OPPRESSION OF ALL PEOPLE, EVEN THE PALESTINIANS.⟩
⟨WHAT ARE YOU **TALKING** ABOUT, RACHEL?⟩
⟨I'M KILLING **NAZIS**.⟩
⟨AH.⟩
⟨WELL, THAT'S OKAY THEN.⟩

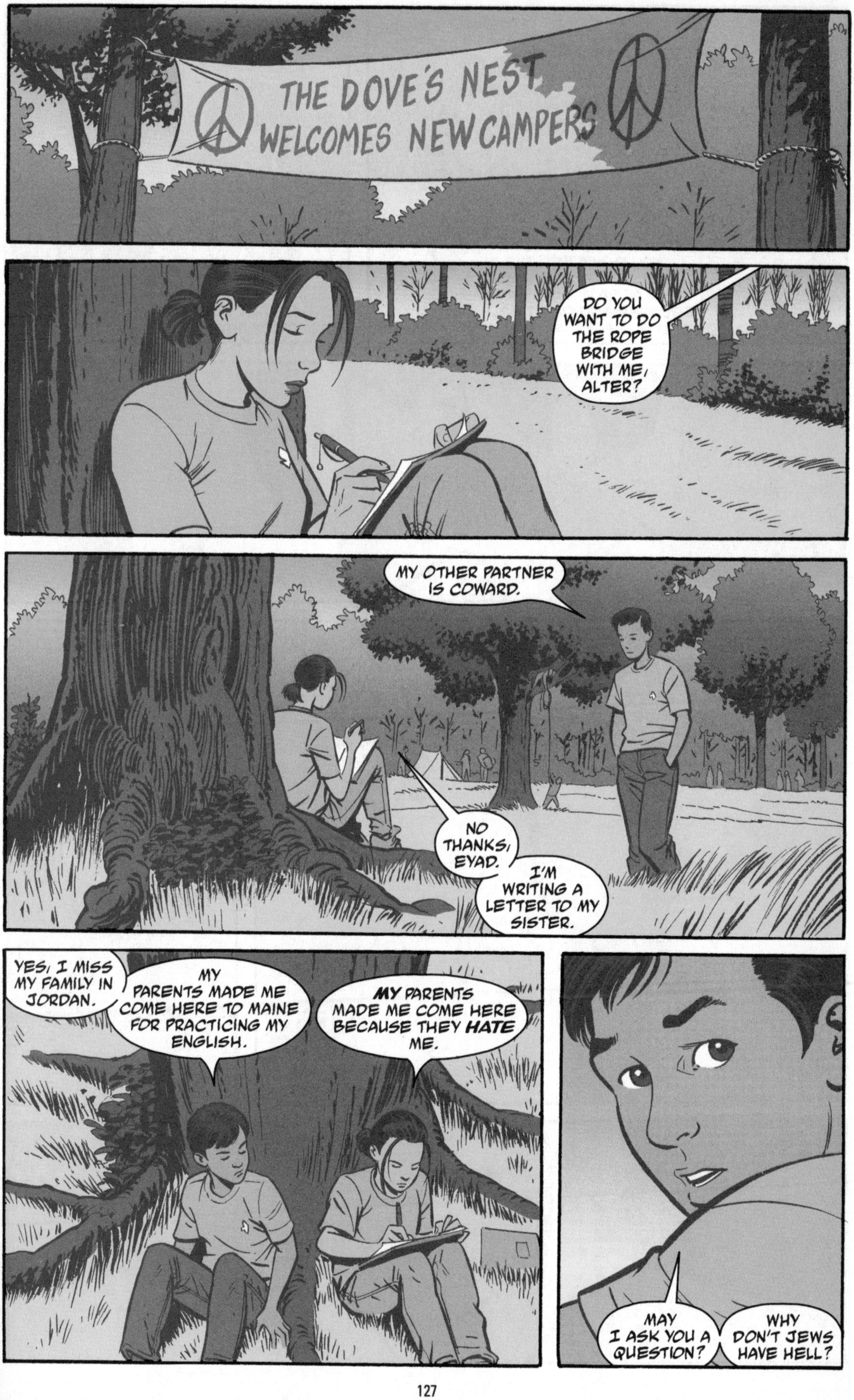
THE DOVE'S NEST
WELCOMES NEW CAMPERS
DO YOU WANT TO DO THE ROPE BRIDGE WITH ME, ALTER?
MY OTHER PARTNER IS COWARD.
NO THANKS, EYAD.
I'M WRITING A LETTER TO MY SISTER.
YES, I MISS MY FAMILY IN JORDAN.
MY PARENTS MADE ME COME HERE TO MAINE FOR PRACTICING MY ENGLISH.
MY PARENTS MADE ME COME HERE BECAUSE THEY **HATE** ME.
MAY I ASK YOU A QUESTION?
WHY DON'T JEWS HAVE HELL?

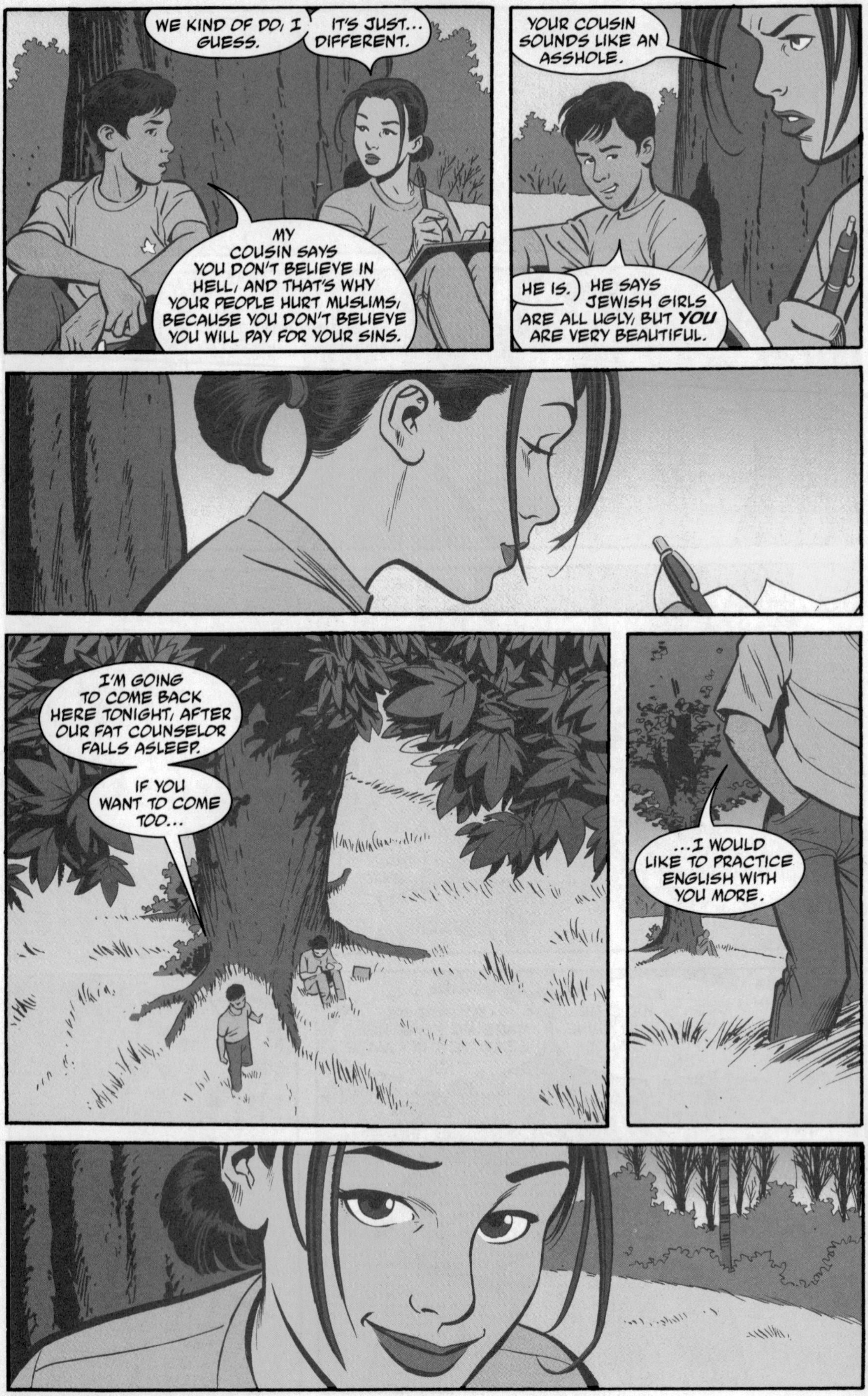
WE KIND OF DO, I GUESS.
IT'S JUST... DIFFERENT.
MY COUSIN SAYS YOU DON'T BELIEVE IN HELL, AND THAT'S WHY YOUR PEOPLE HURT MUSLIMS, BECAUSE YOU DON'T BELIEVE YOU WILL PAY FOR YOUR SINS.
YOUR COUSIN SOUNDS LIKE AN ASSHOLE.
HE IS.
HE SAYS JEWISH GIRLS ARE ALL UGLY, BUT *YOU* ARE VERY BEAUTIFUL.
I'M GOING TO COME BACK HERE TONIGHT, AFTER OUR FAT COUNSELOR FALLS ASLEEP.
IF YOU WANT TO COME TOO...
...I WOULD LIKE TO PRACTICE ENGLISH WITH YOU MORE.

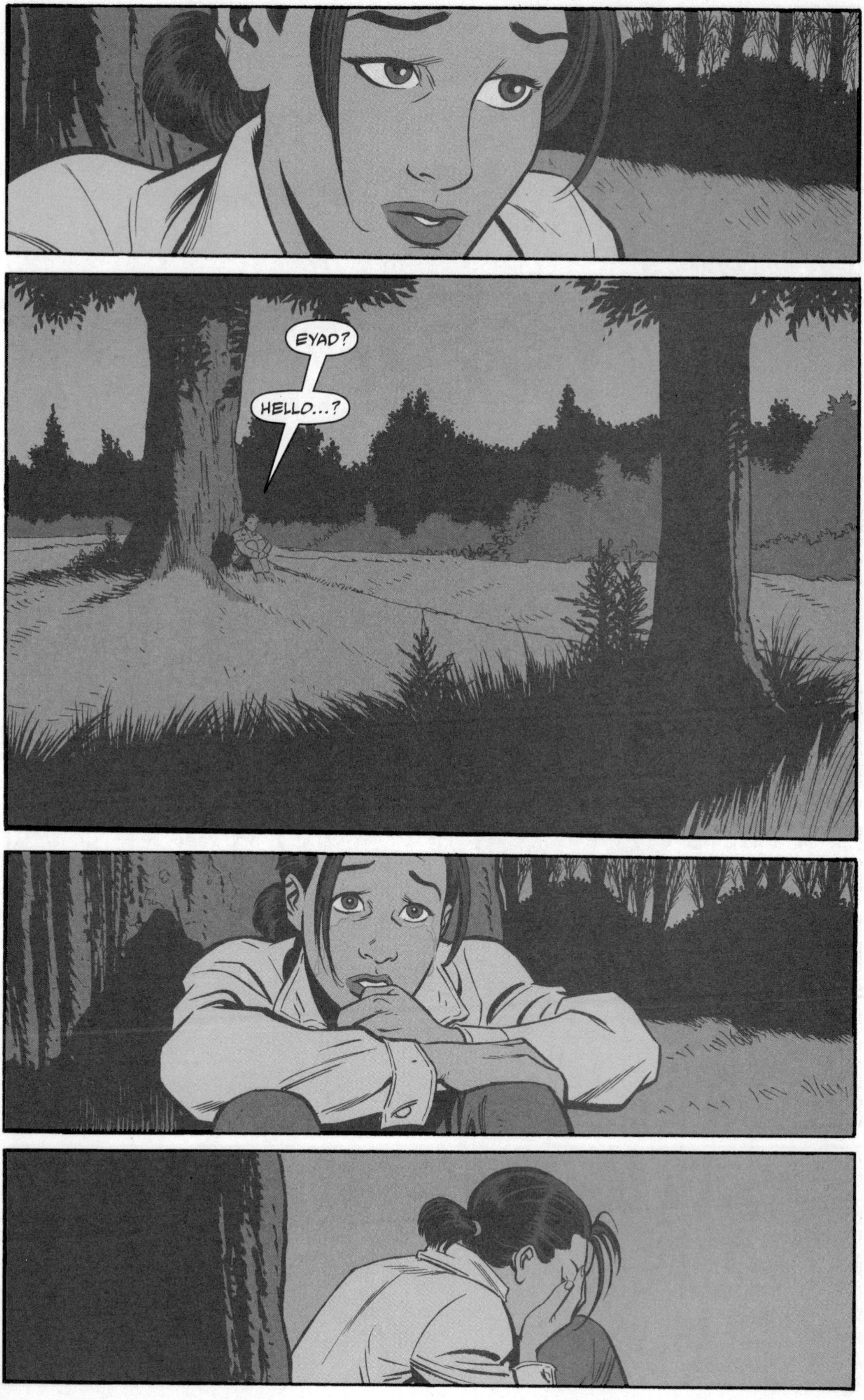
EYAD?
HELLO...?

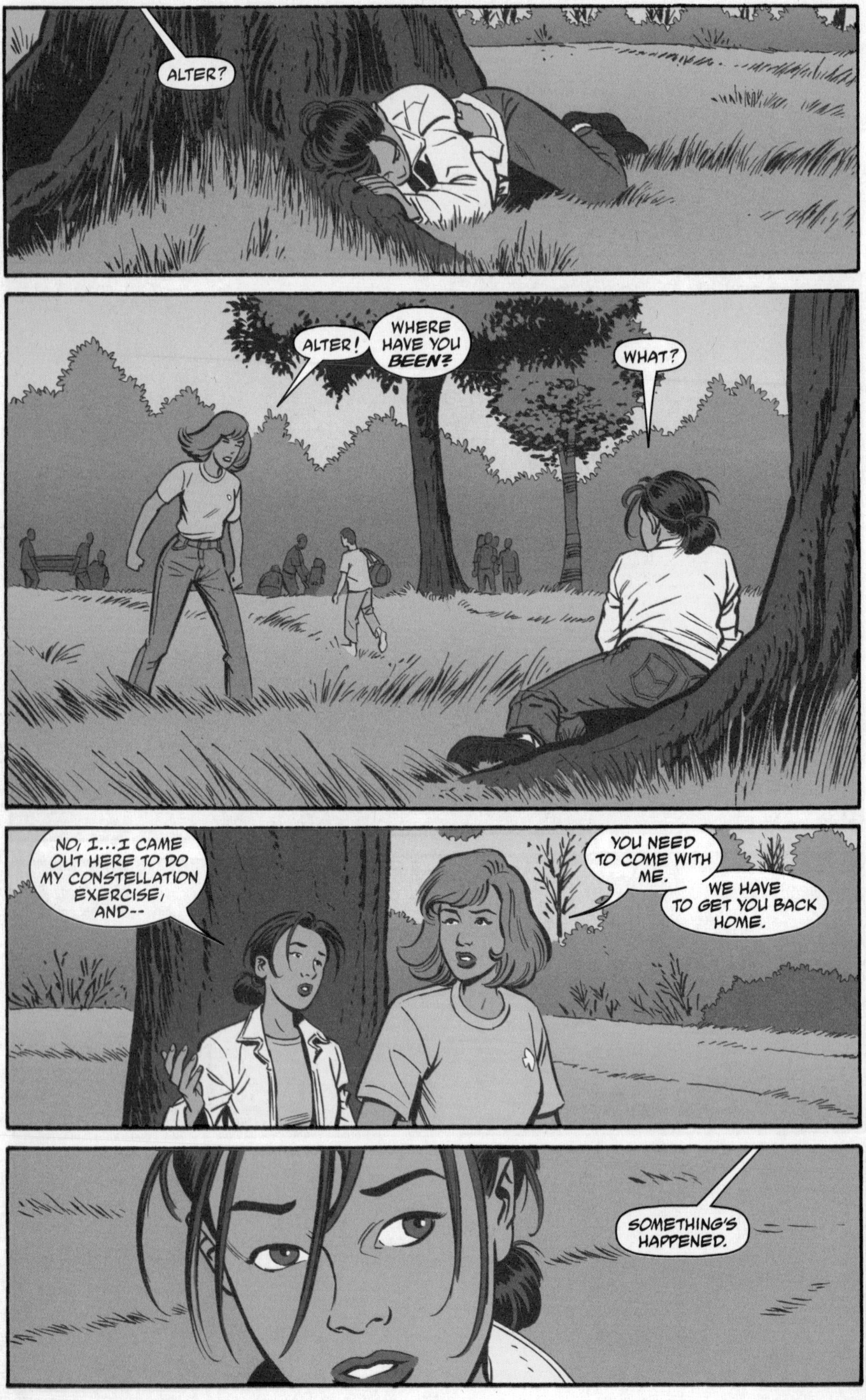
ALTER?
ALTER!
WHERE HAVE YOU BEEN?
WHAT?
NO, I... I CAME OUT HERE TO DO MY CONSTELLATION EXERCISE, AND--
YOU NEED TO COME WITH ME.
WE HAVE TO GET YOU BACK HOME.
SOMETHING'S HAPPENED.

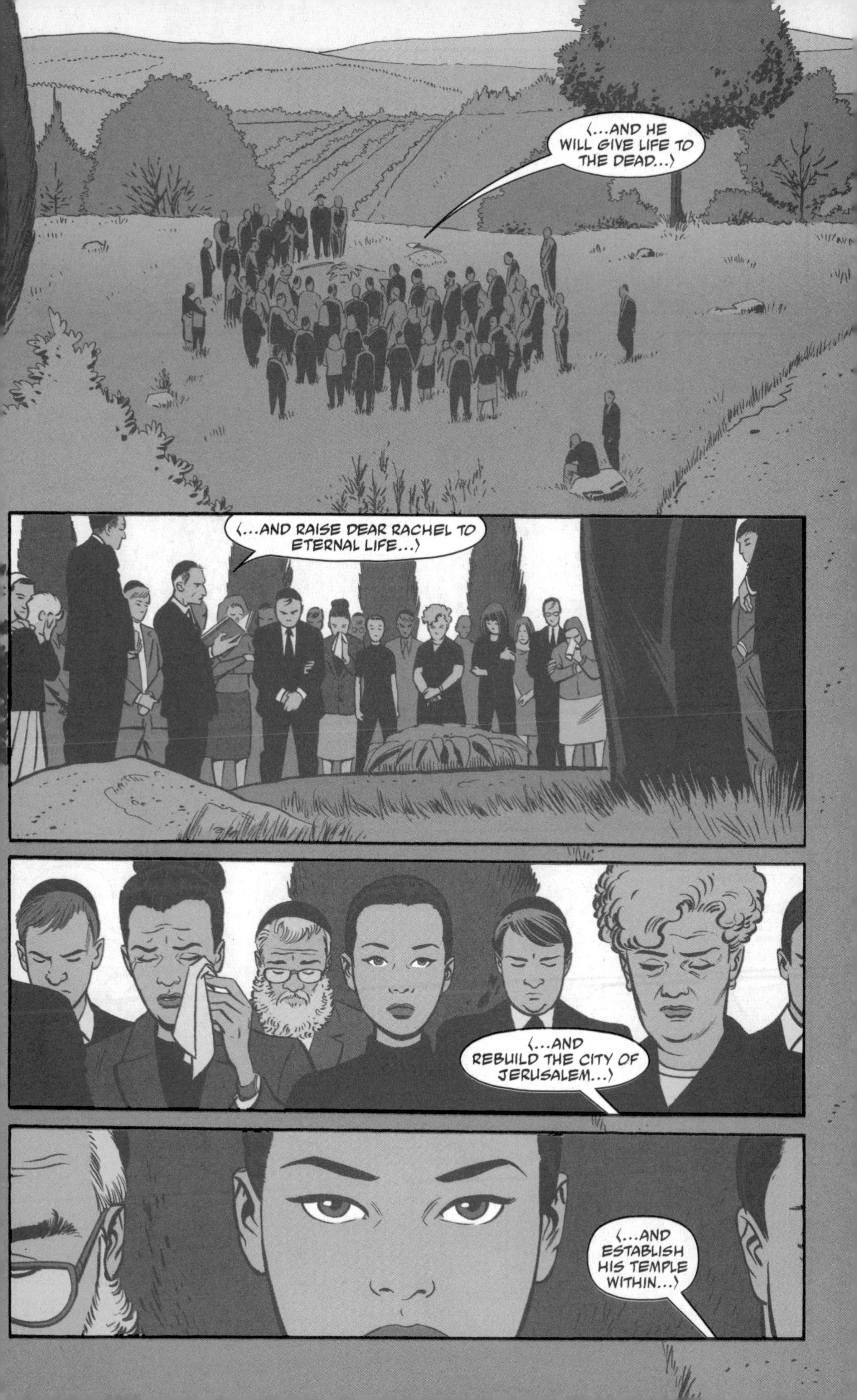

⟨...AND HE WILL GIVE LIFE TO THE DEAD...⟩
⟨...AND RAISE DEAR RACHEL TO ETERNAL LIFE...⟩
⟨...AND REBUILD THE CITY OF JERUSALEM...⟩
⟨...AND ESTABLISH HIS TEMPLE WITHIN...⟩

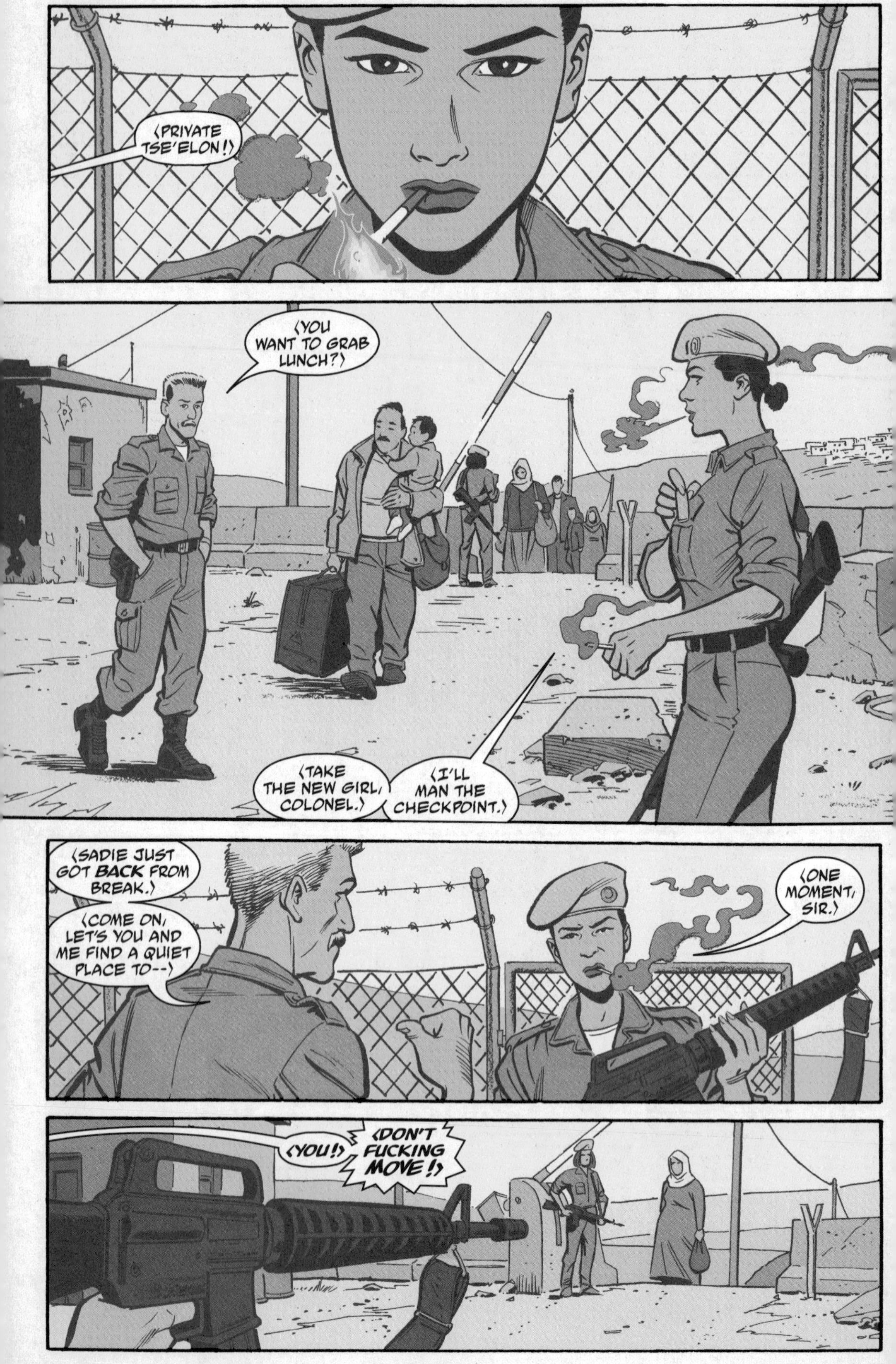
‹PRIVATE TSE'ELON!›
‹YOU WANT TO GRAB LUNCH?›
‹TAKE THE NEW GIRL, COLONEL.›
‹I'LL MAN THE CHECKPOINT.›
‹SADIE JUST GOT BACK FROM BREAK.›
‹COME ON, LET'S YOU AND ME FIND A QUIET PLACE TO--›
‹ONE MOMENT, SIR.›
‹YOU!›
‹DON'T FUCKING MOVE!›

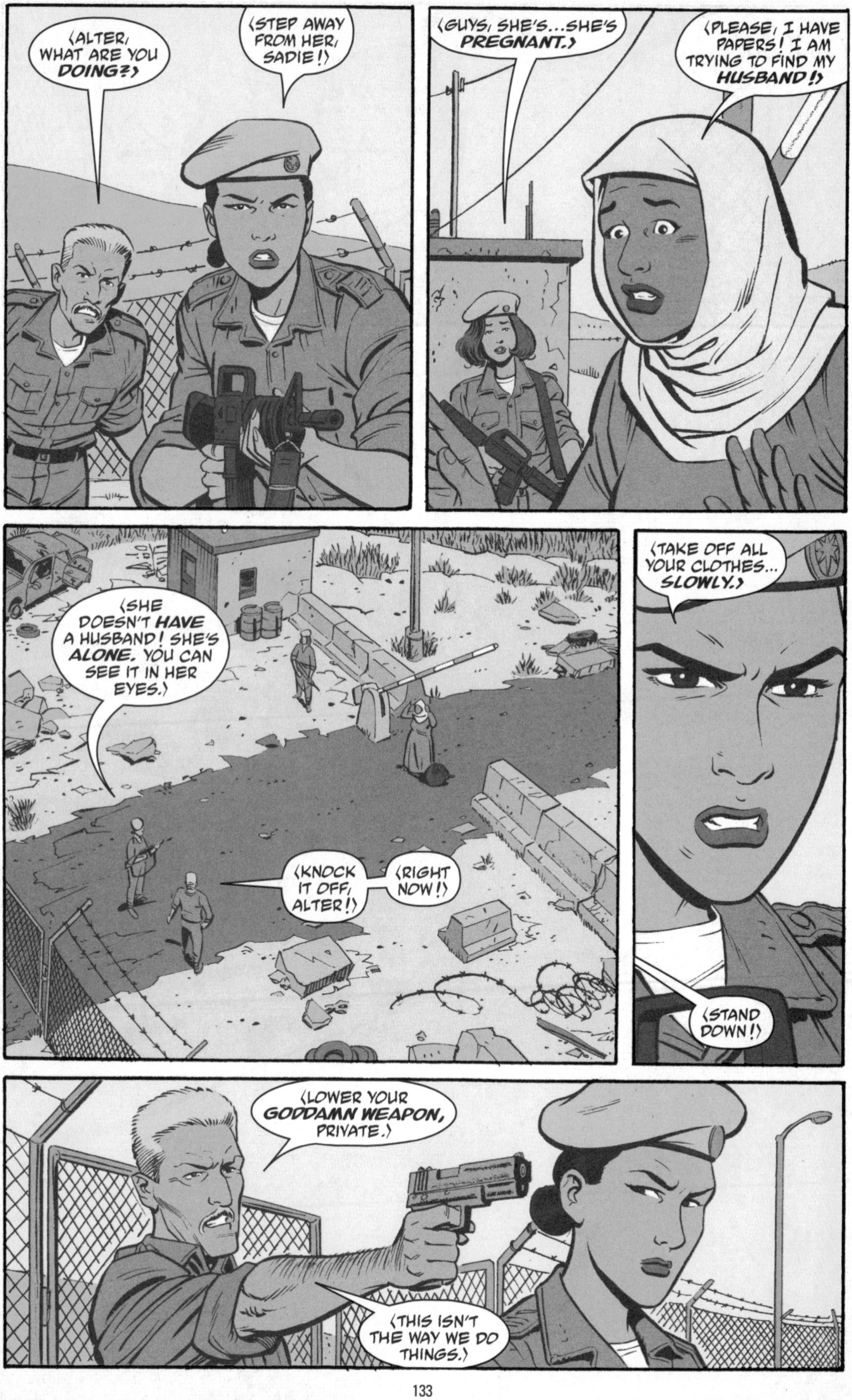
‹ALTER, WHAT ARE YOU **DOING?**›
‹STEP AWAY FROM HER, SADIE!›
‹GUYS, SHE'S...SHE'S **PREGNANT.**›
‹PLEASE, I HAVE PAPERS! I AM TRYING TO FIND MY **HUSBAND!**›
‹SHE DOESN'T **HAVE** A HUSBAND! SHE'S **ALONE.** YOU CAN SEE IT IN HER EYES.›
‹KNOCK IT OFF, ALTER!›
‹RIGHT NOW!›
‹TAKE OFF ALL YOUR CLOTHES... **SLOWLY.**›
‹STAND DOWN!›
‹LOWER YOUR **GODDAMN WEAPON,** PRIVATE.›
‹THIS ISN'T THE WAY WE DO THINGS.›

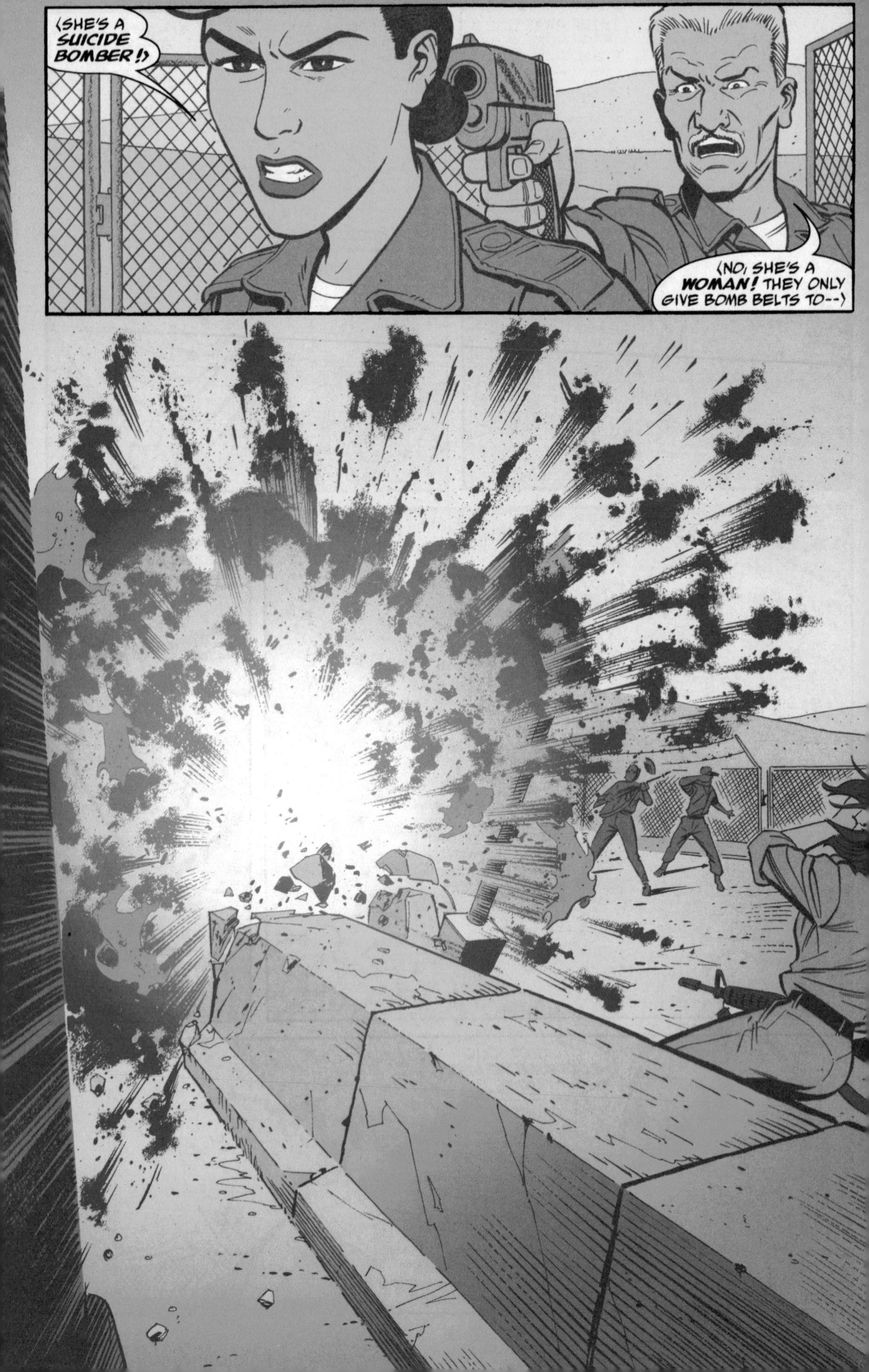
(SHE'S A SUICIDE BOMBER!)
(NO, SHE'S A WOMAN! THEY ONLY GIVE BOMB BELTS TO--)

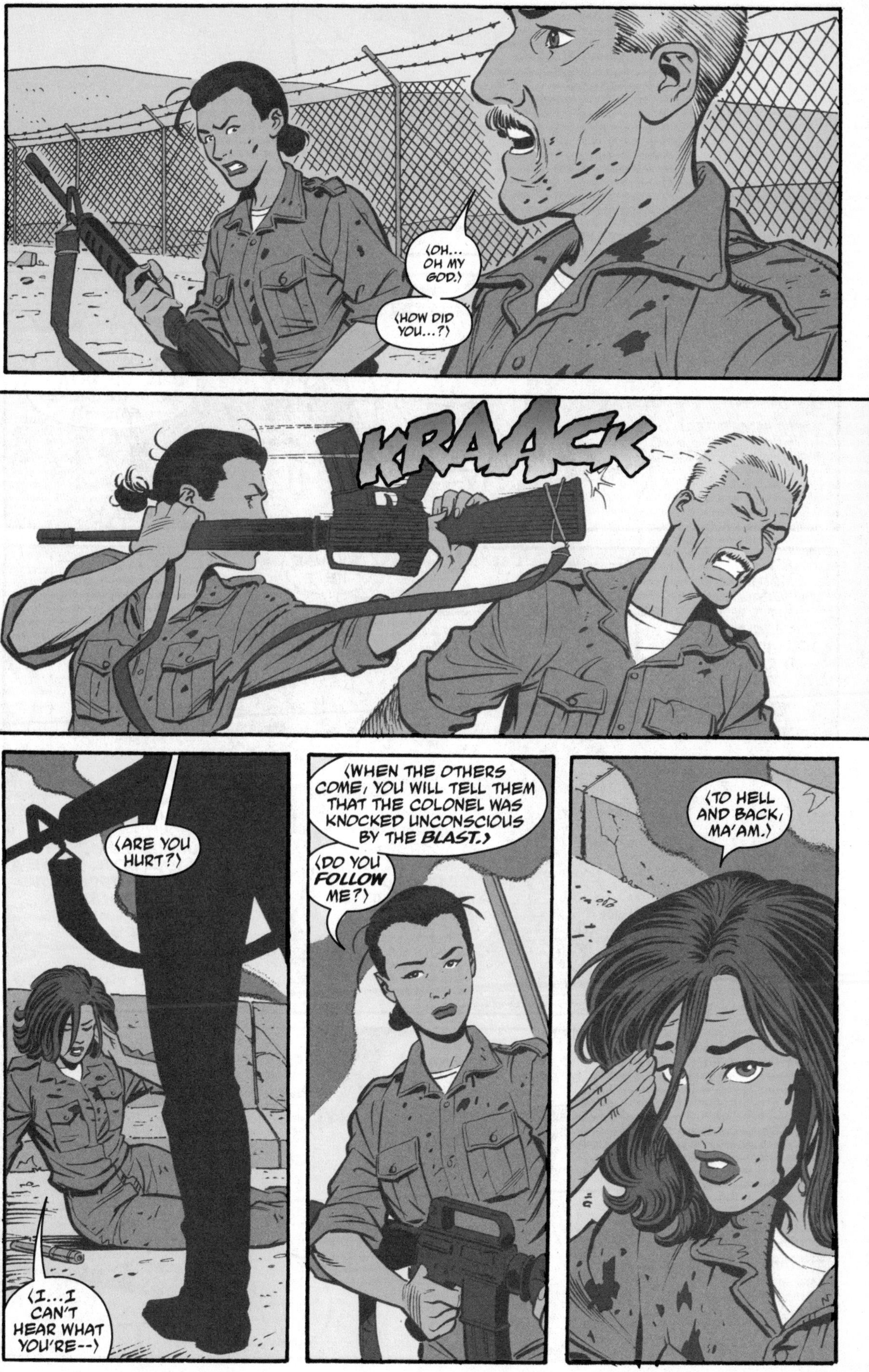

‹OH... OH MY GOD.›
‹HOW DID YOU...?›
KRAACK
‹ARE YOU HURT?›
‹I...I CAN'T HEAR WHAT YOU'RE--›
‹WHEN THE OTHERS COME, YOU WILL TELL THEM THAT THE COLONEL WAS KNOCKED UNCONSCIOUS BY THE *BLAST.*›
‹DO YOU *FOLLOW* ME?›
‹TO HELL AND BACK, MA'AM.›

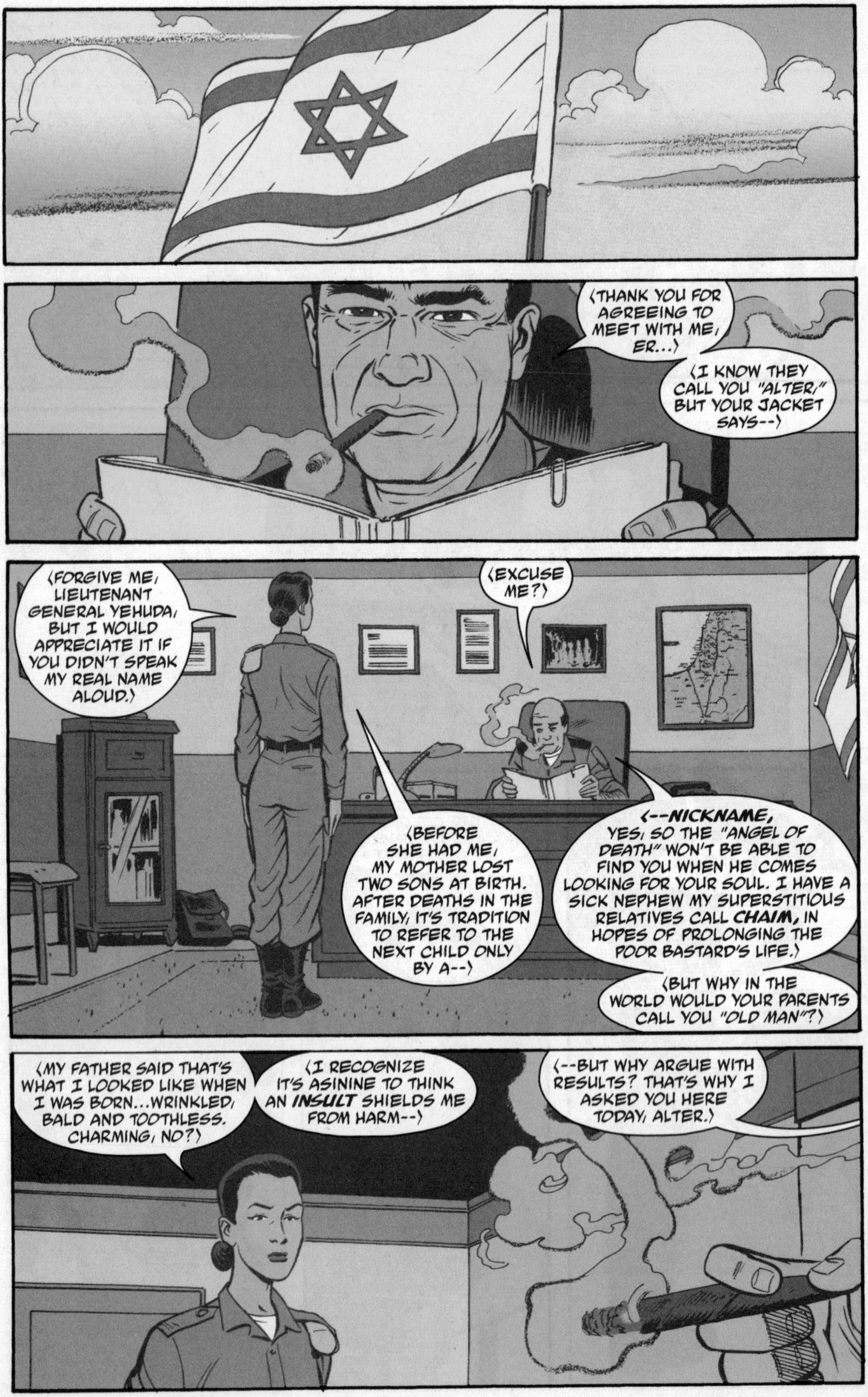

⟨THANK YOU FOR AGREEING TO MEET WITH ME, ER...⟩
⟨I KNOW THEY CALL YOU "ALTER," BUT YOUR JACKET SAYS--⟩
⟨FORGIVE ME, LIEUTENANT GENERAL YEHUDA, BUT I WOULD APPRECIATE IT IF YOU DIDN'T SPEAK MY REAL NAME ALOUD.⟩
⟨EXCUSE ME?⟩
⟨BEFORE SHE HAD ME, MY MOTHER LOST TWO SONS AT BIRTH. AFTER DEATHS IN THE FAMILY, IT'S TRADITION TO REFER TO THE NEXT CHILD ONLY BY A--⟩
⟨--**NICKNAME,** YES, SO THE "ANGEL OF DEATH" WON'T BE ABLE TO FIND YOU WHEN HE COMES LOOKING FOR YOUR SOUL. I HAVE A SICK NEPHEW MY SUPERSTITIOUS RELATIVES CALL **CHAIM,** IN HOPES OF PROLONGING THE POOR BASTARD'S LIFE.⟩
⟨BUT WHY IN THE WORLD WOULD YOUR PARENTS CALL YOU "OLD MAN"?⟩
⟨MY FATHER SAID THAT'S WHAT I LOOKED LIKE WHEN I WAS BORN...WRINKLED, BALD AND TOOTHLESS. CHARMING, NO?⟩
⟨I RECOGNIZE IT'S ASININE TO THINK AN **INSULT** SHIELDS ME FROM HARM--⟩
⟨--BUT WHY ARGUE WITH RESULTS? THAT'S WHY I ASKED YOU HERE TODAY, ALTER.⟩

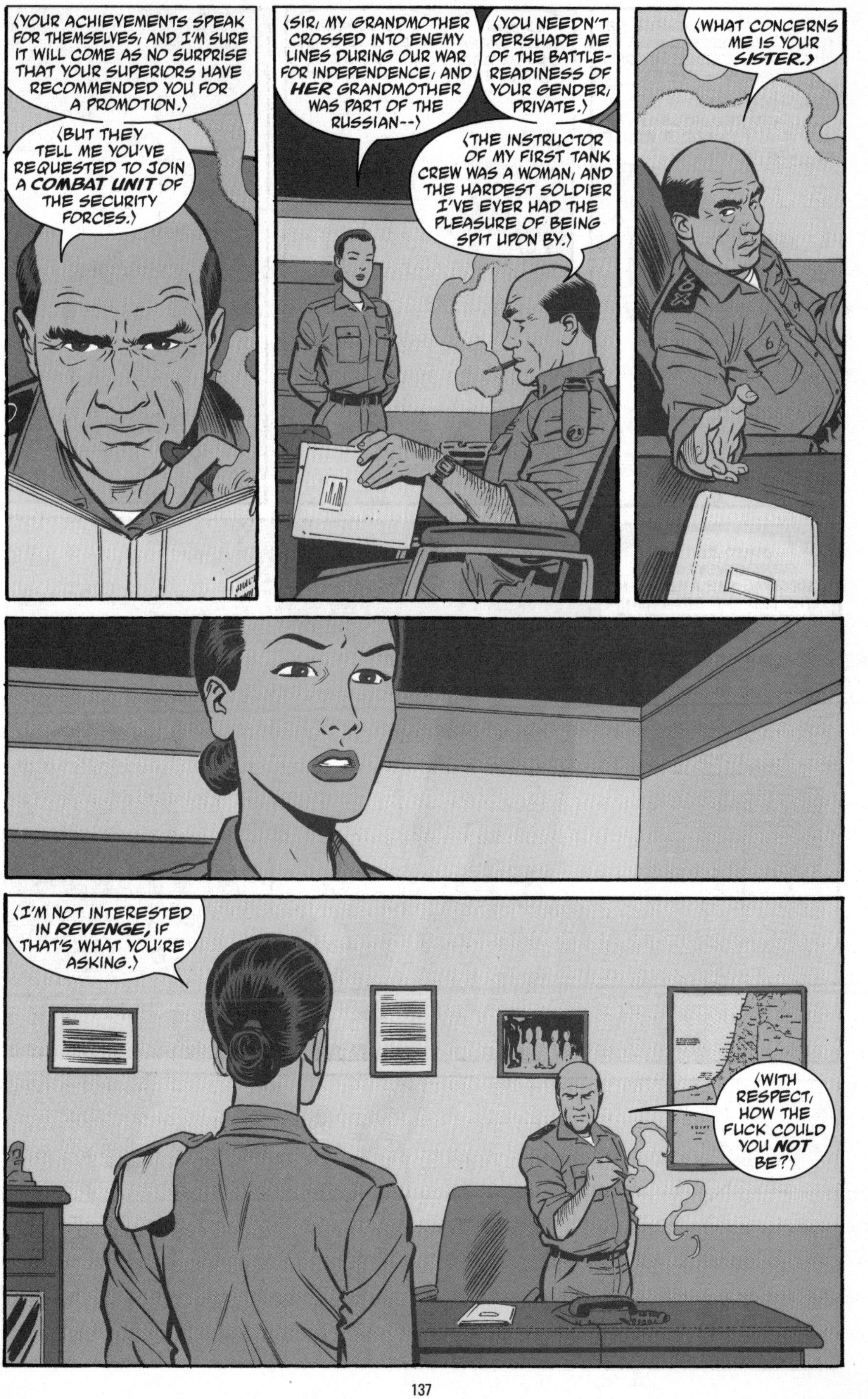
‹YOUR ACHIEVEMENTS SPEAK FOR THEMSELVES, AND I'M SURE IT WILL COME AS NO SURPRISE THAT YOUR SUPERIORS HAVE RECOMMENDED YOU FOR A PROMOTION.›
‹BUT THEY TELL ME YOU'VE REQUESTED TO JOIN A COMBAT UNIT OF THE SECURITY FORCES.›
‹SIR, MY GRANDMOTHER CROSSED INTO ENEMY LINES DURING OUR WAR FOR INDEPENDENCE, AND HER GRANDMOTHER WAS PART OF THE RUSSIAN--›
‹YOU NEEDN'T PERSUADE ME OF THE BATTLE-READINESS OF YOUR GENDER, PRIVATE.›
‹THE INSTRUCTOR OF MY FIRST TANK CREW WAS A WOMAN, AND THE HARDEST SOLDIER I'VE EVER HAD THE PLEASURE OF BEING SPIT UPON BY.›
‹WHAT CONCERNS ME IS YOUR SISTER.›
‹I'M NOT INTERESTED IN REVENGE, IF THAT'S WHAT YOU'RE ASKING.›
‹WITH RESPECT, HOW THE FUCK COULD YOU NOT BE?›

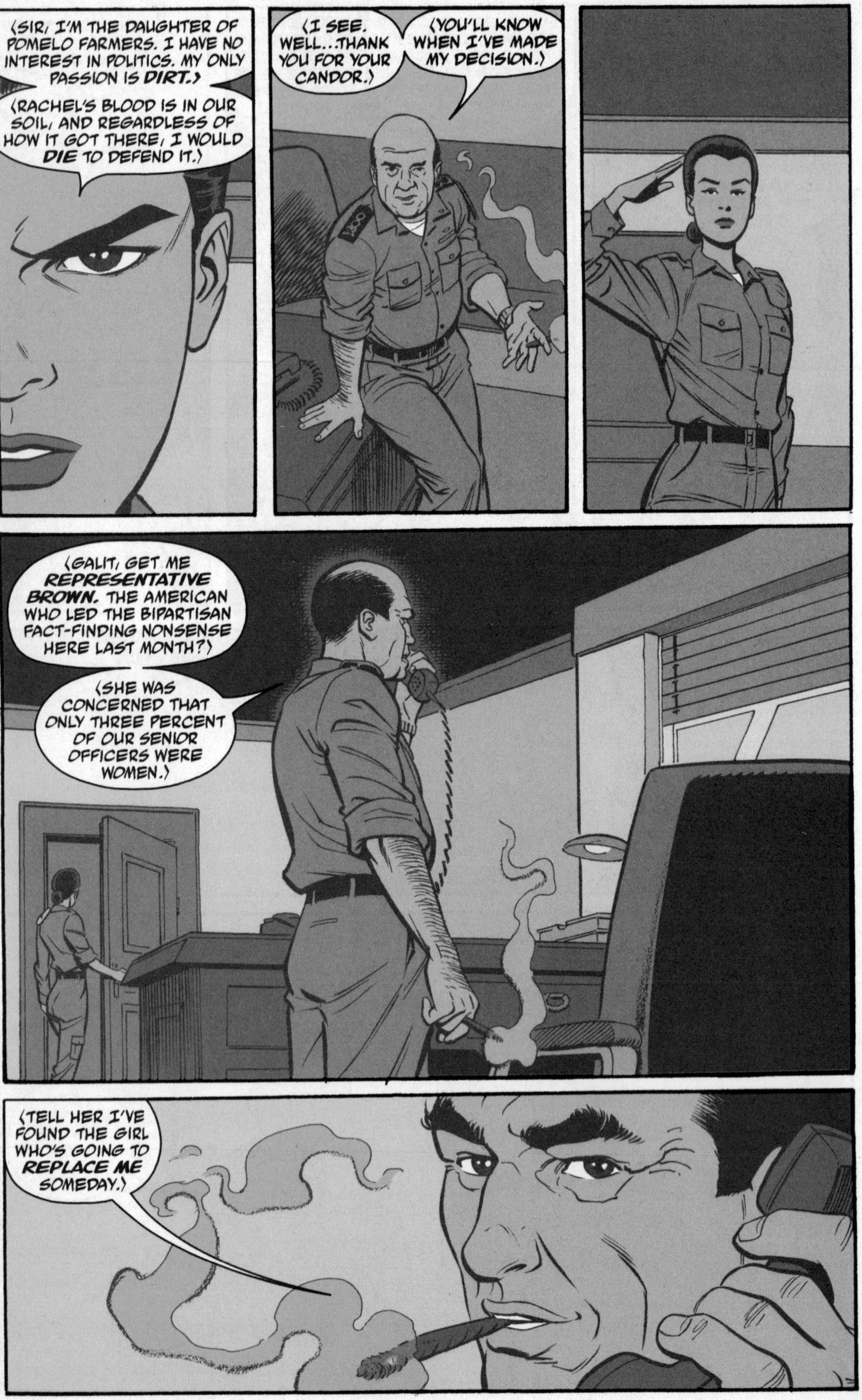
‹SIR, I'M THE DAUGHTER OF POMELO FARMERS. I HAVE NO INTEREST IN POLITICS. MY ONLY PASSION IS DIRT.›
‹RACHEL'S BLOOD IS IN OUR SOIL, AND REGARDLESS OF HOW IT GOT THERE, I WOULD DIE TO DEFEND IT.›
‹I SEE. WELL...THANK YOU FOR YOUR CANDOR.›
‹YOU'LL KNOW WHEN I'VE MADE MY DECISION.›
‹GALIT, GET ME REPRESENTATIVE BROWN. THE AMERICAN WHO LED THE BIPARTISAN FACT-FINDING NONSENSE HERE LAST MONTH?›
‹SHE WAS CONCERNED THAT ONLY THREE PERCENT OF OUR SENIOR OFFICERS WERE WOMEN.›
‹TELL HER I'VE FOUND THE GIRL WHO'S GOING TO REPLACE ME SOMEDAY.›

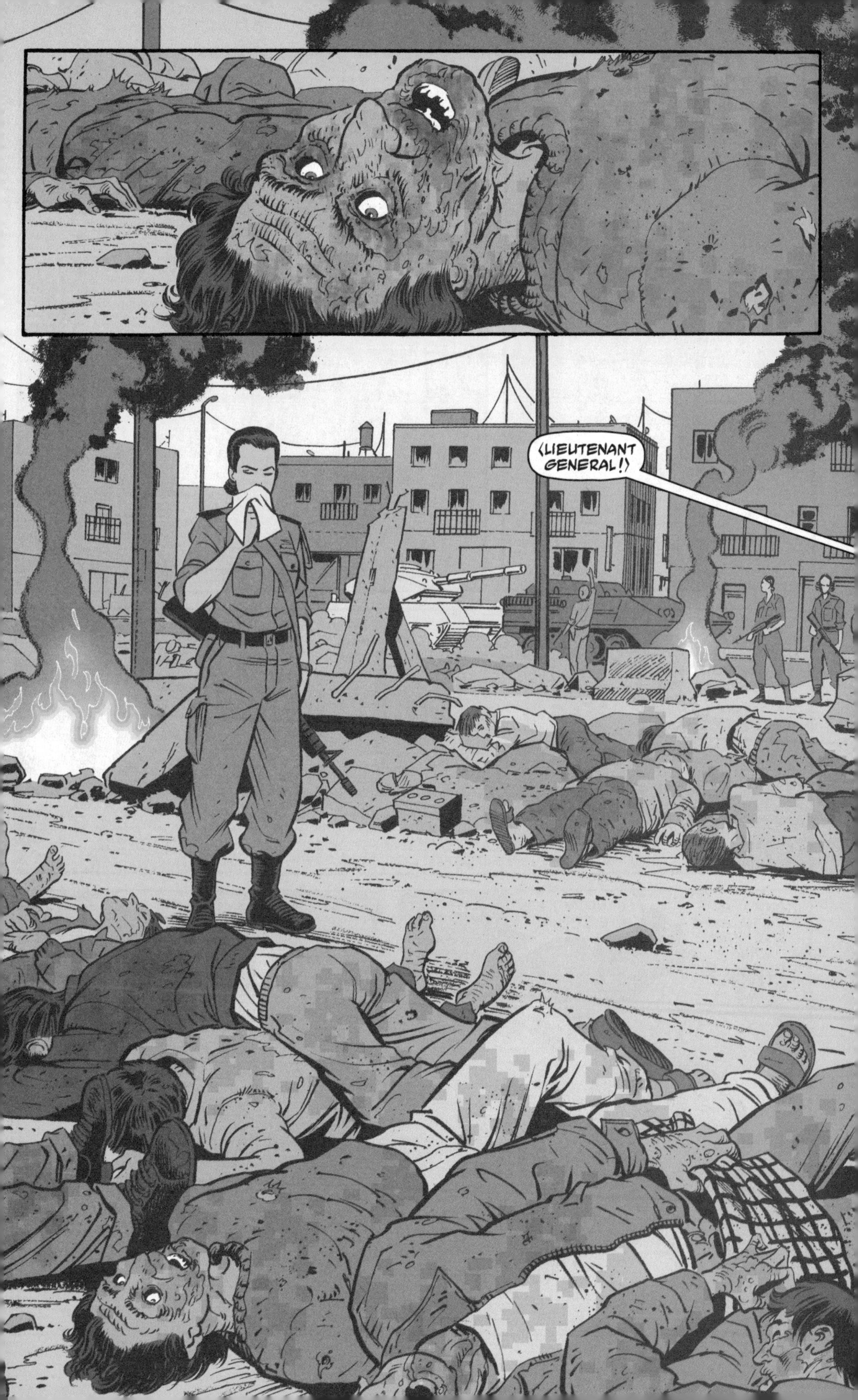
‹LIEUTENANT GENERAL!›

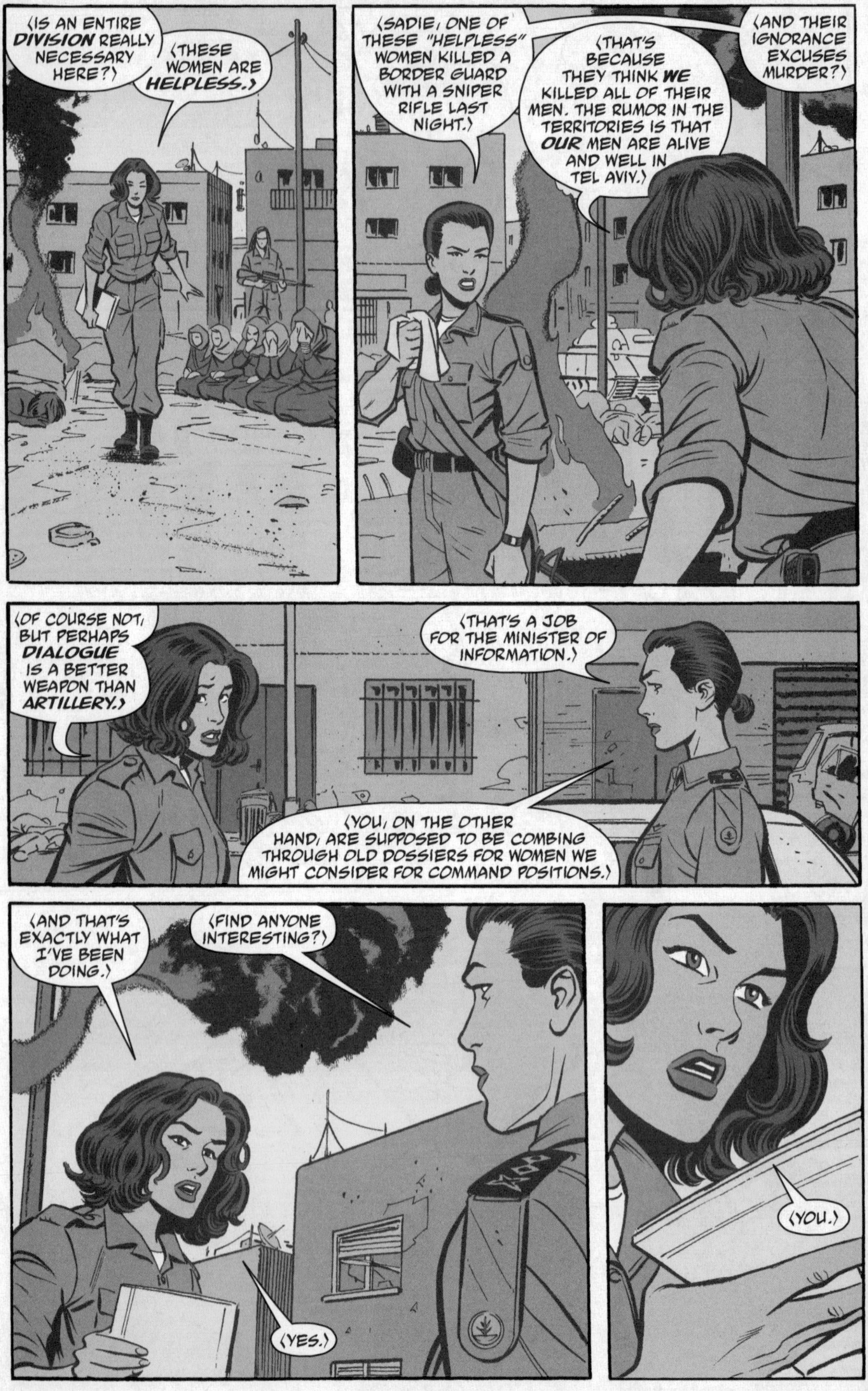
⟨IS AN ENTIRE DIVISION REALLY NECESSARY HERE?⟩
⟨THESE WOMEN ARE HELPLESS.⟩
⟨SADIE, ONE OF THESE "HELPLESS" WOMEN KILLED A BORDER GUARD WITH A SNIPER RIFLE LAST NIGHT.⟩
⟨THAT'S BECAUSE THEY THINK WE KILLED ALL OF THEIR MEN. THE RUMOR IN THE TERRITORIES IS THAT OUR MEN ARE ALIVE AND WELL IN TEL AVIV.⟩
⟨AND THEIR IGNORANCE EXCUSES MURDER?⟩
⟨OF COURSE NOT, BUT PERHAPS DIALOGUE IS A BETTER WEAPON THAN ARTILLERY.⟩
⟨THAT'S A JOB FOR THE MINISTER OF INFORMATION.⟩
⟨YOU, ON THE OTHER HAND, ARE SUPPOSED TO BE COMBING THROUGH OLD DOSSIERS FOR WOMEN WE MIGHT CONSIDER FOR COMMAND POSITIONS.⟩
⟨AND THAT'S EXACTLY WHAT I'VE BEEN DOING.⟩
⟨FIND ANYONE INTERESTING?⟩
⟨YES.⟩
⟨YOU.⟩

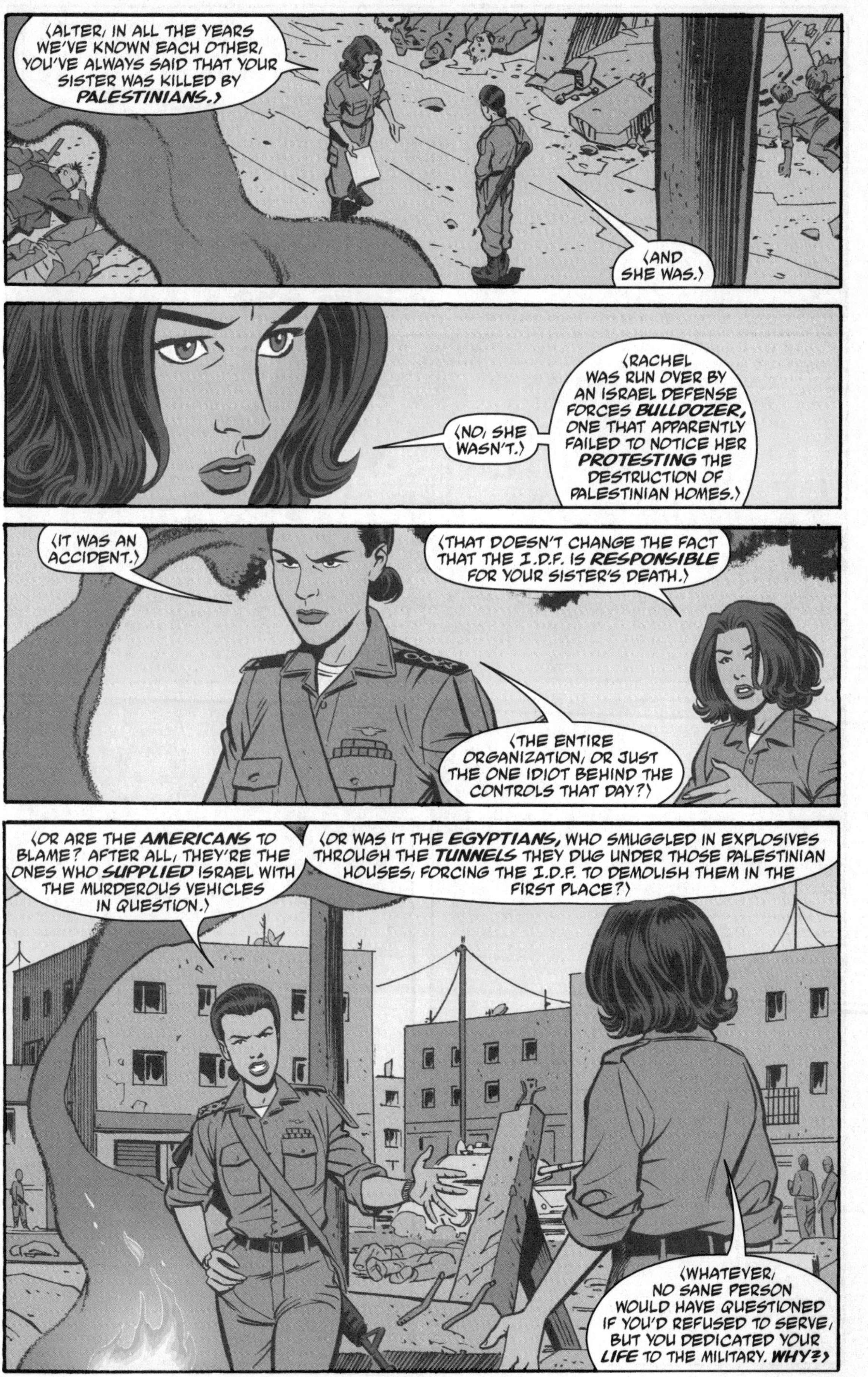
‹ALTER, IN ALL THE YEARS WE'VE KNOWN EACH OTHER, YOU'VE ALWAYS SAID THAT YOUR SISTER WAS KILLED BY **PALESTINIANS.**›
‹AND SHE WAS.›
‹NO, SHE WASN'T.›
‹RACHEL WAS RUN OVER BY AN ISRAEL DEFENSE FORCES **BULLDOZER,** ONE THAT APPARENTLY FAILED TO NOTICE HER **PROTESTING** THE DESTRUCTION OF PALESTINIAN HOMES.›
‹IT WAS AN ACCIDENT.›
‹THAT DOESN'T CHANGE THE FACT THAT THE I.D.F. IS **RESPONSIBLE** FOR YOUR SISTER'S DEATH.›
‹THE ENTIRE ORGANIZATION, OR JUST THE ONE IDIOT BEHIND THE CONTROLS THAT DAY?›
‹OR ARE THE **AMERICANS** TO BLAME? AFTER ALL, THEY'RE THE ONES WHO **SUPPLIED** ISRAEL WITH THE MURDEROUS VEHICLES IN QUESTION.›
‹OR WAS IT THE **EGYPTIANS,** WHO SMUGGLED IN EXPLOSIVES THROUGH THE **TUNNELS** THEY DUG UNDER THOSE PALESTINIAN HOUSES, FORCING THE I.D.F. TO DEMOLISH THEM IN THE FIRST PLACE?›
‹WHATEVER, NO SANE PERSON WOULD HAVE QUESTIONED IF YOU'D REFUSED TO SERVE, BUT YOU DEDICATED YOUR **LIFE** TO THE MILITARY. **WHY?**›

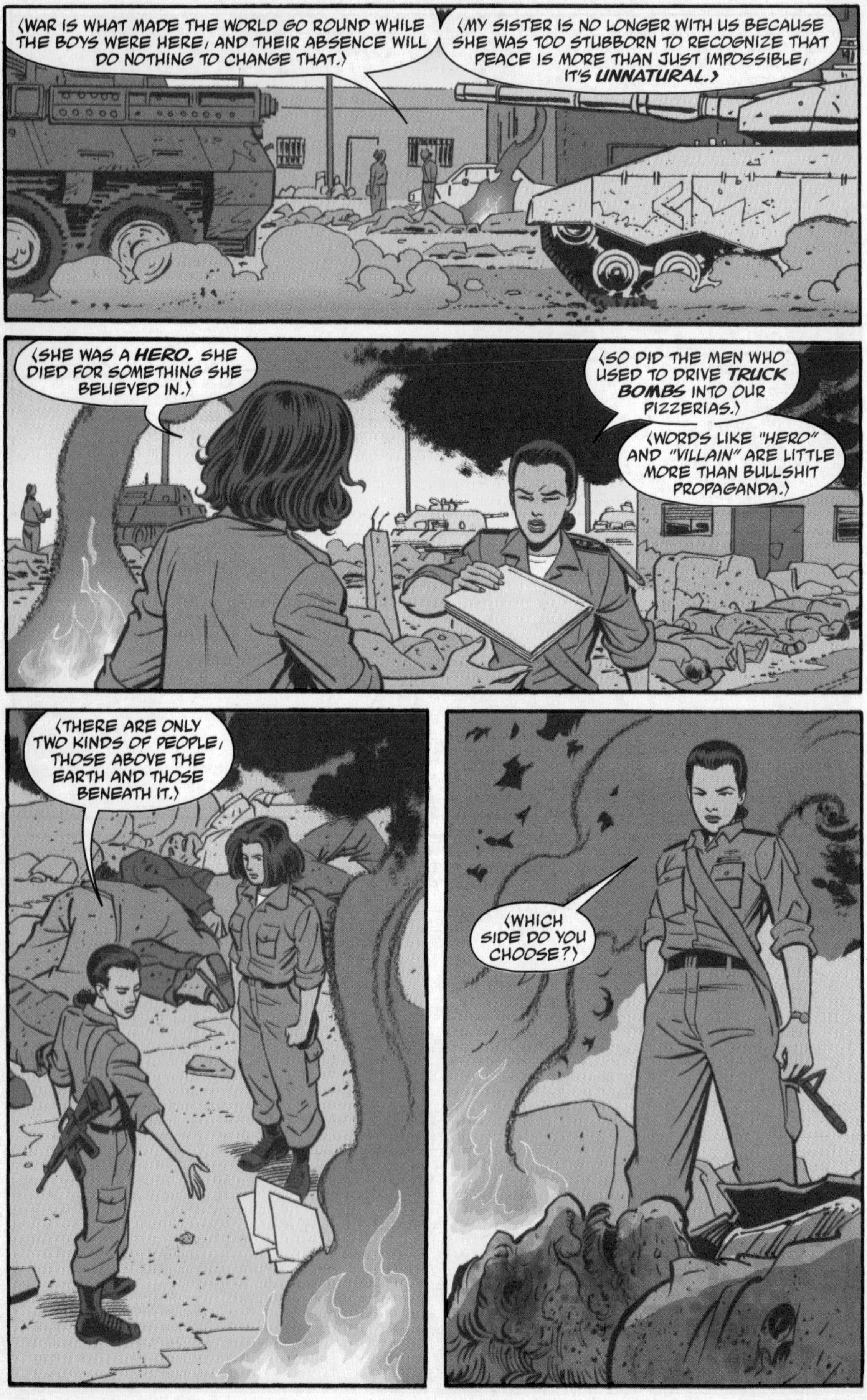
⟨WAR IS WHAT MADE THE WORLD GO ROUND WHILE THE BOYS WERE HERE, AND THEIR ABSENCE WILL DO NOTHING TO CHANGE THAT.⟩
⟨MY SISTER IS NO LONGER WITH US BECAUSE SHE WAS TOO STUBBORN TO RECOGNIZE THAT PEACE IS MORE THAN JUST IMPOSSIBLE, IT'S **UNNATURAL.**⟩
⟨SHE WAS A **HERO.** SHE DIED FOR SOMETHING SHE BELIEVED IN.⟩
⟨SO DID THE MEN WHO USED TO DRIVE **TRUCK BOMBS** INTO OUR PIZZERIAS.⟩
⟨WORDS LIKE "HERO" AND "VILLAIN" ARE LITTLE MORE THAN BULLSHIT PROPAGANDA.⟩
⟨THERE ARE ONLY TWO KINDS OF PEOPLE, THOSE ABOVE THE EARTH AND THOSE BENEATH IT.⟩
⟨WHICH SIDE DO YOU CHOOSE?⟩

YOU'RE A *FUCKING* LUNATIC.

AND YOU'RE ABOUT TO HAVE YOUR SHARE OF THE RATIONS DOWN HERE *DOUBLED*.

DON'T SAY A WORD, HEIDI!

YORICK...HE'S ON HIS WAY TO *FRANCE*, ALL RIGHT? TO FIND HIS *GIRLFRIEND*. THE OTHERS LEFT TO MEET HIM. I'LL PLAY YOU THE CALL RECORDS IF YOU DON'T BELIEVE ME.

JUST PLEASE... DON'T HURT HEATHER.

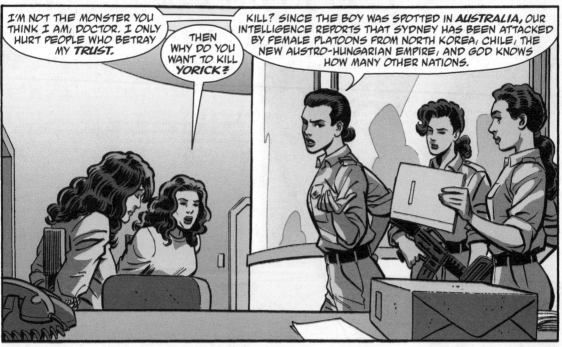

I'M NOT THE MONSTER YOU THINK I AM, DOCTOR. I ONLY HURT PEOPLE WHO BETRAY MY *TRUST*.

THEN WHY DO YOU WANT TO KILL *YORICK*?

KILL? SINCE THE BOY WAS SPOTTED IN *AUSTRALIA*, OUR INTELLIGENCE REPORTS THAT SYDNEY HAS BEEN ATTACKED BY FEMALE PLATOONS FROM NORTH KOREA, CHILE, THE NEW AUSTRO-HUNGARIAN EMPIRE, AND GOD KNOWS HOW MANY OTHER NATIONS.

IF AND WHEN ONE OF THESE ARMIES FINDS MR. BROWN, THE CULPER RING GIRL WILL BE UNABLE TO PROTECT HIM.

I ASSURE YOU, I AM NOT THE LAST MAN'S ENEMY...

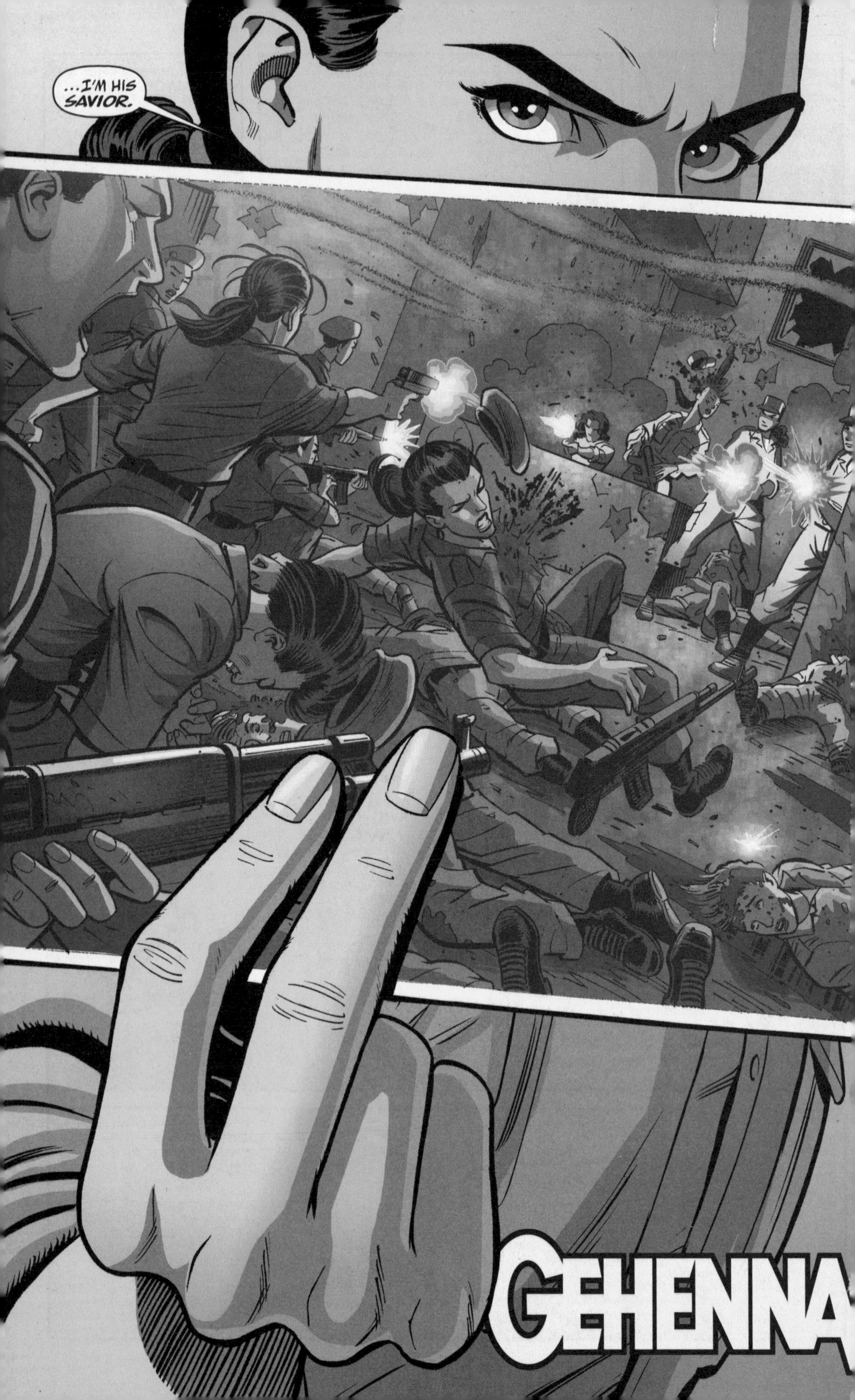
...I'M HIS SAVIOR.
GEHENNA